Educating in Dialog

Dialogue Studies (DS)

Dialogue Studies takes the notion of dialogicity as central; it encompasses every type of language use, workaday, institutional and literary. By covering the whole range of language use, the growing field of dialogue studies comes close to pragmatics and studies in discourse or conversation. The concept of dialogicity, however, provides a clear methodological profile. The series aims to cross disciplinary boundaries and considers a genuinely inter-disciplinary approach necessary for addressing the complex phenomenon of dialogic language use. This peer reviewed series will include monographs, thematic collections of articles, and textbooks in the relevant areas.

For an overview of all books published in this series, please see
http://benjamins.com/catalog/ds

Volume 24

Educating in Dialog. Constructing meaning and building knowledge with dialogic technology
Edited by Sebastian Feller and Ilker Yengin

Educating in Dialog

Constructing meaning and building knowledge with dialogic technology

Edited by

Sebastian Feller
A*STAR - Institute of High Performance Computing, Singapore

Ilker Yengin
A*STAR - Institute of High Performance Computing, Singapore

John Benjamins Publishing Company
Amsterdam / Philadelphia

∞™ The paper used in this publication meets the minimum requirements of the American National Standard for Information Sciences – Permanence of Paper for Printed Library Materials, ANSI Z39.48-1984.

Library of Congress Cataloging-in-Publication Data

Educating in dialog : constructing meaning and building knowledge with dialogic technology / Edited by Sebastian Feller and Ilker Yengin.

p. cm. (Dialogue Studies, ISSN 1875-1792 ; v. 24)

Includes bibliographical references and index.

1. Dialogue analysis--Data processing. 2. Dialogue analysis--Technical innovations 3. Communication in education--Technological innovations. 4. Distance education. 5. Social media. 6. Education--Effect of technological innovations on 7. Educational technology. I. Feller, Sebastian, editor. II. Yengin, Ilker, editor.

P40.5.D53E38 2014

371.35'8--dc23 2014026468

ISBN 978 90 272 1041 8 (Hb ; alk. paper)

ISBN 978 90 272 6934 8 (Eb)

John Benjamins Publishing Co. · P.O. Box 36224 · 1020 ME Amsterdam · The Netherlands

John Benjamins North America · P.O. Box 27519 · Philadelphia PA 19118-0519 · USA

I dedicate this book to my two sons, Ariel and Enzo.
This book is a promise to all our children to hand them every opportunity for a world filled with brilliant thoughts and inspiring ideas.

Sebastian Feller
Singapore, August 2014

Table of contents

Part III. Dialogic knowledge building: Potentials of dialogic technologies for knowledge building and negotiation

Preface

Modern society has rapidly converged upon the 'information society', i.e., a society that constantly shares and uses information in all kinds of daily activities. We create technologies that help us share information amongst each other instantly, anywhere and anytime. The Internet is probably the best example for the excess of information flowing around in our increasingly digitalized world. However, caution is warranted: information alone is not everything, not by a long stretch. We have to use it in meaningful ways in order to arrive at more complex conceptualizations that help us make sense of the world and what is going on around us.

These insights have set in motion some fundamental societal changes. We are now mutating rapidly from the information society to the knowledge society (Mansell and Wehn 1998), a society that uses information and communication technologies for collaborative thinking and problem solving, shaping the ways we act and interact with each other (Livingstone 2008; Zuboff 1988, 2002). In the knowledge society, jointly constructed knowledge "add[s] values" to activities and processes, and thus to society at large (Glibert 2007; Bereiter and Scardamalia 2005; Drucker 1993). In light of these developments, we hold that new pedagogies and learning settings need to be created. As Friesen and Jardine (2009) conclude: "The factory model of schooling we inherited no longer serves our contemporary 21st century knowledge society." What is needed is to integrate knowledge building skills and new technologies into dialogic educational activities both in and outside of schools. Learning environments need to be created in which students are actively involved in collaborative learning activities of building and sharing knowledge using modern technologies designed for this purpose. Simply adding technologies to an old curriculum that is not designed for them (cf., e.g., Bennett 2002; Cuban 2001; Levin and Arafeh 2002; Peck et al. 2002; Reimann and Markauskaite 2010) will lead, sooner or later, to a dead end.

In this context, there are a number of important issues that require our attention. For instance, we should spend more time investigating the particular functions of knowledge, i.e., what knowledge is used for exactly, and the roles of technology in supporting us in our knowledge related activities; we should elucidate in a detailed manner what the skills are that enable people to make sense of information and to jointly build knowledge in technology-driven environments.

This book sets out to investigate the roles and functions that knowledge and education have in our modern, technology driven world. It does so in the context of dialogic education or, more precisely, how we teach and learn things together. We perceive education as a genuinely dialogic enterprise, a view that is also reflected in recent educational discussions, as evidenced by an increasing shift of focus in educational science to the "knowledge community" or the "learning community" (e.g., Kilpatrick, Barrett, and Jones 2006; Smith et al. 2005). In this kind of dialogic learning, different perspectives come together to form deeper explanations. Tackling problems in dialogic interaction encourages learners to use higher order cognitive skills and higher level thinking (cf. Alexander 2004; Craig et al. 2000; Fisher 2007; Swedin and Ferro 2007).

Needless to say, researchers always need a starting point in the attempt to think about, talk, and discuss new ideas. We need tools that allow us to come to grips with abstract concepts like knowledge building, technology supported teaching and learning, cognitive skills, and collaborative learning. In this book, it is Weigand's (2010) Mixed Game Model (MGM), a holistic theory of dialog, which lies at the heart of the chapters to come. The MGM provides a theoretical foundation for dialogic education: it conceptualizes dialog as a complex culturally shaped game between interlocutors, incorporating each individual's world of emotive and motivational states, personal preferences and expectations, beliefs, and convictions. This complex whole is conceptualized in terms of what Weigand calls the communicative action game, a game that at its core consists of two mutually related communicative actions: the active and the reactive speech act. Importantly, the game is not limited to verbal means of communication, rather, it is based on the assumption that speakers integrate different types of communicative means in dialog: verbal, perceptual, and cognitive.

It is not difficult to recognize that the MGM describes the basic things we should find in 21st century education. Learning should not so much be about the *what*, but rather the *what for*, the *why*, and the *how*. Science has taken a similar direction in dealing with reality. The "science wars", for example, have shaken the positivist view of knowledge as being about reality, a reality that exists independently of human thought and perception. Scientists from the constructivist camp have put forward many plausible arguments that reality and knowledge are social constructs, not ultimate truths or facts. We filter whatever "reality" may lie out there with our minds and perceive only a "censored" version that we shape and refine through discussions and interactions with others. Knowledge becomes a dialogically built social artifact that is inherently dynamic, malleable, and probabilistic. It can be challenged, changed, discarded, amended, and built, but not found, verified, or proven. It is dialog that provides us with a suitable framework to engage in these knowledge-building activities, and it is the MGM, which gives us the means to think and talk about these activities. The chapters in this book are all inextricably linked to this theoretical view of dialog.

On the basis of these considerations, the essence of learning should be constructed around how we process information and build knowledge in dialog with the aim of making sense of the world. We need to be able to recognize meaningful information patterns in order to obtain deeper insights. We need to possess the skills to collaboratively select and piece information together to build knowledge in interaction with one another. Moreover, it is thereby important that knowledge is transferable. This is essential in our ever-changing modern world. Education in the 21st century should, thus, support individuals in developing these skills and abilities. Recent research looks into how cognitive skills are transferred between individuals who collaborate in teams to solve problems and build knowledge together (Brown and Campione 1996; Slotta and Najafi 2013; Peters and Slotta 2010). This trend has cumulated in a new pedagogical paradigm: 21st century skills. These skills include creative, critical, and innovative thinking, as well as collaborative learning, critical discussion, and technological versatility, to name but a few.

Another important point is that, since knowledge is created in dialog between different individuals, it becomes pertinent to take into account personal differences between learners. Each and everyone of us is shaped by their individual personalities, cultural and societal backgrounds, as well as their personal histories, interests, and preferences. As Pinker (2002) points out, we are not blank slates but build new knowledge on top of existing concepts and conceptualizations. In his book *Anna, die Schule und der liebe Gott* (2013) the German philosopher Richard David Precht depicts a school system around project-based learning, flipped teaching, and open curricula that respects individual differences and the personal learning preferences of each learner. This shows the increasing importance of learner-centered pedagogies. Fortunately, with the help of emerging technologies in the 21st century, new opportunities are arising to enable us to include the perspectives of different individuals in learning activities. With the advent of sophisticated machines and larger information networks such as the Internet Computer Supported Collaborative Learning (CSCL) has emerged. Nowadays, a vast variety of CSCL software applications are available for a large number of different subjects and learning goals. Pinkwart and McLaren's (2012) *Educational Technologies for Teaching Argumentation Skills* gives an overview of state-of-the-art applications that are used to teach skills like critical thinking, argumentation, and meta-cognitive thinking. These applications are human-in-the-loop, i.e., they assist the learner by highlighting argumentation features that might be important in the discussion. Collaborative learning takes place here not so much between the application and the learner, but rather between the different learners using the application. In addition, intelligent tutoring systems like AutoTutor interact with the learner in natural language using psychometrics and natural language processing to update themselves about the learner's motivational, cognitive, and emotive states, using this information to give the learner real-time feedback on her performance. Although these systems are still a long way from replacing human teachers, their believability and usefulness have been steadily advancing over the last years. All in all, these developments make apparent that dialog is a basic element of personalized learning.

Exploring 21st century education in dialogic interaction, this book provides a vast array of viewpoints from distinct disciplinary backgrounds including educational science, linguistics, dialog analysis, psychology, philosophy, and computer science. The different perspectives combine both theoretical and practical aspects of dialogic knowledge building with technology. The chapters in this book provide essential insights into the why, what for, and how new pedagogies and educational technologies for 21st century dialogic knowledge building should be designed. The first section introduces the key concepts like knowledge, understanding, explaining, and sense-making via social construction. Section 2 applies these concepts to specific teaching and learning contexts encompassing indigenous learning spaces at university, teacher training courses, and vocational training in a company. Section 3 deals with the question of how to translate concepts such as collaborative learning, dialog, knowledge building, learner-centeredness, and 21st century skills into technological applications. The authors provide design models and guidelines that lay the basis for new dialogic educational technologies.

We invite anyone who is interested in education and its relation to technology to join us on this exciting journey through diverse topics and thoughts. We hope this book will kindle new discussions on how to meet the challenges of 21st century education, combining learning and technology in meaningful dialogic ways.

Sebastian Feller and Ilker Yengin
Singapore, 04 February 2014

References

Alexander, Robin J. 2004. *Towards Dialogic Teaching: Rethinking Classroom Talk*. York: Dialogos.

Bennett, Frederick. 2002. "The Future of Computer Technology in K-12 Education." *Phi Delta Kappan* 83 (8): 621–625.

Bereiter, Carl, and Marlene Scardamalia. 2005. "Beyond Bloom's Taxonomy: Rethinking Knowledge for the Knowledge Age." In *Fundamental Change*, ed.by Michael Fullan, 5–22. Netherlands: Springer. DOI: 10.1007/1-4020-4454-2_2

Brown, Ann L., and Joseph C. Campione. 1994. "Guided Discovery in a Community of Learners. In *Classroom Lessons: Integrating Cognitive Theory and Classroom Practice*, ed. by Kate McGilly, 229–270. Cambridge, MA: MIT Press/Bradford Books.

Craig, Scotty D., Barry Gholson, Matthew Ventura, Arthur C. Graesser, and the Tutoring Research Group. 2000. "Overhearing Dialogues and Monologues in Virtual Tutoring Sessions: Effects on Questioning and Vicarious Learning." *International Journal of Artificial Intelligence in Education* 11: 242–253.

Cuban, Larry. 2001. *Oversold and Underused: Computers in the Classroom*. Harvard University Press.

Drucker, Peter F. 1993. *Post-Capitalist Society*. New York: Routledge.

Fisher, Robert. 2007. "Dialogic Teaching: Developing Thinking and Metacognition through Philosophical Discussion." *Early Child Development and Care* 177 (6–7): 615–631. DOI: 10.1080/03004430701378985

Friesen, Sharon and David Jardine. 2009. "21st Century Learning and Learners." Prepared for Western and Northern Canadian Curriculum Protocol by Galileo Educational Network. http://education.alberta.ca/media/1087278/wncp% 2021st% 20cent% 20learning2.

Kilpatrick, Sue, Tammy Jones and Margaret Barrett. 2006. "Learning through Research: A Regional University and Its Community." *International Journal of Pedagogies and Learning* 2(2): 36–49. DOI: 10.5172/ijpl.2.2.36

Leibold, Marius, Gilbert Probst and Michael Gibbert. 2007. *Strategic Management in the Knowledge Economy: New Approaches and Business Applications*. Erlangen: John Wiley & Sons.

Levin, Douglas and Sousan Arafeh. 2009. "The Digital Disconnect: The Widening Gap between Internet-Savvy Students and Their Schools." http://www.pewinternet.org/reports/pdfs/PIP_Schools_Internet_Report.pdf.

Livingstone, Sonia. 2008. "Internet Literacy: Young People's Negotiation of New Online Opportunities." In *Digital Youth, Innovation, and the Unexpected*", ed. by Tara McPherson, 101–121. Cambridge, MA: MIT Press.

Mansell, Robin, and Uta When (eds). 1998. *Knowledge Societies: Information Technology for Sustainable Development*. Oxford, UK: Oxford University Press.

Peck, Craig, Larry Cuban and Heather Kirkpatrick. 2002. "Techno-Promoter Dreams, Student Realities." *Phi Delta Kappan* 83 (6): 472–480.

Pinker, Steven. 2002. *The Blank Slate: The Modern Denial of Human Nature*. New York: Viking.

Pinkwart, Nils, and Bruce M. McLaren (eds). 2012. *Educational Technologies for Teaching Argumentation Skills*. Oak Park: Bentham.

Precht, Richard David. 2013. *Anna, die Schule und der liebe Gott*. Muenchen: Goldmann.

Slotta, James D., and Hedieh Najafi. 2013. "Supporting Collaborative Knowledge Construction with Web 2.0 Technologies." In *Emerging Technologies for the Classroom*, ed. by Chrystalla Mouza, and Nancy Lavigne, 93–112. New York: Springer. DOI: 10.1007/978-1-4614-4696-5_7

Smith, Ken G., Christopher J. Collins, and Kevin D. Clark. 2005. "Existing Knowledge, Knowledge Creation Capability, and the Rate of New Product Introduction in High-Technology Firms." *Academy of Management Journal* 48 (2): 346–357. DOI: 10.5465/AMJ.2005.16928421

Swedin, Eric G., and David L. Ferro. 2007. *Computers: The Life Story of a Technology*. Baltimore: Johns Hopkins University Press.

Weigand, Edda. 2010. *Dialogue: The Mixed Game*. Amsterdam: John Benjamins publishing company. DOI: 10.1075/ds.10

Zuboff, Shoshana, and James Maxmin. 2004. *The Support Economy: Why Corporations are Failing Individuals and the Next Episode of Capitalism*. New York: Penguin.

Zuboff, Shoshana. 1988. *In the Age of the Smart Machine: The Future of Work and Power*. New York: Basic Books.

About the authors

Alexander Bartel studied information systems at the Kempten University of Applied Sciences, Germany. He continued with a research master program in electrical engineering at the Coburg University of Applied Sciences, Germany and joined the research project EVELIN in 2012. As a PhD candidate and a research fellow at the Kempten University of Applied Sciences, his research interests include gamification, mobile learning, (mobile) software architecture and application development for mobile devices.

Jurg Bronnimann has obtained his PhD in German Studies from Massey University in New Zealand. He has been working in the tertiary education sector for more than 20 years; in New Zealand, the Middle East and Australia. Before moving into the field of Teaching and Learning and Curriculum Development, he was a Senior Lecturer for German language and literature and Programme Director for the BA with majors in German, Spanish, Chinese, Japanese and English. In his current role at Batchelor Institute of Indigenous Tertiary Education he is responsible for building organisational capacity and promoting and supporting the achievement of excellence in teaching, learning and engagement. Jurg is a reviewer for the Oman Academic Accreditation authority.

Jasper Doomen is a Lecturer in Law at Leiden University and has previously been active in the same capacity at Utrecht University. He holds an M.A. in Philosophy (Leiden University, 2003) and a J.D. (Utrecht University, 2005). His publications are mainly in the fields of Philosophy and Law.

Sebastian Feller obtained his PhD in English Linguistics from the University of Muenster in Germany. He is currently working for the Social Cognitive Computing Department at A*STAR Institute of High Performance Computing in Singapore where he designs socially intelligent educational technologies. In the past he taught as lecturer at the Department of English Studies at Majan University College in Muscat, Oman and at the Institute for General Linguistics at the University of Muenster in Germany. Sebastian also worked as a school teacher in Germany. He is board member of the International Association of Dialogue Analysis, which investigates dialog from an interdisciplinary standpoint and Assistant Editor for the Benjamins journal *Language and Dialogue* as well as the book series *Dialogue Studies*.

Paula Figas studied pedagogy and psychology at the University of Augsburg, Germany. Since 2012 she works as research fellow in the project EVELIN at the Kempten University of Applied Sciences and is participating in a PhD program at the University of Augsburg. Her research interests concern new learning methods in university context and especially the advancement of creativity of students.

Robert Foster is nearing the completion of his PhD in Computational Linguistics as a member of the Computational Linguistics group within the Research Institute in Information and Language Processing at Wolverhampton University. His research investigates methodologies for generating Multiple Choice Question test items (MCQs), including the application of Controlled Languages, Natural Language Processing, the definition of learning objectives and the relative merits of alternative formats of MCQs. Alongside his PhD studies Robert holds a full time post in industry, as the Manager of Computer Based Training Design for a UK Electricity Distribution Company.

Prof. Dr. Georg Hagel received his PhD in computer sciences from the Eberhard-Karls-University Tübingen, Germany. He is a professor for software engineering, software architecture, design patterns and requirements engineering. His research interests are patterns in software architecture and didactic of software engineering. He is member of the program committee of the special track Technical Didactic of Software Engineering at the IEEE EDUCON conference and of the special track Research and Development of the Embedded Software Engineering Congress.

Henk Huijser has a PhD in Screen and Media Studies from the University of Waikato in New Zealand. His research interests include Online Learning, Problem Based Learning, Learning and Teaching in Higher Education, Social Networking, and Media and Cultural Studies, and he has published widely in all these areas. Henk joined Batchelor Institute in June 2012 after two years at Bahrain Polytechnic in the Arabian Gulf, where he was a Curriculum Developer specialising in Problem Based Learning. He is Associate Editor for the *Journal of Peer Learning*, and a member of the College of Reviewers for *Higher Education Research & Development*.

Daryl Ku is a research associate with the Learning Sciences and Technologies academic group at the National Institute of Education (Singapore). His research interests is in user experience design, with a focus on technology-mediated learning experiences. He has conducted research involving adult learning experiences with technology.

Yiannis Laouris is a social and business entrepreneur, a neuroscientist and systems engineer working as Senior Scientist at the Cyprus Neuroscience and Technology Institute. He holds an MD and a PhD in Neurophysiology from Germany (Leipzig) and an MS in Systems and Industrial Engineering from the University of Arizona. He applied linear/non-linear digital processing to biological signals from experimental animals to study brain signals. He published several books, book chapters, over 60 peered-reviewed publications and > 160 conference papers. In the 90ties, he founded CYBER Kids (www.cyber-kids.net), a chain of franchised computer learning centers (numerous prestigious awards), which introduced IT in the lives of over 15,000 children and 10,000 adults in Cyprus and thousands in 7 other countries.

Jon Mason is a Senior Lecturer within the School of Education at Charles Darwin University in Australia. His professional career has focused on digital learning and information technology standardization and has included independent consultancy, managerial and academic roles within higher education, and senior executive roles for government agencies in Australia. He has served as Australian Head of Delegation to ISO/IEC JTC 1/SC36 on behalf of Standards Australia for over 12 years. He completed his PhD at Queensland University of Technology in education and has Masters Degrees in Knowledge Management and Cognitive Science.

Darlene Ciuffetelli Parker, PhD, is an Associate Professor in the Faculty of Education at Brock University, Ontario, Canada. She researches and uses narrative inquiry methodology to gain insight into the fields of teacher education, literacy, marginalized communities (poverty and schooling), and diversity. Darlene recently has received awards recognizing her teaching and research including: the 2013 recipient of *Brock University's Distinguished Teaching Award*; the 2012 international *American Educational Research Association* (AERA) recipient of the *Early Career Award of the Narrative Research Special Interest Group*, and; the 2012 *Faculty of Education Award for Excellence in Teaching* at Brock University.

Debbie Pushor, PhD, is an Associate Professor in the Department of Curriculum Studies at the University of Saskatchewan in Canada. In her program of research, Debbie has engaged in narrative inquiries into 'parent knowledge' and into 'parent engagement and leadership.' In her undergraduate and graduate teaching, Debbie makes central an often absent or underrepresented conversation about the positioning of parents in relation to school landscapes. Debbie is the recipient of the *Provost's 2013 Award for Outstanding Teaching* in the College of Education and of the Fall, 2013 *Master Teacher Award* in recognition of exceptional pedagogy and excellent teaching at the University of Saskatchewan.

Reynold Redekopp obtained his PhD in technology in education from the University of Oregon. He has taught at the middle years, senior years and university levels. His research interests include best technology practices in the classroom, our local and limited uses of the internet, and the persistence of technique in our cultures. He is a big fan of *Calvin and Hobbes*.

Seng Chee Tan is the Head of the Learning Sciences and Technologies academic group of the National Institute of Education (Singapore). His research interests include computer-supported collaborative learning and knowledge creation in education. He has conducted several intervention projects in Singapore classrooms using knowledge building pedagogy and has been working on building teachers' community for knowledge creation among teachers.

Ilker Yengin (PhD, University of Nebraska-Lincoln) studies the role of technology for learning and its impact on our emotions, cognition, as well as everyday academic life. His expertise focuses on the design of processes that enhance learners' motivation and deep thinking. Currently, he is a scientist for the Situational and Social Awareness (SSA) group of A*STAR Institute of High Performance Computing, Singapore. Yengin develops edutainment applications for a robotic tutor equipped with specialized hardware for teaching language.

PART I

A constructivist approach to dialogic teaching and learning

Knowledge as social construction

Education and our conversations about, with and through technology

Reynold Redekopp
University of Manitoba

This discussion of technology in education considers three aspects of dialogue. The first is a subtle dialogue where students and teachers negotiate the impact of the tacit knowledge inherent in the technology. Every technology carries a bias and has metaphors embedded in both the design and practical use. The second is the conversation we engage in as we try to shape the technology to do our bidding, and as we adapt to what the technology wants us to do. The third idea focuses on how we carry on our conversations with others through the technology and how the medium influences the message. The underlying question is how do we use the technology to move beyond fact gathering to deeper thinking?

1. Introduction

How did technology gain almost complete mastery of modern society? Technology removed its essence from the dialogue and substituted with a dialogue of things. Technology dialogue tends to be limited to new devices and their relative speed, size and current software.

At the most fundamental level technology has become invisible. It is not invisible due to the microscopic dimensions within a computer chip. Precisely the opposite; technology has become so immense and so ingrained into modern society that it is indistinguishable from air. So while the 'things' like computers, cell phones and the internet are ubiquitous, the real influence of technology, the driving force of modern society, has become such a given that it is essentially hidden.

Educators need to be aware of how the ideas of technology have permeated modern society so completely. They need to create a new dialogue with their students about the technological worldview. Teachers and students need to ask questions about technology that go well beyond how to use a new app and into how technology affects their thinking and view of life.

Once educators are aware of this aspect of talking about technology they can enter a dialogue with the technology. They will have some understanding of the negotiations we have with technology as we try to get it to do our bidding while, at the same time, we adapt to the impetus of the technology. Finally, this chapter examines our dialogue with each other through the technology and how the technology mediates and influences the message. These notions of dialogue are artificial distinctions created for the purpose of this discussion but in practice the lines separating them are not clear or straight. Dialogue is thereby conceptualized in terms of Weigand's (2010) Mixed Game Model (MGM), a holistic theory of dialogue which can cope with the complexities that we face in this context. Each part influences another both in theory and in practice and this discussion will attempt to examine both the epistemological and pedagogical implications. As Lopez (1988, 111) puts it,

> While we explore the issue of digital media and technology as it relates to education, youth, and Native America, we need to probe deeply into our own operating paradigm to understand fully what is required to nurture critically engaged youth that will not simply replicate the assumptions of our system, but will be engaged in culturally and locally relevant pedagogy.

What is technology? At its most basic: "If it's not nature, then it's technology" (Hlynka 2013), or as Arthur C. Clarke (1962, in 2013) put it, "Any sufficiently advanced technology is indistinguishable from magic." This discussion focuses on digital technologies as they seem increasingly 'magical' and further removed from our comprehension. This also tends to exempt them from meaningful discussion, which is a problem all its own. The technologies with the greatest influence on education are these digital technologies which are both an extension of previous ideas, but also show a power and influence all their own.

This is not a doomsday report. It is a critique and an attempt to open up seemingly restricted ideas for further dialogue and conversation. The intent is to inspire discussion about the technologies we use and to consider what ways they use us and how we in turn might use them to build better societies for more people. This conversation will be focused on three key themes: conversation *about* technology, conversation *with* technology and conversation *through* technology. The intent of this chapter is to focus discussion on each of these themes.

2. Conversation *about* technology: Technology changes how we think

Technology is not neutral: "We need to understand it as an influence. It doesn't just do what we ask. It tells us what we can do" Redekopp (2011). This is a difficult conversation to have because technology is so ubiquitous that it is part of our assumed environment, and like air or gravity, we find it difficult to frame the terms of reference for the discussion. It simply IS most of the time.

Winston Churchill (1941 in 2013) accurately stated that, "We shape our buildings, and afterwards our buildings shape us." We tend to think of our technologies as merely being 'tools' with which we can do as we please. However our tools have a purpose of their own and we yield to their purpose as often as they yield to ours. We tend to use new tools in all sorts of situations for which they were not intended, but our fascination with, and need to justify them propels us. We need only think of the child who gets a new hammer as a present – suddenly everything needs to be hammered. A pertinent education example of this symptom comes from PLPNetwork (2013), "Dropbox is more of a mega-utility than a simple tool. It begs you to think up new ways to use it, in and out of the classroom." If it's new, we must use it!

The influences of our technologies are usually subtler than this. The tacit knowledge imbued in them directs us and begins to shape our ways of thinking about the world and ourselves. The devices become a part of our language and we build our metaphors around them. From the perspective of the MGM, conversations about technology can be viewed as being embedded in a culture which is significantly shaped by technology itself. We need only think of the phrase "Google it" to see the power of our technology to shape our language and ideas. But these are still surface examples. We will explore some of the deeper aspects that influence our notions of knowledge, the environment, enculturation/globalization, democracy, and equity.

2.1 Knowledge and Ways of Thinking – what is valued and what is lost/devalued

A common assumption is that the only way to progress is through technology and the disciplines that support it:

> Everybody in this room understands that our nation's success depends on strengthening America's role as the world's engine of discovery and innovation. And that leadership tomorrow depends on how we educate our students today – especially in science, technology, engineering, and math.
>
> President Obama to a gathering of CEOs, scientists, teachers, and others. September 16, 2010 (in Crosby 2013, 1)

Jacques Ellul asks us to take a step back from the actual technology to consider the concept of 'technique' which he defines as "… the totality of methods, rationally arrived at and having absolute efficiency (for a given stage of development) in every field of human activity" (1964, xxv). For Ellul technique is not about the machines; it has taken over machines and is turning everything into machines/mechanisms. Technique is so pervasive and influential that it now limits scientific creativity by forcing it into prescribed patterns and purposes in the compulsive search for efficiency and the one best way. Technique defines the assumptions underlying our logic, how we plan, how we organize our communities, how we conduct our medical practices, how we run our businesses, how we conduct our wars. In other words, technique determines how we think – take President Obama's use of the engine metaphor as a clear example. Technique determines to a large extent what is valued and what is not valued.

Technology has a bias, a way of interpreting the world and a set of values that is primarily that of the developed world males who created the technology. Bias is not used pejoratively here. It is simply recognition that technology tends to enhance values such as short-term linear thinking, discrete bits of information, removal of emotion, decontextualized communication, deductive reasoning, objectivity, knowledge as transmission of facts, and individualism. It devalues long-term planning, tacit cultural knowledge, body language, the metaphorical nature of language, knowledge in context, a gestalt view – the whole is greater than the discrete pieces, and the emotional relationship of people with data (Bowers 1988).

Similarly, Aikenhead (1996, 220) lists the attributes of the science 'sub-culture' as: "mechanistic, materialistic, reductionist, empirical, rational, decontextualized, mathematically idealized, communal, ideological, masculine, elitist, competitive, exploitative, impersonal and violent." He compares these with Aboriginal views of science (p. 221): "thematic, survival-oriented, holistic, empirical, rational, contextualized, specific, communal, ideological, spiritual, inclusive, cooperative, coexistent, personal and peaceful." Notice that there are some strong commonalities, and Aikenhead uses to these to promote a new science curricula that tries to avoid a romantic view of Aboriginals peaceful coexistence with nature, but where Western science is interpreted within and guided by a more holistic and connected view of people and the environment.

The unquestioning acceptance of these hidden values lends an undue authority not only to content, but to the technology itself. We still see and feel that in our frequent response to information gathered from the Internet as opposed to print material such as textbooks. We question the value of information from sources such as Wikipedia where we might have access to the author, but still give complete authority to printed encyclopedias (or their online equivalent) even though we know nothing about their authors or the decision making that went into creating an article. We are beginning to identify the web sites that are authoritative; not surprisingly, they are the same ones that we relied on in print, radio and television – the corporate publishers and networks.

One of the significant losses of the values diminished by technology is the contextualization that is so important to our regular communication. We tend to value literacy and the written word over orality. Orality, spoken word or narrative, brings people the tacit knowledge that is critical to full communication: body language, tone, pace, place, humour, etc. We integrate verbal, cognitive and perceptual means in communication from the very beginning (Weigand 2010). There are attempts to imitate the tacit feedback with emoticons such as :) and :-(, bracketed comments, and text expressions such as LOL, but these serve better as reminders of the importance of context rather than adequate replacements (Turkle 2011, 158). These techno-attempts at more complete communication work best with the people we already know and have a shared in-person experience with because we can 'see' their hand movements and expressions and 'hear' their tone of voice and perhaps determine the nuances of sarcasm. We are familiar with these and we interpret what we read within the context of that personal experience.

Bowers (1988) observes that the computer's ability of enhancing the value of discrete bits of data and the ability to manipulate them is promoting yet again the power of literacy that we already find in books. He argues that knowledge is contextual. Knowledge is not independent. It is culture specific and culture bound and it is risky to impose one kind of knowledge into a different cultural situation. This autonomous view of knowledge leads us to believe in an objective reality where 'facts' are important, universal and unchanging. But didn't Pluto used to be a planet? We forget that facts are based on assumptions and a particular way of looking at the world.

The technological view of the world is based on the ideas of progress, speed, newer is better, science will find a solution, and more is better. But there are other ways of viewing the world. Deloria and Wildcat (in Lopez 2008, 114), contrast these ideas with values often found in indigenous societies, "The Western conception and practices of technology are bound up in essentially human-centered materialism: the doctrine that physical well-being and worldly possessions constitute the greatest good and highest value in life. Indigenous conceptions and practices of technology are embedded in a way of living life that is inclusive of spiritual, physical, emotional, and intellectual dimensions emergent in the world or, more accurately, particular places in the world." Lopez (2008) writes about native American tribes meeting the first Europeans and noting that their crucifixes did not have a circle around them. This indicated that the newcomers lacked a holistic view of the world and that their way of life was unsustainable. "By taking our cue from the Native insight on the use of cultural symbols, we could also learn to draw a circle around our cultural cross. For we would be remiss not to learn their valuable insight that technology without holism has disastrous consequences" (p. 124).

How can educators begin to open up a dialogue between technology and students? How do educators help students create a richer set of worldviews? Mander (1991, 49–50) provides some ideas of how to enter a conversation about the technology with his list of attitudes we should adopt about any new technology:

- Be skeptical of all claims of new technology.
- Assume guilty until proven innocent.
- Bear in mind that technology is not neutral or value free.
- Negative aspects are slow to appear and blinded by the attractions of the new and now.
- Look beyond your personal benefits to a more holistic view of its impact.
- How does the new technology fit into the larger technology web?
- Is the control of the technology local or centralized somewhere inaccessible?
- Consider things like isolation, crime, suicide, abuse (drug or economic), jobs, and culture change.
- Rejecting or containing a technology is possible – nothing is inevitable.
- Recognize technological worship for what it is.

None of these are beyond the scope of students at any level but educators must be willing to enter into this conversation with them.

2.2 Technology and control of the environment

Technology does not solve problems; people do. The social and ecological problems we face are problems that require human, political solutions, not technological ones but we need to perceive the problems differently.

Heidegger (1977, 15) describes the tight relationship between technology and science and the corresponding shift in values that results in seeing the earth as a resource or storage facility for our use rather than us being in a relationship with all life. The earth and its parts are simple raw materials. "Air is now set upon to yield nitrogen, the earth to yield ore, ore to yield uranium, for example; uranium is set upon to yield atomic energy, which can be released either for destruction or for peaceful use."

And so we exist in a consumer society distanced from the coltan mines in Zaire that produce, at the cost of many lives, some of the metals we need for our cell phones (Mbubi 2012). We are equally distanced from the piles of electronic waste in China that result from our discarded devices (Pelly 2008). But we believe that there is always a new technology on the horizon to address these problems. Pacey (1983) gives an example of this from an economics point of view: there are plenty of mineral resources available, but they get harder to extract. However, if the demand is there then prices will rise sufficiently to make it worthwhile and our technologies will find a way to do it. This "tells us a good deal about the fundamental beliefs of those who ... have a remarkable faith in technology, and accuse the scientists who foresee a crisis of scarcity of not understanding society, and in particular, of under-estimating the way human-inventiveness can respond to market forces" (Pacey 1983, 60).

Jerry Mander (1991) uses computers as an example of a technology whose long-term effects haven't been considered and which contribute to health issues, shifts in employment (displacement of people), valuing quantification, surveillance, centralization, and automated warfare. He gives a number of examples of how our explicit trust in the technology has had disastrous effects on the environment when computer models were relied on to set policy and quotas, and the advice of local elders was ignored.

Mander (1991) also documents the fight/plight of indigenous peoples against corporations, which are another form of technology. Corporations are a technology, or machine logic, developed to enhance the power of industry and commerce. These are supposedly value-neutral or amoral organizations, but by definition they are obliged to seek profits for their shareholders. This is their value system and this requirement demands competition and growth. Mander suggests that amoral in this context means being moral only about profit and growth and often immoral (or at least short-sighted) in the treatment of people, communities and the environment. Corporations have no responsibility to the local communities in which they work, or to the world as a whole. Mander then cites numerous examples where corporations (and the governments that support them) have broken treaties and driven peoples off their lands in the search for more resources and profits. We now even have corporations trying to patent life forms. The inability to question or properly discuss the role of corporations is further illustration of our acceptance of technique as the natural order. Corporations respond to two things; consumer demand and shareholders. We can educate students to think about these ideas and to engage corporations and our lawmakers in dialogue about changes to corporate structure that make them responsible for individuals, communities and the environment.

As Pacey (1983, 81–82) says:

> It is a great mistake to allow the myth that technology is value-free to blind us to these impulses and values. It is especially mistaken to regard these imperatives as inexplicable and deterministic. Few technologists will acknowledge the 'infixed, unrelenting fangs' that are often the source of their drive; few talk about existential joy. But the fact remain that research, invention and design, like poetry and painting and other creative activities, tend to become compulsive. They take on purposes of their own, separate from economic or military goals.

There is an ability to create a more global classroom. Are educators willing to engage in a dialogue with peoples whose lives have been drastically impacted by our technological drive? Do they have the frame of reference to enter into such a conversation? Do they have a choice?

2.3 Technology as enculturation and globalization

Postman (1995) asks,

> Who, we may ask, has had the greatest impact on American education in this century? If you are thinking of John Dewey or any other education philosopher, I must say you are quite wrong. The greatest impact has been made by quiet men in grey suits in a suburb of New York City called Princeton, New Jersey. There, they developed and promoted the technology known as the standardized test, such as IQ tests, the SATs and the GREs. Their tests redefined what we mean by learning, and have resulted in our reorganizing the curriculum to accommodate the tests.

In education we have certainly been enculturated to this testing point of view. We have bought into the idea that standardization is important and that whatever is measured efficiently is important. Education movements continually attempt to move beyond the kind of testing and measurement that Postman describes but constantly encounter the resistance of technique and its promise of accuracy and efficiency. And it certainly is accurate and efficient in what it purports to measure. Standardized tests are less expensive and more consistent in measuring across disparate groups of students, but the scope of what is measured is so limited. (Standardized Tests ProCon 2013) And while educators want to assess more than facts, that is so easily done with tests, and is so convenient that little progress happens. We are not prepared to pay the price in terms of time or money, and so we remain stuck in the world of 'technique' in assessment. The education audience or stakeholders (parents and administrators) desire measurable, comparable results that focus on economic value.

As I have expressed previously,

> The way of thinking currently represented in the images, texts, curricula and organizational structures of education, is that individuals are free to use data or information to think in any manner they choose. This is not how teachers experience the reality of teaching however; they are aware of a variety of influences on the thinking of each student. From this experiential basis, the view of the student (and teacher) as a social and cultural being seems inherently obvious. On the other hand, in the practice of teaching, the teacher's experiential knowledge conflicts with the idea of the rational individual that is embedded in the images, texts, curricula and organizational structures of education. (Redekopp 1990, 48)

The process of enculturation can be briefly summarized as:

- Authority – the operations of most of our devices are now beyond our comprehension and so we ascribe to them an authority because of their mystical nature and ability to please us.
- Language – specialized terminology lends an authority to a culture or discipline and the people who are able to speak the language. This also includes the metaphors that we develop using the new technology as the model.
- Literacy – we develop dependencies on anonymous authorities shifting from textbooks to Google searches.
- Problem Definition – since it is difficult to challenge technology in any meaningful way we find ourselves only able to define problems using the language and tools of our technologies.
- Process – the rituals and models of using technology limit what we consider to be important and what can be questioned, especially concepts so ingrained as the nature and value of time, work, freedom and democracy.
- Tools and models – we tend to focus our investigations on what our tools and models allow us to do; a tool first mentality.

Nathan Ensmenger (2012) notes the infiltration of technique into our language for describing ourselves and placing us within the technique model. Our metaphors, in part, determine our approach to solving. The metaphors become our reality.

> Lily Kay, among others, has documented the ways in which concepts from computer science and information theory disseminated throughout the biological sciences in the late twentieth century. It is now commonplace, for example, to talk about the human genome as a code to be decrypted, the brain as a neural network, and disease as a "subspecies of information malfunction or communications pathology." These are not mere metaphors, but statements about ontology. As the noted biologist Richard Dawkins described it, "genetics has become a branch of information technology. The genetic code is truly digital, in exactly the same way as computer codes. *This is not some vague analogy, it is the literal truth.*" For many working in the modern biological sciences, living cells are not *like* computers – they *are* computers. While the long-term utility and durability of this computational turn in biology might still be an open question, the existence of the phenomenon is undeniable.

Unless educators and their students become aware of the enculturation process of technique and the power of metaphor, the knowledge they are constructing will be insufficient to deal with the problems they will encounter.

2.4 How technology interferes with democracy

> Technique cannot be otherwise than totalitarian.
> Everything is its concern.
> (Ellul 1964, 125)

Darin Barney (2007) in his lecture, *One Nation Under Google*, makes the case that when you can't question something, it is no longer democratic, it is fundamentalist. We must set the goals of education without the influence of technique and technology and only then examine their relative worth and possible contributions. Barney maintains, "Citizenship, like science and technology, is a way of knowing and acting, a way of being in the world, a practice" (2007, 11). But while we think that more access to information is automatically a good thing, we find that increased access is mainly used for "spectacular entertainment; docile recreation; habituation to the rhythms of capitalist production and consumption; cultural normalization" (p. 21). As a result we cannot equate access to information with better quality citizenship. If we think of technology as being apolitical we cannot enter into a dialogue about the direction it is leading us.

And if greater access to technology and information supposedly enhances citizenship and participation in democracy, it is interesting to note that in Canada (Elections Canada 2012) voter turnout in federal elections generally remained at about 70% from 1945 until 1988 and then dropped precipitously to 60% in 2011, and by far the lowest turnout in 2011 were the age groups of 18–24 (39%) and 25–34 (45%), presumably the most connected of all groups. Results in the United Kingdom (UK Political Info 2011) are similar, dropping to 60% in 2001 but rising to 65% in 2010. Idea.int (2013) shows voter turnout for most countries and while in some, Australia and Belgium, voter turnout levels remain constant, many countries with high levels of access to information such as France, Finland, United States, and the Republic of Korea have seen remarkable drops in voter turnout. Access does not seem to equate to active citizenship in terms of voting. Educators can have an influence on how students view their role in a democratic society. Barney's ideas can give us some insight into the need for creating politically motivated and involved citizens.

Barney also refers to Andrew Feenberg's assertion that "technology should be considered a new kind of legislation, not so very different from other public decisions" (p. 24). Barney makes the case that citizens are never asked which technologies should be created or funded by their tax dollars. He makes a list of questions that we might ask – not so different from Mander's list:

> And what questions might you have about these technologies? What are the possible unintended consequences? Will some people benefit more than others? How could they possibly know? And what venue would be right for asking these questions? An election? A committee meeting? An online opinion poll? The challenge that technology poses for citizenship is not just that we do not treat technology as an object of political judgment, but that it is difficult to imagine how we possibly could. (pp. 25–26)

Barney suggests that the general population, although they may not understand the technical details, can make sound judgments about the direction of technological development and should be involved in decisions about "design, development and regulation of technology" (p. 23). "The alternatives are the fundamentalism of technology, or the fundamentalism of its opponents" (p. 45). Educators have an opportunity to teach students about the need for this dialogue and hopefully avoid these divisive either/or scenarios.

Mander (1991) also argues along these lines. While there are some benefits for individuals using the technology, we need to look at who benefits most from any technology. For example, the internet brings access to information and the ability for individuals to express themselves, but brings much greater freedom of speech for the wealthy. And while we argue that the internet is free, it **most** certainly is not free either in terms of money (cost of computers, internet access) or in terms of web savviness (Search engine optimization, design, word crafting, use of images, ad revenue generating, etc.). Mander argues that we need to have open debate about the true costs of technologies that are introduced to us – not just one-sided advertisements extolling their benefits.

Fowler (2000) summarizes Ellul's view of technique and democracy in this way:

> Technique became the defining force, the ultimate value, of a new social order in which efficiency was no longer an option but a necessity imposed on all human activity. Technique became universally totalitarian in modern society as rationalistic proceduralism imposed an artificial value system of measuring and organizing everything quantitatively rather than qualitatively. Like cancer in a living organism, the systematization of technique pervades every cell of our modern technical and technological society.

Similarly, Postman argues that, "When a technology become mythic, it is always dangerous because it is then accepted as it is, and is therefore not easily susceptible to modification or control."

Educators can help their students demythologize technique and perhaps engage their students in the political process as full participants.

2.5 Technology and equity

To discuss equity and digital technologies Mander's (1991) key question is, "Who benefits most?" Is it individuals, aboriginals, corporations, local businesses or governments?

We tend to look at how we benefit from technology as individuals rather than look at societal impacts. Technology allows the larger social/environmental impact to be hidden or distanced from the individual and while technology can bring us images and video and facts from these distant places, we are still viewing the problem at a distance. It is still a problem in someone else's backyard and therefore easily forgotten in our daily routines.

A summary of Neil Postman's (1998) "Five Things We Should Know About Technological Change:"

1. There is always a trade-off – we gain and we lose.
2. Things are never distributed equally.
3. Embedded in every technology is at least one very powerful idea (often hidden)
   "The writing person favors logical organization and systematic analysis, not proverbs. The telegraphic person values speed, not introspection. The television person values immediacy, not history. And computer people, what shall we say of them? Perhaps we can say that the computer person values information, not knowledge, certainly not wisdom. Indeed, in the computer age, the concept of wisdom may vanish altogether."
4. "A new technology does not add something, it changes everything."
5. A new technology tends to become 'mythic' or larger than life.

So what are educators to do? Begin the conversation by making students aware that there is a conversation to be had. Creating a space for questioning and dialogue within all of our curricula about the bigger questions is critical. What kind of society do we want? What are our foundational priorities? Where have these come from? Will these priorities be sustainable in terms of politics, lifestyle, the environment? How do we try to set long term goals in democracies when we hold elections frequently and politicians use short term incentives to get elected?

These are high level discussions which don't have ready made answers and which should first be discussed without reference to technology. This is more than just a math word problem in a textbook where two trains meet at some fictitious place or creating a work of exploratory art. This is more than a Google search can answer. This is not just a topic for social studies or language arts. The influences are found in math and science and art and physical education – our values are evident in all of these. What are some of the questions we should ask?

In terms of what kind of society do we want we perhaps need to make students and ourselves aware that "... the structures of our world and its real norms represent diametrically the opposite" [of brotherly relations]. The fundamental rule of today is the rule of economic, political, and class competition." (Ellul 1964, 333). We need to be aware of the consequences of making decisions based on the short-term goals of these priorities. This is difficult work. Whether a teacher or education system chooses to approach this from a radical viewpoint or not, these conversations are critical.

There are broad questions that we should ask to facilitate this dialogue. Neil Postman (1998) suggests the following:

> The questions, then, that are never far from the mind of a person who is knowledgeable about technological change are these: Who specifically benefits from the development of a new technology? Which groups, what type of person, what kind of industry will be favored? And, of course, which groups of people will thereby be harmed?

There are diverse points of view that we can consider. One is the impact on women, in developed nations and in developing nations. Some laud the anonymity of the internet as an equalizer for women to express their views without prejudice. And although women do have greater access to publishing, publishing anonymously seems eerily similar to female writers who had to use masculine pseudonyms to be published and taken seriously.

An example of women and the influence of technology in the developing world comes from Anoja Wickramsinghe (1993, 59) who writes about the meaning of women's daily efforts in Sri Lanka. "Technologies that have been developed and used in the past by women were not meant to be "labour saving," but were primarily aimed at (1) eliminating drought-induced shortfalls of food availability; (2) ensuring the diversity of food supplies; (3) efficiently using products which are available in large quantities during specific seasons; (4) facilitating the storage of the products." But when more modern technologies came along, control of these was given to the men and their goals became more outward looking and more in line with the goals of economics. And Wickramsinghe observes that "The social and environmental changes that are taking place in these communities have not improved the lives of women" (61).

As mentioned early this is not intended to be a condemnation of technology as we currently understand it. As Aikenhead (2006, 4) states, "Eurocentric Western ST [science and technology] is a powerful predictor of events in several contexts of natural phenomena, which makes it an attractive tool for medical, industrial, corporate, and military interests." This needs to be balanced by a broader perspective that values multiple points of view if we are to make progress in creating the world we want.

> Thus, future scientists and engineers need a foundation in a rich, culturally diverse ST education because if they continue to try to solve today's problems with the same kind of thinking that caused the problems in the first place, the quality of life on this planet is in jeopardy. (p. 4)

And so, in terms of science education for First Nations Canadians, Aikenhead (2002, 10) proposes establishing an aboriginal viewpoint of the natural world as part of any science unit. He describes how aboriginal youth must move among various ways of understanding the world. We have noted the attributes of modern science and technology, but aboriginal students must also negotiate with another worldview which emphasizes a relationship with the natural world, that relies on observation more than experimentation, that sees progress as cyclical rather than linear. Aikenhead calls these cultural border crossings and notes that while this should benefit aboriginal students, it should equally benefit those students who are so immersed in the technological society that they need a more balanced worldview.

After the unit is firmly grounded in an Aboriginal framework (accomplished in one to three lessons), the next move is to introduce students to relevant Western science content from the Saskatchewan [Canada] science curriculum. An introduction to Western science content is an explicit border crossing event into a different culture. This cultural border crossing is acknowledged by *consciously* switching:

1. values (e.g. from harmony with nature, to power and domination over nature),
2. language (e.g. from mahihkan to *Canis lupis),*
3. conceptualizations (e.g. from "Who is that animal?" to "How is it classified?"),
4. assumptions about nature (e.g. from the observer being personally related to what is observed, to the observer being objectively removed), and
5. ways of knowing (e.g. from holism to reductionism). (p. 296)

Equity does not mean internet access for all or a computer in every classroom. Equity has to respect difference and a true attempt to understand difference and how it may enable educators and students to embrace and act with multiple views of the world.

President Obama described success in terms of science, technology, math and engineering. This definition of success is insufficient as it is based on the assumptions of technique that are creating many of the most serious local and global problems our students will face. These assumptions cannot stay hidden and out of reach of classroom discussions. Teachers and students need to be engaged in conversation about technique and about alternate worldviews if they are to become reengaged in the political process and begin to solve some of the world's dilemmas.

3. Conversation *with* technology: Trying to negotiate with and control the technology

We tend to recognize obliquely the biases, limits and tendencies of our technologies discussed in the previous section. Primarily we see them in our expectations, disappointments and frustrations. These frustrations are not only with getting the right device or getting it to function the way it was advertised, but also in our overarching search for all that technology promises but never quite delivers: where is all that extra leisure time or effortless learning? We also see it in the unintended problems that the technology creates: pollution, abuse of natural resources, health issues. And yet we find it hard to question the assumptions of our technology and remarkably continue to struggle to make it be the dream that we expect it to be. In many ways we try to address these issues indirectly by working incredibly hard and creatively to restore the things we lost by adopting the technological way. To understand this process we need a brief exploration of the development of digital technology.

3.1 Design drives the logic and bias of technology

We often forget (or never knew) that computers brought into prominence the use of another mathematical language (or number system) called binary (base 2), which coordinates easily with another system called hexadecimal (base 16). The use of base two was required because computers were developed with only the two states of actual light bulbs; 'on and off' or 'zero and one'. This is both an extension, and reinforcement of our dualistic way of thinking. Since the first computers were designed to calculate quickly and help break code, the logic system that was therefore developed was simple and designed to accomplish those purposes. There is no 'malicious intent' on the part of the designers to impose dualistic thinking on users, but this is the bias built into the machine. The values of the digital machine are speed, computation, facts and discrete bits of information (things that are computable). One only need look at a low-level language such as Assembly (Swanson 2013) to understand this. There is a very limited set of commands – only 10 areas – designed to manipulate numbers.

The design devalues factors such as context and emotion since these are much harder to quantify. Computers were designed and used by large corporations and the military to manipulate data but moved into the mainstream. With them came these inherent values and enhanced ideas of efficiency and centralized data collection, analysis, and decision-making. There was also a huge emphasis on the value of text since images, music and video were not possible.

The other factor of note is the development of ARPANET, the US precursor of the internet. A result of the cold war, this network connected the military with research institutions in a distributed manner so that a nuclear bomb hitting one node would not bring down the whole network. This network became the basis for the current Internet, and was originally expanded for the distribution of scientific research. Tim Berners-Lee saw the need for a language designed to make this scientific exchange easier and more consistent. Thus he created HTML (Hyper-Text Markup Language). HTML is a simple framework and the design elements include basic text functions such as headings, sub-headings, tables, superscript and subscript; all the elements needed to write and read scientific papers. The point is that the 'web' was not created for the average home user or student.

Building the basis of the "Information Society" and the current internet has been a Herculean task for those who wanted to create an Internet for the 'masses.' The developers took a very limited system, designed for very specific purposes and made it interesting and relatively easy for the common person to use. They have been adding layers onto this limited, and limiting, structure. And while the upper levels of the structure have adapted somewhat (HTML is now in version 5) the underlying processes are the same. What is most interesting is what these developers have been trying to produce. They are trying to replicate all the things that the original designers were trying to eliminate. Social media and Web 2.0 are attempts to restore all that was lost – images, audio, video recording and live video. They are attempting to find ways to reproduce aspects of the tacit knowledge that numbers and text do not communicate. They are jerry-rigging the technology to overcome the limits of the technology. This need, which is fundamental for natural language use (Weigand 2010, 85), has been evident even in the text-only stage where we use emoticons to try and express emotions or use easily misinterpreted abbreviations such as LOL (Laugh Out Loud, sometimes awkwardly misconstrued as Lots Of Love). Interestingly these attempts at restoring the tacit knowledge work best among real friends who have personal experience with each other. They are able to interpret the symbols because they can 'hear and see' the person behind the text. Video conferencing restores some of the pace, tone and facial expressions that are lost in text, but someone else is always choosing (consciously or not) the time, place, and camera angles.

In the process of these rapid attempts to make things work in this layering scheme, the standards that are set are less than optimal but often get locked in. Lanier (2010) is a strong advocate for good design. One of his examples of poor 'locked in' design is a common format for music, MIDI, developed in the early 1990's, which became popular and embedded, but was not a great design. It was however the first workable solution and so MIDI became the standard and a whole industry has been built around it.

What has not clearly emerged yet is a sense of where 'authority' lies in this new world of information. Academics are quick to condemn crowd-sourced knowledge sites such as Wikipedia. But the crowd seems to be quite willing to invest a measure of authority in these crowd-created information sites. In the areas of popular culture (and there are many other cultures) people find websites they have confidence in to help choose music, movies, hotels and online shopping sites. In other areas, such as news, editorial opinion and current affairs, they tend to turn back to the web-based version of the same sources that they relied on previously; the websites of newspapers and TV and radio networks. Our notion of authority has become rather fluid, shifting according to popularity, personal relevance, search engine rankings, and some old habits.

3.2 Technology steers the conversation to facts

Facts are a priority – technique demands this.

Currently, for most people, dialogue with computers is limited to simple questions and answers using search engines such as Google, Yahoo or Bing. Most of the questions are fact seeking, from the lower orders of Bloom's taxonomy, and are for immediate and temporary use. The internet and our related devices are fantastic at finding bits of information to answer our fact based questions such as:

- Where is Bangalore?
- What is the exchange rate from Euros to Yen?
- When does my train leave?
- How much is a ticket?
- Who is the president of Angola?

But these are primarily needed only for travel, a dinner conversation or crossword puzzle and do not have a context in which we might embed them. They are quickly lost. This does not diminish their value for their intended purpose, but as educators we want our students to reach further and develop most robust ideas. Postman (1998) commented "the computer person values information, not knowledge, certainly not wisdom." And while Postman may have originally been pointing to the people developing and operating computers, we can now see this applied to the broader population and how they (we) have bought into the idea of these random pieces of information being valuable. And while they certainly are momentarily valuable to the individuals seeking them, they add little or nothing to our collective wisdom or ability to solve real political or social problems while adding enormous advertising revenues to corporations.

So how do we move from facts to knowledge and perhaps even to wisdom? If one of the inherent ideas embedded in technology is the value of discrete bits of information and problem solving on a micro level, what do educators have to do to balance this and incorporate this technological strength to our advantage?

3.3 Relationships are mediated by technology

For many, the internet and ability to access all this information is indeed instructional as they use the resources to learn how to do new things: play a musical instrument, sew an outfit or create a garden. Again these are valuable to the individual. We also join social groups where we meet friends and colleagues and fellow learners. But we tend to only read, watch and listen to what affirms our current beliefs, mindsets and biases. Will Richardson (2006), a noted American blogger and technology-in-education promoter states,

> Whether it's blogs or wikis or RSS, all roads now point to a Web where little is done in isolation. The biggest, most sweeping change in our relationship with the Internet may not be as much the ability to publish as it is the ability to share, connect, and create with many, many others of like minds and interests.

This is amazing, and a good start but our students need to go beyond simply reaffirming their current beliefs to develop a more enlightened view of their world. In Maslow's (1943) terms they are stuck at the level of 'Love and Belonging.' Internet isolation will not serve us well. And as Google, Bing, Yahoo and the other search engines try to personalize our searches to fit our interests, they are limiting our experience rather than enhancing it. Perhaps search engines should have a two-column results page with the second column entitled, "Here are some different/alternate views."

It would seem that we don't naturally seek out new ways of thinking. My own preliminary research with teacher candidates indicates that most of them limit their internet use to a few familiar places. They search for facts of immediate value, engage in their social networks with like-minded friends and predominantly read/watch news and get entertainment from very few sources. The only time they tend to move out of their comfort zone is when they have to do research for university courses or for work.

And while this co-construction of knowledge within our social networking groups is a fantastic way to learn, can we achieve this co-construction with those whom we don't know or with whom we disagree? Can we learn to explore different ideas along with others while not necessarily abandoning our core beliefs and values? Can we examine 'facts' but from different perspectives and interpretations – including math and science where we think there are no alternatives. Can we learn to dialogue with others using new metaphors to shift and enhance our thinking? Metaphor shifts are critical because as Schon (in Ortony 1979, 255) suggests, metaphors "have more to do with problem setting than with problem solving, more to do with ways in which we frame the purposes to be achieved than with the selection of optimal means for achieving them." Or as Einstein (2013) put it, "The significant problems we face cannot be solved at the same level of thinking we were at when we created them."

We still have a predilection for facts and not for a diversity of opinion. Again, part of the reason for that is in the nature of the machine. McLuhan (1964) stressed that "The medium is the message," and whereas the message of the TV might be, "Sit down, be quiet and watch me," the message of digital technology is, "never leave me, interact with me and embrace my speed and access to fact-type information." Students also have to cope with the operant conditioning reinforcement their devices provide which can make them extremely addicting.

Another example of the 'medium is the message' principle is found in multitasking. As computers have developed in processing capability, the ability to run multiple programs simultaneously and use multiple processors promotes the notion that multitasking for humans is a positive practice as well. In the computing world it is good practice. But whether you call it multitasking or continuous partial attention research has shown that it is not helpful for humans who need to accomplish a task that requires significant cognitive energy. Gallagher (2009) argues that what we pay attention to matters, and Small (2008) explains how our ability to perform on a task decreases significantly when we try to multitask. Small also points out that our ability to multitask is one of the last things to develop in childhood and one of the first to go in the very old. Not surprisingly those who are best at it are teens and young adults who can jump from task to task with very little recovery time as they resume a prior task, but their task performance still suffers when they multitask. Background music seems to be an exception and is often useful to block out other distractions.

So what is valuable for the functioning of a computer may not be as good for humans and yet we choose to embrace the metaphor for ourselves and think of it in positive terms. Certainly for mundane and routine tasks, multitasking is great. But building those routines and muscle memory takes a concerted effort somewhere along the way, and at that point multitasking is limiting. We need to help students sort out which is which and learn when to commit to a task.

A subtler example of 'the medium is the message' is how we are letting the technology redefine our social worlds. The notion of what teens and young adults mean by social interaction, friends and networks is being defined by the technology they use. Facebook, Google+, Twitter, LinkedIn and Diigo allow us potential contacts around the world that we never had the chance to work with previously, and the opportunity to expand our point of view. This appears to have enormous benefits, but also has the potential to isolate us from our immediate social scene, friends who can provide physical help, and the local networks we rely on to manage our day-to-day lives. Can we learn to balance these or do we end up like the extremely isolated people on the planet Solaria in Isaac Asimov's novel *Naked Sun* (1957)?

A final example of 'the medium is the message' can be found by exploring a concept that may have more of a positive aspect to it – sharing. Digitization, networks and the Internet promote sharing, legally or illegally. The technology makes it possible and now demands it of us. The technology is asking us to redefine sharing in terms of the capability of the machine: digitizing and sharing is possible therefore it must be done. Obviously this has caused much grief in the music, software, and movie industries, but has been an incredible benefit in the sharing of knowledge, research and opinion. The quality of what is being shared is often questionable, but those who promote sharing are willing to trust the crowd (and the search engines) to direct us to the best of the internet. The crowd will be the editors and judges of internet information and opinion and supposedly will lead us, through reviews, recommendations and links to the best material.

The crowd may work well for basic information but for student projects we already have problems dealing with all the information available and the time it takes to find the quality we expect. We do need to teach students how to 'converse' with a search engine, but we also need teachers and librarians (cybrarians) to help direct students to places that will stretch their point of view. To move from facts to knowledge students need guidance to find a number of differing views so that they move beyond the facts and a single interpretation of those facts. This will not likely happen without teacher assistance and intervention.

How do we educate students (and ourselves) about their conversation with the technology? Should we teach low-level programming to all students so they understand somewhat the dialogue between themselves and the machine? That seems a bit extreme, but we can engage them in a dialogue about the technological influences in their lives. Educators can also illustrate for them the way that technology tends to emphasize its value to the individual and how this can be a distraction to confronting societal issues and taking social action.

Educators may argue that they don't have time for this. But the increasingly popular concept known as the flipped classroom may give them some of the flexibility they need. In the flipped classroom model students watch the content videos at home instead of having teachers lecture during class time. Classes are then devoted to group work, problem solving and projects. This is an interesting approach in that it may allow for some class time to deal with bigger issues but it also highlights the human-machine conversation in a slightly different way. This dialogue includes the ability to take direct instruction (the video) and make it personal and interactive. The user can stop, skip forward or back, and take breaks. The student is asking questions that they might be reluctant to ask in class such as, "can you repeat that please, can you slow down, what does that mean again?" Watching videos they can ask the questions of the instructor without fear of looking foolish or slowing down the whole class while they take notes or need an idea repeated.

3.4 Actions for educators

Ultimately as we try to move from facts to knowledge and wisdom we need to work with students on understanding the strengths and limitations of their technologies.

- Students feel they have a bigger social world, but do not really if their bigger world is homogeneous.
- The internet is not 'colour-blind' or homogeneous. There is room for lots of cultural and social groups to thrive. Ethan Zuckerman (2010) illustrates this in his TED talk.
- Some tacit knowledge (facial cues, tone, tempo) is being reintroduced but we are still limited to what others choose to show.
- Access to lots of information is great, but students (and educators) need to learn to interpret that information through multiple lenses. We need to read, watch and listen to other points of view.
- A common language (currently English) is convenient, but also limits a conversation to the words and metaphors of that language.
- Sharing is great, sharing is risky.
- Multitasking is exhilarating but less effective.
- Technology is about rapid change. There are social, political, and environmental consequences connected to rapid change which students and educators should be aware of. Good examples are Bandi Mbubi's (2012) TED talk about the devastating effects of coltan mining in Congo and the CBS *60 Minutes* (2009) report on the poor disposal or recycling of our used gadgets in *The Electronic Wasteland.*

4. Conversation *through* technology: How we dialogue with each other using technology

Our ability to dialogue with others has changed dramatically since the mid 1990s through the use of digital technologies and the advent of high-speed internet, cell phones and tablets. We will discuss how technology mediates and filters our conversations in terms of distance, time, and audience.

4.1 Distance

Our ability to communicate with people around the world at any time is phenomenal on a personal and professional level. The digital age has eliminated many of the barriers from global communication for many of us. Physical distance is hardly an issue when there is internet access or a cell phone connection. A classroom can now easily connect to classrooms around the world leading to a call for a global or flattened classroom. There is no doubt that this gives students a wonderful opportunity to learn about different cultures as they exchange text, view images, share video and hear voices. This is not the genuine experience but does allow for amazing collaboration among groups of students to create projects and to collect and share data as well as local interpretation of the data. In many ways this can enhance the point of view of all the participants.

This begs the question of who benefits most from the supposed removal of distance barriers. Even within the context of classrooms, is what we are sharing a new form of imperialism as we introduce a first world way of life and consumption to students in developing countries? Is the very nature of using the technology to minimize distance and time an intrusion into a different way of perceiving the world? Are we introducing a false sense of urgency and highly structured time into a culture that may not measure or value time in the same ways? These are not questions that should stop educators from creating global experiences for their students. They should be questions to reflect on with students as they participate in flattening the classroom.

4.2 Time

Time can still be an issue, but time differences can be managed through convenient scheduling or using asynchronous communications. Asynchronous, or one way, communication such as texting, email and posting content on web pages means that information can be sent or posted without necessarily disturbing the receiver. This is reminiscent of regular mail or newsletters, but now the distribution is instantaneous and the potential audience is immense. There is still a time lag between sending and when the audience may choose to view the content, but it is generally measured in minutes or hours rather than days, weeks or months.

Technology has also changed our ideas of the separation between in-class and out-of-class time. Students and educators participate in discussions that are extensions of class time, mainly through asynchronous technology such as texting, Twitter and the class web space. A significant benefit is that students who are reluctant to participate in live class discussions have the time, space and possible anonymity to allow them the confidence to contribute to the online dialogue (Redekopp & Bourbonniere 2009, 34). Students may be adding further insights or questions or sending links of relevant information, all of which can be collected and added to the pool of information. Sending thoughts and information when they occur rather than waiting for class reduces the chances of losing the ideas, but more importantly it means that students are in fact engaged in the conversation and trying to place the information they are gathering into a new context, perhaps moving them from facts to knowledge.

4.3 Audience

Technology has increased the speed at which we operate, but interestingly digital communication also allows users to potentially use time to hide behind their devices in ways that are impossible in face-to-face conversation. So while programmers struggle to bring more subtlety to our communication by reintroducing more visual and audio cues to our conversations, Sherry Turkle's (2011) research indicates that not all of our students are comfortable with that. She finds that a large number of students would rather text than use their phone. They deem texting to be safer because you are less likely to give away your true feelings or to make 'mistakes.' In a live conversation you don't always have time to think about your responses or control your body language. Some find this very disconcerting and prefer the time delay, lack of facial cues, and ability to edit when they are texting. If your significant friend says, "I love you" in a face-to-face conversation your body language and how long it takes you to respond is going to say more than your words. However if this message comes as a text, you have time, even if it is only a minute or two, to compose a measured response and you can even add an emoticon or text abbreviation to represent the body language and tone you wish to convey.

From another perspective this ability to hide behind the device, either through time lapse or through anonymity, affords many users the opportunity to express themselves in ways that they would never do in public. Setting aside momentarily the problems of rude or harassing comments, digital technologies, with their potential anonymity and time lag provide many students with the time and space to compose their thoughts and post them without the intimidation or time pressure that they feel in the classroom. Many students use this feature to participate in discussions and activities that they would avoid in public. Some test out different personalities on their social media sites to see what kind of reactions they get to the different personas or avatars they create.

Even in-class participation can sometimes be enhanced by anonymity or at least the ability to give your opinion without having to speak. Instant response through the technology is much preferred by students who will not regularly participate in classroom discussions. This is certainly a mediated dialogue, but does provide opportunities for many more students. Mark Sample (2010) writing on *The Chronicle of Higher Education* website, proposes a framework for teaching with Twitter that is applicable to other media as well (Figure 1). The framework highlights a movement from a passive, monologic use of technology to an active dialogic way of integrating technology into education. Students move from being strictly consumers of information to active contributors before, during and after class.

Dialogic	**In-class back channel** *Uses:* ad hoc class discussions, real-time commenting, recording divergent viewpoints *Benefits:* engages less vocal students, archives otherwise ephemeral comments	**Outside of class discussions** *Uses:* extend class discussions, exchange comments about readings or questions about assignments *Benefits:* community building, continuity between class sessions	**In-class directed discussion** *Uses:* Open or guided questions with student responses collected for later ananlysis *Benefits:* engages all students in discussions in large lecture classes
	Tracking activities *Uses:* find and follow instructor, experts in the field, or key topics *Benefits:* expossure to the larger cultural conversation about the class material	**Lightly structured activities** *Uses:* solicit course feeback, offer ambient office hours, poll class, language or writing practice *Benefits:* flexibility, availability, scalability	**Metacognitive/Reflective activities** *Uses:* students report in self learning, articulate their difficulties, recap the most valuable lesson of the day *Benefits:* fosters critical thinking
Monologic	**Institutional communication** *Uses:* community outreach, alerts, announcements	**Instructor communication** *Uses:* announcements, syllabus changes, reminders	**Pedagogical comuunication** *Uses:* sharing timely links and resources

Passive ← **Student activity** → Active

Figure 1. A framework for teaching with Twitter (by Mark Sample)

When we create opportunities for more students to participate, whether through in-class 'back channels' or through the ongoing post-class discussions we also are expanding the audience for our students. These alternate types of dialogue allow students to hear the 'voices' of classmates who never talk in class and expand their point of view to some degree. Further, for students to know that the work they create and submit online will have a wider audience than just their teacher can potentially increase their motivation and the quality of their work. This can be intimidating for some, but perhaps less so if educators practice the idea of posting one's work online as the beginning of a conversation on a topic where viewers get to comment and ask questions and the student is allowed to respond and adapt.

Also significant in the discussion of audience is the idea that technology, and especially the internet, is not 'colour-blind' or culture free. Students can tune their contributions to a particular group, whether it is a forum specifically related to aboriginal concerns, a particular genre of writing or a Twitter hashtag. In his TED talk Ethan Zuckerman (2010) provides statistics that show that while the US might have the most Twitter users, China and Brazil combined have as many Twitter users, and these two countries each have higher percentages of Twitters users among people who have internet access. Within the US, African-Americans are represented on Twitter nearly twice as much as their actual population in America. Zuckerman points out that on most days many highly trending topics are African-American topics and white Americans know nothing about these. "What happens on a social network is you interact with the people you have chosen to interact with" (3:38). But he points out that if we want to find out about other people's interests it is only a click or two away.

Lopez (2008, 110) writing about Canadian aboriginal education says,

> As advocates of digital media education, we understand that it is important to be cognizant of alternate modes of engagement, and to design programming that is appropriate and sensitive to these differences, not out of a tokenistic desire for multiculturalism, but out of a real engagement of difference that is positive and constructive.

4.4 Implications for educators

Students have very specific audiences for the content they produce and they will want to produce good content for that perceived audience. This means educators should give them more creative choice in presenting their ideas. They will want to use more than text and words. They will incorporate images, audio, video and animation. This doesn't diminish the importance of learning to write formal essays, but acknowledges that there are opportunities for more students to present their ideas in ways that work best for them. If educators want to know what students have really learned they will have to, at times, allow them more freedom to choose the medium and with whom they will collaborate.

Technology is sometimes seen as a possible replacement for memorization and fact recall. This is indeed a strength of technology at present, but this is not necessarily the best use of technology in education. Technology as a fact-replacement tool is much too limiting and does nothing to move students from facts to knowledge and wisdom. Educators can use the technology more effectively to encourage higher levels of thinking and student involvement. Some suggestions to promote these goals are listed below.

Some of the best uses of technology in education are:

1. Participation of those who voice is typically not heard in a regular classroom.
2. Allowing space and time for students to gather thoughts and communicate them – especially for the non-vocal, shy students.
3. Students being able to dialogue with the audio/video lecture; asking for the pauses, repetition and other questions that they would not ask in person.
4. Collaboration among students and with teachers.
5. Classes being collaborative and inquiry based if the flipped classroom model is used effectively.
6. Collecting facts and giving them a context. Constructing knowledge with the socio-cultural individual in mind.
7. Assessment – allowing students to demonstrate their learning through media other than writing.
8. Finding alternate viewpoints and alternate media assignments. Questioning the very technologies we use.
9. Creating work for a public audience and making more student work available for a broader audience to comment. This could be just students and parents or completely public.

Actions that should be minimized or avoided:

1. Over reliance on the technology – thinking everything has to be 'flipped' or recorded or done via technology. The technology bias leads us to a linear, context independent view of the world and problem solving.
2. Using audio/video in the purely 'transmission' mode of learning. Make it part of the dialogue.
3. 'Flipping' a classroom without making radical changes to in-class time. Class time has to be an active intentional problem investigation arena.
4. Throwing out the socialization and face-to-face communication aspects of education. Students need good real-time communication skills.
5. Confusing creativity with random, poorly composed ideas. Good content still matters.
6. Neglecting good organization and writing skills. Essays and other types of good writing are still necessary.
7. Devaluing a factual knowledge base. Having good information at hand is a necessary context for any good discussion or presentation.
8. Multitasking when an important task needs to learned or done. Learning and mastering new skills requires focus.

5. Conclusion

Technology dominates our way of thinking in the modern world. Dialogue is limited by the pervasiveness of the ideals of technique; they are as natural as air and simply a part of being. What's to discuss other than the odd irritation when one of our devices is too slow? As educators we need to bring these ideals of technique into the dialogue with our students – to allow them to talk *about* the technology.

The conversation *about* technology aides us in understanding our negotiation with the technology, trying to make our machines function more naturally while fighting the pressure to submit ourselves to the logic of the device. This is the conversation our students and we need to have *with* the technology – how do we get beyond the facts and linear thinking to those places of thought and wisdom?

Finally, educators need to develop a critical awareness of knowing how the technology shapes and partly defines our communication with each other. Technology mediates, influences and occasionally defines our conversations and relationships by the tools we create. Our dialogue with each other *through* the technology is not neutral. Students are capable of understanding this and educators must illustrate for students the various strengths and weakness of communicating *through* our devices as opposed to real-time interpersonal communication.

The technological way of thinking and problem solving has led to many great achievements and conveniences. It has also brought the earth to the brink of disaster. The larger question is whether educators are willing to enter into a dialogue with their students that considers the bias of technique and seriously considers alternative ways of thinking and problem solving to balance their worldview.

Educators can move their students from facts to knowledge by finding and collaborating with those who hold alternate worldviews. Awareness, not necessarily acceptance, of these dialogues is the beginning of the path to wisdom.

"Education no longer has a humanist end or any value in itself; it has only one goal, to create technicians" (Ellul 1964, 248). If Ellul is correct how are we to change this perceived goal, or perhaps better still, how can we create, not technicians, but enlightened, thoughtful citizens? We need to acknowledge our presence in a technological society, and we must move toward making it a society of conscious choice rather than one driven purely by the impulse of technique. We need to sustain the dialogues *about*, *with* and *through* technology.

References

Abumrad, Jad, and Robert Krulwich. 2009. "Numbers." *Radiolab*. http://www.radiolab.org/archive. (last date of access 26 March, 2013).

Aikenhead, Glen. 2010. "Cross-Cultural Science Teaching: Rekindling Traditions for Aboriginal Students." University of Saskatchewan. http://www.usask.ca/education/people/aikenhead/cjsmte.htm. (last date of access 26 March, 2013).

Aikenhead, Glen. 2006. "Science and Technology Education from Different Cultural Perspectives." *12th Symposium of the International Organization for Science and Technology Education*. Lecture conducted at the International Organization for Science and Technology Education, Penang, Malaysia, July 30, 2006.

Aikenhead, Glen. 2002. "Cross-cultural Science Teaching: Rekindling Traditions for Aboriginal Students." *Canadian Journal of Science Mathematics and Technology Education* 2 (3): 287–304. DOI: 10.1080/14926150209556522

Anderson, S. E. 1997. "Worldmath Curriculum: Fighting Eurocentrism in Mathematics." In *Ethnomathematics Challenging Eurocentrism in Mathematics Education*, ed. by A. B. Powell, and M. Frankenstein, 292–307. Albany: State University of New York Press.

Asimov, Isaac. 1957. *The Naked Sun*. Garden City, N.Y.: Doubleday.

Barney, Darin. 2007. "One Nation Under Google." *Hart House Lectures*. www.mcgill.ca/files/arts/barney_2007HartHouseLecture.pdf. (last date of access 29 March, 2013).

Bowers, Chet A. 1988. *The Cultural Dimensions of Educational Computing: Understanding the Non-neutrality of Technology*. New York: Teachers College Press.

Churchill, Winston. 1941. "Famous Quotations and Stories." *Welcome to WinstonChurchill.org*. http://www.winstonchurchill.org/learn/speeches/quotations. (last date of access 26 March, 2013).

Clarke, Arthur C. n.d. "Hazards of Prophecy." *KU Libraries Electronic Reserve*. www.sfcenter.ku.edu/Sci-Tech Society/futurists_hazards_of_prophecy.pdf. (last date of access 20 March, 2013).

Crosby, Brian. 2013. "Going Deep: STEM in the Connected Classroom." *Powerful Learning Practice*. http://plpnetwork.com/2013/03/15/time-stem-education-reform. (last date of access 21 March, 2013).

Einstein, Albert. n.d. "Einstein Quotes – Quotes by Albert Einstein." *Albert Einstein Site Online*. http://www.alberteinsteinsite.com/quotes. (last date of access 10 April, 2013).

Elections Canada Online. 2012. "Estimation of Voter Turnout by Age Group and Gender at the 2011 Federal General Election." *Elections Canada On-line – Élections Canada en ligne*. http://www.elections.ca/content.aspx?section=res&dir=rec/part/estim/41ge&document=report41&lang=e. (last date of access 30 March, 2013).

Ellul, Jacques. 1964. *The Technological Society*, 1st American edn. New York: Knopf.

Ensmenger, Nathan. n.d. "The Digital Construction of Technology." *eTC: About T&C*. http://www.techculture.org/2012_oct/etc_ensmenger.html (last date of access 29 March, 2013).

Fasheh, Munir. 1997. "Mathematics, Culture, and Authority." In *Ethnomathematics Challenging Eurocentrism in Mathematics Education*, ed. by A. B. Powell, and M. Frankenstein, 273–291. Albany: State University of New York Press.

Fowler, James. n.d. "A Synopsis and Analysis of the Thought and Writings of Jacques Ellul." *Christ In You*. http://www.christinyou.net/pages/ellul.html. (last date of access 22 March, 2013).

Gallagher, Winfried. 2009. *Rapt: Attention and the Focused Life*. New York: Penguin Press.
Heidegger, Martin. 1977. *The Question Concerning Technology, and Other Essays*. New York: Harper and Row.
Hlynka, Denis. 2013. "Thinking about Technology." *Teaching in the Senior Years*. Lecture conducted at University of Manitoba, Winnipeg, February 7, 2013.
International IDEA. n.d. *International Institute for Democracy and Electoral Assistance | International IDEA*. http://www.idea.int/vt. (last date of access 30 March, 2013).
Lanier, Jaron. 2010. *You Are Not a Gadget: A Manifesto*. New York: Alfred A. Knopf.
Mander, Jerry. 1991. *In the Absence of the Sacred: The Failure of Technology and the Survival of the Indian Nations*. San Francisco: Sierra Club Books.
Maslow, Abraham. n.d. "Classics in the History of Psychology – A. H. Maslow (1943) A Theory of Human Motivation." *Classics in the History of Psychology*. http://psychclassics.yorku.ca/Maslow/motivation.htm. (last date of access 12 April, 2013).
Mbubi, Bandi. n.d. "Bandi Mbubi: Demand a Fair Trade Cell Phone. Video on TED.com." *TED: Ideas Worth Spreading*. http://www.ted.com/talks/bandi_mbubi_demand_a_fair_trade_cell_phone.html. (last date of access 12 April, 2013).
McLuhan, Marshall. 1964. *Understanding Media; the Extensions of Man*. New York: McGraw-Hill.
Ortony, Antony. 1979. "Generative Metaphor: A Perspective on Problem-Setting in Social Policy." In *Metaphor and Thought*. Cambridge: Cambridge University Press.
Pacey, Arnold. 1983. *The Culture of Technology*. Cambridge, Mass.: MIT Press.
Pelley, Scott. 2009. "The Electronic Wasteland – 60 Minutes – CBS News." *Breaking News Headlines: Business, Entertainment & World News – CBS News*. http://www.cbsnews.com/video/watch/?id=4586903n. (last date of access 12 April, 2013).
Postman, Neil. 1998. "Five Things We Need to Know About Technological Change." *Neil Postman*. https://www.student.cs.uwaterloo.ca/~cs492/papers/neil-postman-five-things.html. (last date of access 22 March, 2013).
Redekopp, Reynold. 2011. "RR Sept 27 Response." *rredekopp*. http://rredekopp.pbworks.com/w/page/46258533/RR%20Sept%2027%20Response. (last date of access 26 March, 2013).
Redekopp, Reynold. 1990. *A Socio-Cultural Investigation of Long-Range Goals for Mathematics Education*. Eugene, OR: University of Oregon.
Redekopp, Reynold, and Elizabeth Bourbonniere. 2009. "Giving Reluctant Students a Voice." *Learning and Leading with Technology* 36 (7): 34–35.
Richardson, Will. 2006. "Tech Learning: The Social Web." *Classroom Technology News | Techlearning.com*. http://www.techlearning.com/features/0039/the-social-web/43387. (last date of access 6 April, 2013)
Sample, Mark. 2010. "A Framework for Teaching with Twitter – ProfHacker." *The Chronicle of Higher Education*. http://chronicle.com/blogs/profhacker/a-framework-for-teaching-with-twitter/26223. (last date of access 6 April, 2013).
Small, Gary W., and Gigi Vorgan. 2008. *IBrain: Surviving the Technological Alteration of the Modern Mind*. New York: Collins Living.
Standardized Tests – ProCon.org. n.d. *Standardized Tests – ProCon.org*. http://standardizedtests.procon.org/. (last date of access 21 June, 2013).
Swanson, William. n.d. "Introduction to Assembly Language." *Swanson Technologies*. http://www.swansontec.com/sprogram.html. (last date of access 8 April, 2013).
Turkle, Sherry. 2011. *Alone Together: Why We Expect More From Technology and Less From Each Other*. New York: Basic Books.

"Using Dropbox in the Classroom." n.d. *Powerful Learning Practice*. http://plpnetwork.com/2012/08/10/dropbox-a-superb-classroom-tool. (last date of access 20 March, 2013).
UK Political Info. 2011. "Voter Turnout at UK General Elections 1945–2010." *UK Political Info. Easy Access to Political and Electoral Data*. http://www.ukpolitical.info/Turnout45.htm. (last date of access 30 March, 2013).
Weigand, Edda. 2010. *Dialogue: The Mixed Game*. Amsterdam: John Benjamins. DOI: 10.1075/ds.10
Wickramsinghe, Anoja. 1993. "Women and Indigenous Technology." *Canadian Woman Studies* 13 (2): 59–61.
Zaslavsky, Claudia. 1997. "World Cultures in the Mathematics Class." In *Ethnomathematics Challenging Eurocentrism in Mathematics Education*, ed. by Arthur B. Powell, and Marilyn Frankenstein, 308–321. Albany: State University of New York Press.
Zuckerman, Ethan. 2010. "Ethan Zuckerman: Listening to Global Voices | Video on TED.com." *TED: Ideas Worth Spreading*. http://www.ted.com/talks/ethan_zuckerman.html. (last date of access 12 April, 2013).

Author's address

Reynold Redekopp
421 Education
University of Manitoba
Winnipeg, MB, Canada R3T 2N2
Phone: +1 204 474 9144
rredekopp@gmail.com

Understanding and explaining

Jasper Doomen
Leiden University

The quest to provide a fundamental understanding and explanation of reality is an ambitious one. Perhaps it is too ambitious. The possible restrictions for such an enterprise to be successful must be inquired in order to determine the issue. Section 1 explores one's understanding in reaching (scientific) conclusions: to what extent does a successful account testify to understanding? Section 2 focuses on the other side of such an account: does it provide an explanation in a more fundamental sense than pointing out causes of phenomena, or is it restricted to such a task? A critical stance vis-à-vis the (scientific) enterprise of unearthing reality's structure remains necessary in order not to confuse a consistent and productive theory with one that demonstrates an understanding and explanation in the sense of this article.

Introduction

A solid basis for a (scientific) theory in general and for learning in particular seems to require both understanding and explaining. One must understand one's findings, since otherwise the theory would be no more than a result one has stumbled upon, as if one were to express a correct reasoning in a language one does not master, merely being able to pronounce the phones, following the syllables' sequence without knowing the meaning of the words, not being able to acknowledge the reasoning's correctness. Philosophers and scientists are supposed to have a more extensive grasp on their fields than the straw man just mentioned, not acting as mechanically as he does. Likewise, a result haphazardly reached is not said to attest to an explanation: if a result is presented, it is not sufficient that it be correct; one must also be able to make it clear *why* it is correct.

In this article, the merits of what are considered to be understanding and explaining are critically examined in that the ability to grasp a meaning may be said to constitute a necessary condition for understanding, just as the presence of an account is a necessary condition for an explanation, but that in neither case a sufficient condition is provided for respectively an understanding and an explanation. In a modest sense, an understanding and an explanation *may* be said to occur, namely if one limits oneself to that which is empirically available. It would, however, testify to a somewhat superficial stance if one might thereby be considered to know how reality is constituted and what the fundamental reason behind a phenomenon is (unless the possibility for such 'deeper' accounts is dismissed, a possibility that is taken seriously in this article). Reality is rather co-constructed in dialog and the interlocutors negotiate their viewpoints on what might count as an explanation and an understanding (Weigand 2010, 43).

In order to distinguish between the sorts of understandings and explanations, 'understanding' and 'explanation' are used in the relatively unproblematic way outlined above and illustrated in Sections 1 and 2. By contrast, 'comprehensive understanding' and 'comprehensive explanation' will refer to a complete account, 'grasping' nature or reality, not limiting oneself to pointing out one or more causes of phenomena concerned with the epistemological abilities of actual beings. (That does not mean that this enterprise is entirely academic, by the way, for once the question is raised whether actual beings act on the basis of something else than factors – something I cannot imagine – those who would affirm this will need to make it clear how (if at all) this is possible (if it all).) Factors are the things that determine ('make'[1]) an action if nothing else is involved. This sounds somewhat abstract, perhaps, but that is in fact unavoidable, since I cannot, being myself factor-determined, indicate which factors are actually decisive. To nonetheless illustrate the matter, presuming that an object such as a stone that is pushed down a hill is fully determined by factors such as the impulse and its shape, the factors determine the stone's path.[2]

A stone is a relatively simple object, one may say, compared with animals and human beings. Strictly speaking, I do not know whether human beings, animals or even stones are factor-determined and know only myself to be of that nature (finding no faculty within me to act alternatively from a determined way, be it on the basis of innate or empirical factors or a combination of both). Still, for the sake of convenience, I will presume the agents mentioned in the present article to be factor-determined. Actors (putatively) acting in a non-factor-determined way, on the basis of what is sometimes called 'free will', is, for me at least, unimaginable, 'free will' only having a meaning if the freedom of movement of the will is expressed.

This means that the will can be focused on a great number of things, not being limited (which is where the freedom of movement becomes clear) in this respect.

1. 'Factor' originally (in Latin) means 'creator'.

2. It is clear that this is a tautological position. That is one of the reasons why I cannot say which beings (if any) besides myself are factor-determined.

That is something different, however, from 'free will', which is usually being used to express the agent's (as far as I am concerned incomprehensible) freedom in acting, 'freedom' meaning something else than the freedom of movement, which is, by contrast, of course easily acknowledged. There is (*ex hypothesi*) no way for such a being not to be factor-determined; if it should reach the same outcome as someone who comprehensively understands and/or is able to comprehensively explain, it has merely stumbled upon that result and does not really find itself in the required state.

A factor-determined being would, in order to comprehensively understand, have to be able to balance the factors themselves, which is of course only possible from a factor-free position, and this is precisely what is lacking. For example, if such a being has adopted some interpretation of quantum mechanics on the basis of an education process and the independent study of authors who promote it (or oppose it, in which case this being in turn opposes *their* interpretation), the education and the result of studying are factors, as is the way the being deals with these sources of information (which may itself be the result of one or more innate or cultivated factors). This being would have to reach a temporary state of suspension of judgment with respect to these factors, which means that it should reach a state in which their influence should – temporarily – be cancelled, and then have access to the means to acquire a comprehensive explaining and a comprehensive understanding. It may – in that case, again on the basis of one or more factors – be able to doubt its knowledge and the path that has led to it, but this will be insufficient to reach the desired result; the only result that is reached is this beings' acknowledgement of its own limitations.

This little excursion, which must now, because this is not a topic to be explored here in depth, be terminated, lest the reader should be left confused with respect to the main issues to be expressed here, was merely necessary to gain some clarity on agents' position when they set out to understand and explain matters. Should they not be considered factor-determined, their acts – and therefore judgments – would be completely inexplicable (and not only in the special sense addressed in the second section of this article).

In the remainder of the article, I will first, in Section 1, indicate what (scientific) understanding in reaching (scientific) conclusions means; comprehensive understanding is the crucial conception here. In line with what is observed there, Section 2 inquires whether a comprehensive explanation might be realized. Section 3 points out the consequences of these observations. From a practical point of view, no world-shaking results ensue; many scientific activities are not affected at all. Those who aspire to realize an account that fundamentally explains reality, however, must confront the objections presented here.

Understanding

Scientific theories usually receive their value upon being proved on the basis of experience; mathematical and logical theories are proved deductively. Two aspects with respect to this issue are addressed here. The first is the perspective of the scientist when (s)he validates a theory, or, in the context of teaching and learning, that of the learner. Do they 'grasp' some 'truth', and what does this mean? This issue will be explored in the present section. The second is the proof's merit, dealt with in Section 2. To differentiate, I will use 'comprehensive understanding'[3] to indicate the grasp of reality and 'understanding' to indicate the ability to use theories.

What does someone's understanding something mean? Is this to be taken to reflect a 'grasp' of reality in that one knows how part of reality is constituted? I will argue that understanding rather means that one is able to utilize theories for some goal, without thereby penetrating fundamentally into reality, considering it as it is in itself (Kant 1781/1787, A 42/ B 59; B 303), whatever that may mean. Even if a theory should in some way reflect reality (in itself), it would still not be clear to the observer why reality is constituted thus and not alternatively. In this sense, understanding remains the output of processes of dialogic negotiation, in which knowledge is co-constructed between the dialog partners (Weigand 2010, 72, 272). Dialog may range from intra- to interpersonal. From this point of view, thinking is also a type of dialog, in which we communicate with different voices within ourselves.

The best examples to start with are logic and mathematics. What is it that one comprehensively understands (i.e., what occurs apart from being able to use the theory) if one knows that contradictions cannot occur, in line with the principle of contradiction, expressed by the formula '$\neg (p \wedge \neg p)$'?[4] It is clear[5] that one needs this information to be able to produce a valuable account at all; if one should, for example, argue that a stone that lies on top of a hill when pushed will both roll down the hill and at the same time remain where it now is, this would result in a theory that would not exclude any outcome and thus be without practical value. After all, if a theory is to be of any use, it must indicate which outcomes can be used, which simultaneously means that it must indicate which alternative outcomes must be dismissed.

3. Avoiding the more poetic but perhaps less clear alternative 'comprehensive comprehension'.

4. This principle is, incidentally, compromised (or at least not evident) on the basis of the existence of alternative views, which acknowledge the existence of contradictions (e.g., Priest 1989, 141).

5. I do not, of course, myself hereby express the occurrence of a comprehensive understanding.

Quantum mechanics does manifest a number of results that conflict with basic logic (e.g., Schrödinger's paradox (Schrödinger 1935, 812)), but whether one should therefore give up some of the laws of logic or part of quantum mechanics (or at least reject some interpretations) – whether such a choice must be made at all depends again on the question whether one should adhere to the principle of contradiction, so the question may not have been put fairly thus – is something to be decided on the basis of other factors than comprehensive understanding (and rather by, e.g., the desire to have a consistent account).

Does someone who understands the necessary exclusion of mutually contradictory propositions comprehensively understand why this is the case? No. Their simultaneous occurrence simply doesn't work: it fails to produce viable results.[6] Besides, if one were to comprehensively understand why it is the case, alternative accounts would *a priori* have been refuted. In mathematics, one cannot penetrate beyond the first definitions and axioms that must be posited, such as those in Euclid's *Elements*. There is no comprehensive understanding here, either: the insights – if one wants to use that term – are not confirmed by a comparison with reality, since no such comparison is available.

This can perhaps best be illustrated on the basis of the (initial) position of Wittgenstein,[7] sometimes designated 'logical atomism', a theory whose scope is not limited to that of mathematics, but includes it. Wittgenstein states that one must compare a picture with reality in order to come to know whether the picture is true or false (Wittgenstein 1921, 2.223). Reality is the existence and nonexistence of states of affairs (Wittgenstein 1921, 2.06), while the world is the whole of the *existing* states of affairs (Wittgenstein 1921, 2.04) (the whole of facts (Wittgenstein 1921, 1.01, 2, 2.04)), which entails the (idiosyncratic) position that reality comprises more than the world, a difficulty that is increased by the statement "The complete reality is the world." ("*Die gesamte Wirklichkeit ist die Welt.*") (Wittgenstein 1921, 2.063.) The difference in scope between 'reality' and 'the world' is apparently not maintained here.

This contradiction is difficult to account for, but, more importantly, it is propagated that a fact and a picture must have something in common for a fact to be a picture (Wittgenstein 1921, 2.16; cf. 2.12: "The picture is a model of reality." (*Das Bild ist ein Modell der Wirklichkeit.*). That means that reality is approached in a

6. Cf., in a different context, Rorty 1979, 157, 158: "The idea of "necessary truth" is just the idea of a proposition which is believed because the "grip" of the object upon us is ineluctable. [...] The objects of mathematical truths will not *let* themselves be misjudged or misrepresented."

7. Wittgenstein subjects his own theory to severe criticism, of course (e.g., 1953, part 1, §114, where the contention in *Tractatus Logico-Philosophicus* that through language nature is ascertained is criticized).

somewhat procrustean manner – if something does not fit the model, it cannot be accounted for –, which is, however, not problematical as long as this model is acknowledged to be what it is: an *a priori* exclusion of that which cannot be expressed in language and logic (Wittgenstein 1921, 5.4711, 5.6, 5.61). In order to ascertain whether Wittgenstein attests to this limitation, the following is illuminating: "The state of affairs is a union of objects (things)." ("*Der Sachverhalt ist eine Verbindung von Gegenständen* (Sachen, Dingen).") (Wittgenstein 1921, 2.01). A proposition of the form 'aRb' is perceived as a picture (Wittgenstein 1921, 4.012). (e.g., "Colorado Springs lies to the south of Denver", if 'a' is 'Colorado Springs', 'b' is 'Denver' and 'R' is 'lying to the south of').

The problem here is that "we make pictures of facts for ourselves" ("*Wir machen uns Bilder der Tatsachen.*") (Wittgenstein 1921, 2.1) (the picture itself, incidentally, being a fact (Wittgenstein 1921, 2.141)), and in order to come to know whether the picture is true or false it must be compared with reality. So the pictures that are made of the facts are compared with reality, the positive part of which is the world (the whole of facts): the pictures made of the facts are compared with the facts. In the most antagonistic interpretation, this amounts to a circle, in which the outcome is a result of one's own contribution.

In the most forthcoming interpretation, Wittgenstein's insistence that everything is experienced within the boundaries of logic and language results in a conceptual prison from which one is unable to escape. This does mean that speaking of 'the world' and 'reality' as unreservedly as Wittgenstein does is not justified (unless this is itself said to follow from one's limitations – being able to use another expression would counter these limitations); it leaves room for remarks on the 'mystical' (Wittgenstein 1921, 6.44, 6.45, 6.522) and propositions as "how the world is, is completely indifferent for what is higher. God does not manifest himself in the world." ("*Wie die Welt ist, ist für das Höhere vollkommen gleichgültig. Gott offenbart sich nicht in der Welt.*") (Wittgenstein 1921, 6.432). The meaning of such sentences depends on how far Wittgenstein's observation is taken that the answer to the problems of life lies in the actual absence of such problems once the possible scientific questions have been answered (Wittgenstein 1921, 6.52).

The first interpretation leads to an untenable result, 'the world', whatever it may be in this case, remaining undisclosed. The same outcome applies in the second interpretation, but it is not equally untenable. In the latter case, the limits of knowledge are rather acknowledged, 'the world' meaning the world insofar as it can be grasped (through logic and language). In any event, logical atomism (in this guise) can merely point to one's limitations in comprehensive understanding.

To return to mathematics: it can be applied, e.g. in construction engineering. Still, that only proves the *application* and not an insight into reality: one knows what to do in order to produce a desired result, but that is all. The stability that is ever observed (the process works in this situation as it has worked in the past, because of the conformity in nature which has hitherto been present, as far as one can tell) is not itself comprehensively understood and may come to an end without the observer being able to account for such an event, something that will be dealt with in Section 2. The regularity is, in other words, observed and then posited to be present in the future. This is of course no critique of the procedure that scientists follow; no engineer or doctor would be able to perform any action without resorting to such a regular pattern. I merely want to indicate that scientists do not comprehensively understand the regularity's presence and cannot therefore be assured that it will last (cf. Hume 1748, Section 4, part 2 (32, 33): "Let the course of things be allowed hitherto ever so regular; that alone, without some new argument or inference, proves not, that, for the future, it will continue so."). That doesn't detract from the need to act.

In physics, the problems are even greater than in mathematics and logic. A vague notion, or rather – since not only comprehensive understanding but even understanding is absent here – word such as 'force' is used.[8] This does not invalidate the results that have been produced any more than in the cases above, but invoking notions or words that cannot be understood means that its practical outcomes constitute its sole merit. If something's cause is provided, the question 'why' it occurs or exists is not answered,[9] but merely the question 'because of what'. Indeed, Hume rightly points to *a priori* reasoning's' insufficiency to lay bare the reason why things are as they are in matters of fact, 'cause' itself being a problematical notion (e.g., Hume 1748, Section 7, part 2 (60)), a view that needs to be complemented with the position that on the basis of experience such an account cannot be produced either (which Hume, incidentally, seems to acknowledge (Hume 1748, Section 4, part 1 (26–28), part 2 (29, 30); Section 5, part 1 (36))).

Physics' *applications* are not in the least struck by the present observations and these are not their focus. A lack of comprehensive understanding with its practitioners follows, however, from the mere given that they have to resort to words that only describe a process, such as 'force', 'gravity' and 'attraction', the introduction of which does not testify to a comprehensive understanding but to the fact that the limits of the ability to understand have been reached.

An even more radical account may be rendered, according to which the perspective that a theory can be said to reflect an insight (even if one grants that a comprehensive understanding is lacking) is forsaken and man's entire enterprise

8. This point will receive additional attention in Section 2.

9. Which is not to imply that it necessarily *can* be answered; perhaps the idea that such an answer is possible is merely a human imagination.

to make sense of the world that is encountered is a mere consequence of his need to survive. In that case, one may also be said to delude oneself in supposing that the problems that are solved point to a comprehensive understanding, when they are rather to be considered outcomes of an attempt to control his surroundings (an attempt that is doomed to fail, as long as there is no comprehensive understanding; any unexpected event may, after all, thwart one's plans, however carefully they may have been outlined and implemented); one may at most achieve a provisional theory, whose sole merit lies in its applicability.

What I have argued in this section is that comprehensive understanding is not realized (at least not by factor-determined beings). This means that a fundamental insight into the nature of reality is not forthcoming. Even 'foundational' sciences such as physics and mathematics were shown not to provide accounts to realize any such feat.

This result will presumably lead to some modesty from scientists, but its purport should not be misjudged. Comprehensive understanding is not the same as understanding, and the latter is not at all affected by the foregoing considerations. Learning processes and scientific processes lose none of their practical value; Section 3 will deal with this in some detail. Before dealing with that issue, however, something else remains to be discussed. The focus of the present section was on the aspect of understanding, the 'subjective' part of an account. The 'objective' part, the aspect of explaining, merits attention as well, so in order to complete the analysis, it will receive the required attention in the next section.

Explaining

In a similar fashion as in Section 1 with respect to 'comprehensive understanding' and 'understanding', I will discern between 'comprehensive explaining' and 'explaining', 'explaining' meaning that an account is provided in which one or more causes (keeping in mind the problems associated with this mentioned in Section 1) for a phenomenon are discerned, and 'comprehensive explaining' meaning that the question '*why*' something occurs or exists is answered. The link between the present section and the previous one is easily established. If there is no comprehensive understanding, scientific theories do not comprehensively explain anything, although they may be said to explain some phenomena, if they are successful, which is the criterion for their continuity and development.

Scientists do not proceed from a comprehensive understanding, but rather collect data on the basis of which a theory is constructed, ever in the context of the relevant background knowledge (e.g., Kuhn 1996, 10). A scientific explanation is, accordingly, fundamentally contingent, which means that it does not necessarily reflect reality; the fact that one thinks in some way does not entail that one *has* to think thus. (The word 'necessarily' is used here; of course, I cannot say that the explanation does not reflect reality sec, since this would imply a point of view on my part that is not the case, viz., that I would myself comprehensively understand and from that perspective be able to notice such a discrepancy.)

For example, nature could have been constituted in such a way that objects randomly appear and disappear. It (presumably) does not behave thus,[10] at least not at the macroscopic level, but science cannot comprehensively explain why this is the case. It can merely discern regular patterns in nature as it actually presents itself. Logic and mathematics are no less contingent in this sense, by the way, despite their claim to necessity and universality. They may apply necessarily and universally, but even if that is the case, it does not derogate from their being contingent in the present sense.

A clear sign that scientific theories do not provide comprehensive explanations is the fact that they resort to words that are merely used because the analysis cannot proceed any further. As Berkeley poignantly observes:

> That a stone falls to the earth, or the sea swells towards the moon, may to some appear sufficiently explained [by gravity]. But how are we enlightened by being told this is done by attraction? [...] [N]othing is determined of the manner or action, and it may as truly (for aught we know) be termed *impulse* or *protrusion* as *attraction*." (Berkeley 1710, part 1, §103 (86); cf. Hume 1748, Section 7, part 1 (50): "There are no ideas, which occur in metaphysics, more obscure and uncertain, than those of *power*, *force*, *energy*, or *necessary connexion*, of which it is every moment necessary for us to treat in all our disquisitions."). It is also important to realize that attraction is adhered to by Newton as a mathematical hypothesis rather than a "true and physical quality." (*qualitatem veram et physicam*)
>
> (Berkeley 1721, §17 (15); cf. Newton 1726, Def. VIII (5))

Indeed, Newton himself insists that he does not seek to penetrate into the nature of things:

> Up to now I have exhibited the phenomena of the heavens and our sea by the force of gravity, but I have not yet pointed out the cause of gravity [...] I do not contrive hypotheses. For whatever is not inferred from phenomena must be called a *hypothesis*; and hypotheses, whether they be metaphysical, physical, of occult qualities or mechanical, have no place in *experimental philosophy*. In this philosophy theorems are inferred from phenomena and rendered general through

10. I say 'presumably' since I can only say something about nature as it appears to me.

induction. […] And it is satisfactory that gravity in fact exists and acts according to the laws that have been demonstrated by us, and suffices for all motions of the celestial bodies and our sea." (*Hactenus phaenomena caelorum et maris nostri per vim gravitatis exposui, sed causam gravitatis nondum assignavi.* […] *[H]ypotheses non fingo. Quicquid enim ex phaenomenis non deducitur, hypothesis vocanda est; et hypotheses seu metaphysicae, seu physicae, seu qualitatum occultarum, seu mechanicae, in philosophia experimentali locum non habent. In hac philosophia propositiones deducuntur ex phaenomenis, et redduntur generales per inductionem. […] Et satis est quod gravitas revera existat, et agat secundum leges a nobis expositas, et ad corporum caelestium et maris nostri motus omnes sufficiat).*

(Newton 1726, Book 3, Scholium Generale 530)

'Force' ('vis') is a vague word (Berkeley 1721, §5 (12)) and gravity itself is not observed (Berkeley 1721, §4 (12)), the cause of a body's being brought downwards not being grasped (Berkeley 1721, §22 (16)). One may, then, say that explanations are given, but no comprehensive explanations. Berkeley does not himself draw this conclusion, by the way, stating that metaphysics can provide "truly active causes" ("*causae vere activae*") (Berkeley 1721, §72 (52); cf. §34 (19)).

The Newtonian theory of gravity (Newton 1726, Def. V (3, 4); Book 3, Regula 3 (388, 389)) may be considered superior to that of Aristotle (Aristotle ± 350 BCE, Book 8 (255b)), but only because it can account for phenomena more precisely and provide a better (in the sense of encompassing) description (or explanation) than the former. As for a comprehensive explanation, neither theory provides one, "gravity" ("heaviness") remaining an opaque word. A comprehensively explanatory distance between one's theory and one's object may also be said to follow from the inclusion of thinking aids in one's theory that make reality *a priori* inaccessible, however useful such aids may be.

This can be argued for the branch of physics that deals with subatomic particles. 'Subatomic' supervenes on 'atomic', of course ('indivisible' or, literally, 'uncuttable'). The atom is not observed but rather postulated as – in the pre-subatomic theories – the smallest possible unit. The atom is indeed postulated: "The atom is no *discovery* of natural science, but an *invention*." ("*Das Atom ist keine naturwissenschaftliche Entdeckung, sondern eine Erfindung*.") (Vaihinger 1922, part 1, Ch. 21 (150).)

The value of the carefully constructed atomic and subatomic models must be acknowledged, but also the corollary of their introduction, namely an absence of comprehensive explanation.[11] This entails that a 'theory of everything' in the sense

11. Fine's conclusion is more radical than mine: "If pressed to answer the question of what, then, does it *mean* to say that something is true (or to what does the truth of so-and-so commit one), NOA [the natural ontological attitude] will reply by pointing out the logical relations engendered by the specific claim and by focusing, then, on the concrete historical circumstances that ground that particular judgment of truth. For, after all, there *is* nothing more to say." (Fine 1986, 134.)

of a theory that aims at unlocking "[...] the cardinal secrets of nature so as to render physical reality comprehensively intelligible." (Rescher 2000, 74), may consist in an account that explains all phenomena (or at least all physical phenomena), but not in a definitive theory in the sense that it would offer a comprehensive explanation for all aspects of reality.[12] After all, physics is characterized by an empirical approach no less than the other sciences, collecting data and constructing a theory by integrating them into a meaningful synthesis.[13] For a comprehensive explanation, another model would be needed as a necessary condition; whether it would also be a *sufficient* condition would depend on the sort of model.

Those who aspire to establish a 'theory of everything' as an alleged reflection of the structure of reality seem, then, to be confined to the metaphysical stage as Comte describes it:

> In the metaphysical state [...], the supernatural agents are replaced by abstract forces, veritable entities (personified abstractions) inherent in various beings of the world, and conceived as capable to engender by themselves all observed phenomena, the explanation of which consists, then, in assigning to each the corresponding entity (*Dans l'état métaphysique [...], les agents surnaturels sont remplacées par des forces abstraites, véritables entités (abstractions personnifiées) inhérentes aux divers êtres du monde, et conçues comme capables d'engendrer par elles-mêmes tous les phénomènes observés, dont l'explication consiste alors à assigner pour chacun l'entité correspondante*). (Comte 1830, Lecture 1 (3, 4))

12. As Duhem observes, "Explaining, *explicare*, is to reveal the *reality* of *appearances* that cover it like veils, in order to see this reality stripped and face to face. The observation of physical phenomena does not put us in touch with reality hidden behind the sensible appearances, but with these sensible appearances themselves, taken in a particular and concrete form. The experiential laws no more have material reality for their object; they deal with these same sensible appearances, albeit taken in an abstract and general form." ("Expliquer, *explicare*, c'est dépouiller la *réalité* des *apparences* qui l'enveloppent comme des voiles, afin de voir cette réalité nue et face à face. L'observation des phénomènes physiques ne nous met pas en rapport avec la réalité qui se cache sous les apparences sensibles, mais avec ces apparences sensibles elles-mêmes, prises sous forme particulière et concrète. Les lois expérimentales n'ont pas davantage pour objet la réalité matérielle; elles traitent de ces mêmes apparences sensibles, prises, il est vrai, sous forme abstraite et générale.") Duhem 1906, 6. Physical theories do not provide a comprehensive explanation (Duhem speaks of 'explanation' (so without 'comprehensive'), of course) (Duhem 1906, 26, 38; cf. 171, 361, 362).

13. One may even be more critical and say that such a methodology cannot even lead to an explanatory account, a holistic theory being necessary for such a result (Rescher 2000, 78–80).

Indeed,

> the final term of the metaphysical system consists in conceiving, instead of multiple particular entities, a single great entity, *nature*, considered as the unique source of all phenomena (*[…] le dernier terme du système métaphysique consiste à concevoir, au lieu des différentes entités particulières, une seule entité générale, la nature, envisagée comme la source unique de tous les phénomènes).*
>
> (Comte 1830, lecture 1 (4)

Once the level of application is considered, the same analysis pertains. From the fact that one knows how to reach a desired result, no comprehensive explanation follows.[14] If a doctor manages to treat a patient successfully, or even cures a disease, all (s)he does (which is not to imply that this is a slight task) is to combine several observations to find one or more causes of a disease that can subsequently be abated or removed. An appeal to notions that cannot be further elucidated, such as 'cell' or 'gene',[15] remains necessary.

Moreover, from the observation that certain behavior is prone to lead to a disease, or, conversely, its absence, no answer to the question 'why' that is the case ensues, and one remains in the realm of explanations in the sense of 'because of what' as mentioned in Section 1. All that is provided in medicine is a generalized observation. Even if some cure exhibits universal results (the cure being effective in each instance encountered hitherto), one still has not comprehensively explained why. A comprehensive explanation would bring with it that doctors could not be surprised by a new case in which the cure would prove not to be effective (in which case a lack of universality would in hindsight be established). Such a state of affairs is not the case in medicine,[16] some new situation that had not been considered being ever possible.

Doctors only discern a regular pattern, oblivious why certain diseases occur in certain cases, only able to observe causes. Apparently, some behavior leads to a disease; somewhere, the explanation ends (so that no comprehensive explanation is given), the difference with previous theories being that one is now able to give a better explanation in the sense that the deepest cause one can find is

14. Cf. Rorty 1991, 5: "On an antirepresentationalist view, it is one thing to say that a prehensile thumb, or an ability to use the word "atom" as physicists do, is useful for coping with the environment. It is another thing to attempt to *explain* this utility by reference to representationalist notions, such as the notion that the reality referred to by "quarks" was "determinate" before the word "quark" came along […]."

15. Cells' and genes' internal structures can of course be uncovered, but that does not lead to a comprehensive explanation.

16. Or other fields of research, for that matter.

further removed from the surface than the deepest ones that appeared before, evidenced in doctors being better equipped to combat illnesses than their precursors were. For medicine's purposes, a comprehensively explicative account may not be required (although its presence would probably be welcomed), but it does question the justification of placing this discipline on a pedestal.[17]

Of course, Molière's discrediting of doctors, *inter alia* on account of their (obviously circular) appeal to a 'dormitive virtue' ('*virtus dormitiva*') to explain why opium makes someone sleep (Molière 1673, Intermede III (443)), is not fully pertinent, at least not anymore, especially since they do know how to cure some patients, as opposed to those derided by him for not being able to do so (Molière 1673, Act III, Scene III (397)).

Presuming that animals (all varieties, from ants to chimpanzees) are factor-determined beings and can be said to use their abilities for survival purposes only, acquiring no comprehensive explanations (and not even explanations, perhaps[18]), this consideration may be extended to human beings (if they are factor-determined beings), so that any theory they constitute does not represent reality, but only serves to (very modestly) control nature.[19] This approach may, in the light of what has been said hitherto, be more convincing than one which does adhere to such a representation.[20] The fact that the theories that are proposed and corroborated may be ever so intricate and impressive takes away nothing of the divide that separates them from a comprehensive explanation, which would only be possible if another approach than the prevailing one were available. The difference between a description and an explanation may, accordingly, be said to be gradual, if such a difference can be upheld at all.

17. Rorty 1989, 8: "From our point of view, explaining the success of science, or the desirability of political liberalism, by talk of "fitting the world" or "expressing human nature" is like explaining why opium makes you sleepy by talking about its dormitive power. To say that Freud's vocabulary gets at the truth about human nature, or Newton's at the truth about the heavens, is not an explanation of anything. It is just an empty compliment – one traditionally paid to writers whose novel jargon we have found useful."

18. I say 'perhaps', since this depends on the scope of the notion 'explanation'; it may be man's prerogative to explain matters, animals being unable to do so, but only if reason is supposed to be a special faculty vis-à-vis the other faculties inherent in man and the animals rather than the apex (as far as I can tell) of a hierarchy of skills to (modestly) control nature.

19. Cf. Rescher 2000, 134–140.

20. In addition, the idea that phenomena can be described and explained in a single, correct way, one creature having the privilege of being capable to do so, may be deemed "merely mythology" (Rescher 2000, 131).

Concluding this section, (scientific) explanations are available, but should be distinguished from comprehensive explanations, which are not accessible to factor-determined beings. Explanations, which are focused on the question of how to reach a (desired) result, or on providing the cause(s) of phenomena, are provided on the basis of scientific analyses, but that does not mean that a comprehensive explanation is offered, as this would require an answer to the question of why phenomena occur, or even why nature itself exists.

These result have no significant impact on the educational process. It does suggest that a somewhat modest stance should be adopted by both learners and teachers, but the issues discussed here have a philosophical rather than a scientific nature, the outcomes of scientific research being evaluated rather than being refuted. The evaluation of any explanation thereby rests on dialog and processes of negotiating knowledge and reality (Weigand 2010, 3). The same observation applies to scientific practice, as will be argued in the final section.

Consequences

It appears that no attempt to gain a comprehensive understanding or a comprehensive explanation has been successful. The two appear to be interrelated in that the acquisition of one entails the other. Whether this is indeed the case remains, strictly speaking, a matter of speculation until the stage of comprehensive understanding or comprehensive explanation is reached. One may, however, doubt the possibility of such a result, not only whether this is feasible for factor-determined beings but whether it is possible at all. Are endeavors to gain a comprehensive understanding as a more fundamental understanding and a comprehensive explanation as a more fundamental explanation than those provided by the sciences not *a priori* doomed to fail, since they are directed at something that is not available, from any perspective whatsoever?

Perhaps that is the most viable way to approach these issues. Perhaps, then, it must be said, with James:

> Purely objective truth, truth in whose establishment the function of giving human satisfaction in marrying previous parts of experience with newer parts played no rôle whatever, is nowhere to be found. The reasons why we call things true is the reason why they *are* true, for 'to be true' *means* only to perform this marriage-function. (James 1907, Lecture II (37))

Whether this is correct cannot be said by a factor-determined being, since it would otherwise already have transgressed its conceptual limits and have entered the realm that is, *ex hypothesi*, undisclosed to it, and whether other beings than factor-determined ones (can) exist is just as speculative, at least for a factor-determined being, let alone the answer to the question whether those beings would be able to reach such a state if they did in fact exist.

For the practical sciences, this result has but few consequences, as was remarked specifically with regard to comprehensive explaining in Section 2. For those sciences that aim to unravel nature's secrets, however, a need to reflect on the validity and possibility of their pursuit arises. Unless a means to construct an alternative method to the one prevalent in the scientific method, viz., a construction of a theory on the basis of empirical input, a model that works quite well in practice but provides neither a comprehensive understanding nor a comprehensive explanation (the contents of which model I am of course unable to provide, not even being able to indicate whether such a model is possible at all), is found, the realm of comprehensive understanding and comprehensive explaining is unattainable. Such a result is obviously unsatisfactory, but the only one that can warrantably be said to follow from the foregoing analysis.

It is tempting to say that a domain of comprehensive understanding and a domain of comprehensive explaining are unreachable *a priori* since they are illusions, fantasies created to have something to aspire to, and that the regular patterns scientists discern are all there is. First of all, this means the acknowledgement of science's limitations. Second, as I mentioned, this is, from the viewpoint of a factor-determined being at least, just as speculative as positing such a realm. One is unable to determine whether nature holds great secrets (whether they be ultimately inaccessible or not) or rather merely presents the material to fabricate the illusion that such secrets would exist, just as it is impossible (for now at least) for a factor-determined being to grasp such secrets if they do in fact exist.

In any event, it is unwarranted to identify discovering a regular pattern in data with comprehensive understanding and comprehensive explaining; all this points to is a regularity, the basis of which remains elusive if all one is able to do is observe it. As long as scientists' activities are limited to induction (or, in mathematics in logic, deduction), however intricate their pursuits may be, no comprehensive understanding or comprehensive explaining is realized.

The results of what was presented in the first two sections are not as devastating, then, to scientific practice as might appear at first sight. It is clear that scientific developments, insofar as they are focused on practical results, are desirable – one would, presumably, be more comfortable with a physician using the latest insights than with one basing the treatment on theories developed centuries ago –, but to conclude from the fact that progress has been made (in the sense that modern techniques produce more desirable results than previous ones) that comprehensive understanding and/or comprehensive explaining takes place would not be justified.

Conclusion

The foregoing easily leads to the conclusion that one is delivered to a forlorn skepticism. No fundamental comprehensive understanding or comprehensive explanation of that which is encountered is provided. Since this situation is inescapable for a factor-determined being, won't an unbridgeable chasm to reality (or nature) remain forever? That depends on one's position. The very notion of a realm of reality existing independently of reasonable inquirers, waiting to be discovered, understood, explained or – according to others than myself – comprehensively understood and comprehensively explained, may have to be relinquished. But where one door closes another one opens up. Dialogic co-construction of knowledge gives reasonable inquirers an opportunity to deal with the world they are part of and to make progress through shared discovery and shared understanding. As Weigand (2010) puts it:

> It is in the end their competence-in-performance or the *ability to experience and negotiate meaning and understanding in dialogue* which enables them to develop societies, institutions, complex cultural systems, or, in general, civilization.
> (p. 272)

This is not problematical in practice for most sciences, whose practitioners will unencumbered continue their pursuits, and whose successes are undisputed, as long as they provide actual results, nor is the teaching process significantly affected. Those sciences that aim at comprehensively explaining reality, however, will need to reflect the very possibility of such a goal. It cannot *a priori* be said to be fruitless – also because I am factor-determined –, but considering the (necessarily empirically uncorroborated) notions they have smuggled in (or, less unfavorably, posited), the need to temper their ambitions appears to be a given.

References

Aristotle. 1960 [± 350 BCE]. *Physica*. Aristotelis Opera, vol. 1. Darmstadt: Wissenschaftliche Buchgesellschaft.

Berkeley, George. 1949 [1710]. "A Treatise Concerning the Principles of Human Knowledge." In *The Works of George Berkeley*, vol. 2, ed. by A. A. Luce, and T. E. Jessop. London: Thomas Nelson and Sons.

Berkeley, George. 1951 [1721]. "De Motu." In *The Works of George Berkeley*, vol. 4. ed. by A. A. Luce, and T. E. Jessop. London: Thomas Nelson and Sons.

Comte, Auguste. 1968 [1830]. *Cours De Philosophie Positive*, part 1. Œuvres d'Auguste Comte, vol. 1. Paris: Éditions anthropos

Duhem, Pierre. 1906. *La Théorie Physique. Son Objet et sa Structure*. Paris: Chevalier and Rivière.

Fine, Arthur. 1986. *The Shaky Game. Einstein, Realism and the Quantum Theory*. Chicago, IL/ London: University of Chicago Press.

Hume, David. 2000 [1748]. *An Enquiry Concerning Human Understanding*. ed. by T. Beauchamp. Oxford: Clarendon Press.

James, William. 1975 [1907]. *Pragmatism. A New Name for Some Old Ways of Thinking*. Cambridge, MA/London: Harvard University Press.

Kant, Immanuel. 1904 [1781/1787]. *Kritik der reinen Vernunft*. Kant's gesammelte Schriften. Erste Abteilung: Werke. Band 3 (Kant's collected writings. First section: Works. vol. 3). Berlin: Georg Reimer.

Kuhn, Thomas. 1996. *The Structure of Scientific Revolutions*. Chicago, IL: University of Chicago Press. DOI: 10.7208/chicago/9780226458106.001.0001

Molière. 1886 [1673]. *Le Malade Imaginaire*, ed. by E. Despois and P. Mesnard. Œuvres de Molière, vol. 9. Paris: Librairie Hachette

Newton, Isaac. 1726. *Philosophiæ Naturalis Principia Mathematica*. London: Apud Guil. and Joh. Innys.

Priest, Graham. 1989. "Classical Logic *aufgehoben*." In *Paraconsistent Logic. Essays on the Inconsistent*, ed. by Graham Priest, Richard Routley, and Jean Norman, 131–145. München, Hamden, Wien: Philosophia Verlag.

Rescher, Nicholas. 2000. *Nature and Understanding. The Metaphysics and Method of Science*. Oxford: Clarendon Press.

Rorty, Richard. 1989. *Contingency, Irony, and Solidarity*. Cambridge: Cambridge University Press. DOI: 10.1017/CBO9780511804397

Rorty, Richard. 1979. *Philosophy and the Mirror of Nature*. Princeton, NJ: Princeton University Press.

Rorty, Richard. 1991. *Objectivity, Relativism, and Truth*. Philosophical Papers, vol. 1. Cambridge: Cambridge University Press.

Schrödinger, Erwin. 1935. "Die gegenwärtige Situation in der Quantenmechanik." *Die Naturwissenschaften* 23 (48): 807–812. DOI: 10.1007/BF01491891

Vaihinger, Hans. 1922. *Die Philosophie des Als Ob*. Leipzig: Felix Meiner.

Weigand, Edda. 2010. *Dialogue: The Mixed Game*. Amsterdam: John Benjamins. DOI: 10.1075/ds.10

Wittgenstein, Ludwig. 1997 [1953]. *Philosophische Untersuchungen*. Working edition, vol. 1. Frankfurt am Main: Suhrkamp.

Wittgenstein, Ludwig. 1997 [1921]. *Tractatus Logico-Philosophicus*. Working edition, vol. 1. Frankfurt am Main: Suhrkamp.

Author's address

Jasper Doomen
Leiden University
Steenschuur 25
2311 ES Leiden
The Netherlands
0031 71527 8515
jasperdoomen@yahoo.com

The *why dimension*, dialogic inquiry, and technology supported learning

Jon Mason
Charles Darwin University, Australia

This chapter introduces a number of theoretical perspectives in presenting an analysis of why the *why dimension* of inquiry – *asking, learning, understanding, knowing,* and *explaining why* – presents challenges and opportunities for the design and implementation of technology supported learning environments. Central to this theoretical discussion are epistemological constructs such as 'becoming to know' (Jakubik 2011) and 'sense-making' (Dervin 1998; Weick 1995; Snowden 2002). Supporting this theoretical discussion is a number of sense-making models representing relationships between learning and knowledge and the characteristics of *why*-questioning. Reasoning, reflection, and dialogue are all identified as embedded within dialogic inquiry and these activities provide the context for consideration of how the *why dimension* in technology supported learning environments may be supported.

Introduction

This chapter can be read as beginning and ending with *inquiry*: it is intended to raise questions and stimulate discourse rather than serve as a commentary of closure. The underlying concern motivating its content is an investigation of *why*-questioning in technology supported learning environments. This concern is explored in terms of sense-making models that represent the relationships between learning and knowledge and the characteristics of *why*-questioning during inquiry. Dialogue, and here especially dialogue in the form of Weigand's (2010) Mixed Game Model (MGM) integrating verbal, cognitive and perceptual means of communication, is identified as a defining characteristic of inquiry initiated by *why*-questioning,including activities involving reflection and reasoning. In pursuing this topic through research spanning a number of years numerous intersecting perspectives from diverse discourses have been drawn upon – discourses such as e-learning theory and practice, educational theory, information science, knowledge management, computational linguistics, communications theory, standards development, and anthropology. Intersecting discourses are nothing new to academic research; however, the consequences of developments in information and communications technology (ICT) since the invention of the Web can be seen as transformational for many domains of activity with ICT providing a common and convergent infrastructure. Such developments have few historical precedents. In many ways, in such a context, it makes more sense to embrace interdisciplinary perspectives than not.

As we move through the second decade of the twenty first century a number of trajectories are clearly evident in the ongoing development of technology supported learning environments. A dominant feature of the last decade has been social media in the mix of technologies that promote interaction, collaboration, networking, and knowledge sharing – at scales never before possible (Williams et al. 2011). Also prominent within a broadening discourse is the movement that has positioned itself to articulate what "21st century skills" might be; skills that place emphasis upon digital literacies, critical thinking, and problem solving in equal measure (Kuhlthau 2004; Griffin et al. 2012; Casey and Bruce 2011). There are strong drivers for an "open agenda" connecting various sub-movements that advocate open source software, open access, open learning, open data, and open educational resources (Leeson and Mason 2007). For some, data itself is the new currency – whether it is exposed, linked or linkable for research purposes, or part of a "data-driven" classroom (Mandinach and Jackson 2012). Mobile technologies are also making their mark in education, providing new opportunities for engagement in learning activities harnessing much more than convenience and personalisation through engaging interfaces that provide a sense of intimacy (Berge and Muilenburg 2013; Bruck and Rao 2013). For many practitioners the pace of innovation and the growing options that involve technology devices have consequences on how we make sense of the world. And so it is that "sense-making" is a term that has entered the discourse on e-learning (Johnson et al. 2010). Through embracing this term and focusing on dialogic inquiry this chapter investigates how sense-making models might inform how ongoing technological innovation can support learning. Issues concerning semantics are raised; importantly, the rich ambiguity of the semantics of the simple one-word question "*why?*" Among its many functions this question provides a trigger for dialogue, a stimulus for reasoning, and a prompt for explanation or elaboration. While semantic ambiguity presents unique problems for information science and software engineering focused on data mining it also presents opportunities for innovative technology to support and stimulate reasoning skills and deep inquiry, and the co-construction of knowledge. As meaning is not fixed but is negotiated between the dialog partners (Weigand 2010, 72), innovative technology should scaffold processes of meaning negotiation and the co-construction of knowledge.

Through first focusing on inquiry itself, the following discussion provides an exposition of dialogic inquiry in the context of technology enabled learning. Issues concerning the nature of content are raised which introduces discussion on philosophical considerations concerning knowledge and how to represent it. A model is introduced to distinguish *explanation* from *information* and other models from cited literature are used to situate *sense-making* as a key activity in learning. The semantics of *why* are analysed from a linguistic perspective and five key activities – *asking, learning, understanding, knowing,* and *explaining* – are represented as the *why dimension* of inquiry and dialogue.

The chapter concludes with discussion of emerging innovations and opportunities for the design and implementation of technology supported learning environments that tackle the challenges associated with the *why dimension.*

Inquiry and learning

Inquiry takes place when an individual, group, or organisation set out to find out something – to satisfy curiosity, discover new information, acquire new knowledge, resolve a problem, or uncover the truth. Importantly, while *learning* may be a by-product or outcome, it is not necessarily the key focus as in the case of finding an answer to a question (Wells 2000, 62). Of course, for an educator where learning is the primary goal, supporting and cultivating student curiosity and inquiry represents good pedagogical practice from constructivist perspectives (Bruner 1966; Vygotsky 1978; Rothstein and Santana 2011). Importantly, inquiry is also very much a *process* that can involve a sequence of activities, as is represented in Figure 1 – an ideal representation of key activities that support inquiry-based learning.

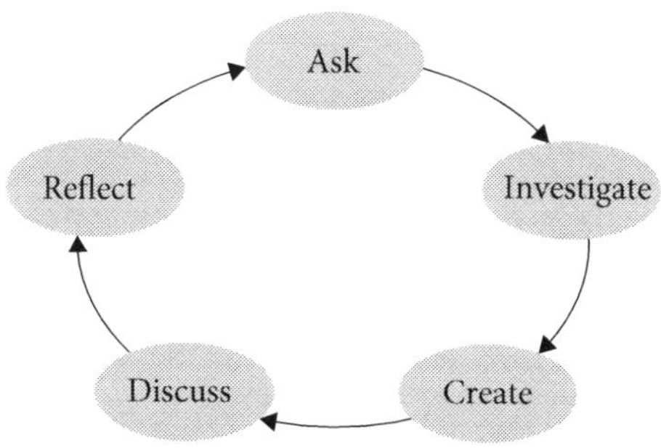

Figure 1. The Inquiry Cycle (Casey and Bruce 2011) – reproduced with permission

The Inquiry Project (2010) at the University of Illinois used Figure 1 in its advocacy for inquiry-based learning spanning a period of ten years together with a motto "learning begins with questions". In many situations this will be so, although Wells (2000) contends:

> Inquiry does not have to start with a clearly formulated question. In fact some of the most absorbing questions arise only after some preliminary work on the topic has been carried out, or as a by-product of trying to answer some other question. (62)

Thus, while representations such as Figure 1 can communicate a strong message they can also be seen to mask detail that may be relevant in specific cases. As such, inquiry is also contextually bound as it may only involve a single act of investigation or reflection, the asking of a question, or even initiation of a technology supported search query. A virtuous circle of inquiry may take place but such a sequence is not a precondition for inquiry.

In her work on "Guided Inquiry", Kuhlthau (2007) describes a pedagogical approach that emphasises inquiry in which "five kinds of learning are accomplished [...] information literacy, learning how to learn, curriculum content, literacy competence and social skills. An inquiry approach is a most efficient way to learn in the 21st century" (Kuhlthau 2009, 4). Underlying this focus is a model developed in earlier work (Kuhlthau 2004) called the Information Search Process (ISP). The ISP is also sequential in that it "describes thoughts, actions and feelings in six stages of inquiry: initiation, selection, exploration, formulation, collection, and presentation" (Kuhlthau 2009, 3). While this earlier (ISP) model is informed largely by *information* seeking a key characteristic of *Guided Inquiry* is relationships with others and, as such, it can be seen as a dialogic approach to learning.

However, and this is both a key argument and assumption of this chapter, while digital technology search tools may be powerful in processing information and enabling social networks they are also (currently) limited in terms of sustaining inquiry or even enabling inquiry that needs to probe deeper into reasoning, problem solving, and interacting with *explanatory* content. This is a significant constraint that exists with most mainstream Internet search tools primarily because they are configured to parse data and information that is calibrated from the *aboutness* of content – descriptive or identifiable information such as keywords and key phrases, date published, the author, and weightings associated with how many back hyperlinks can be determined. In other words, mainstream search engines can be seen as privileging "factoid" information that can be reduced to expressions of *who, what, when,* and *where* information (Verberne 2010; Mason 2008). Such information may satisfy basic information seeking and may even establish a basis for further investigation but it does not necessarily stimulate reasoning, reflection, problem solving, critical thinking, and dialogue – all activities so fundamental to inquiry.

Dialogue, learning and technology

The connection between dialogue and learning was most famously established by Socrates over twenty-five hundred years ago (Guthrie 1989, 723; Stumpf 1983). For Socrates, spoken dialogue was paramount in revealing poor argumentation and prejudice, particularly where ethical or moral issues were concerned. By encouraging the student as the protagonist of an argument the so-called *Socratic Method* places emphasis upon the instructor choosing probing questions that help guide or cultivate reasoning skills and a moral compass in the student. As Tokuhama-Espinosa (2011) observes, this dialectic and dialogic approach to learning not only has a proven track record but has currency in "prestigious law and medical institutions around the world, and … it is successful because it focuses more on the "*whys*" of information then the "*whats*" (Tokuhama-Espinosa 2011, 104 [*my emphasis*]).

In many ways contemporary educational literature on scaffolding (Teo 2003; Wood et al. 1976; Lipscomb et al. 2004) demonstrates a strong link with the Socratic approach. Likewise, the roots of the critical thinking movement in education can also be traced to Socrates, for its goals of clarity of thought and the pursuit of truth are similar, although the literature on critical thinking is more explicit about the importance of *metacognition*, or thinking about thinking (Paul 1990).

It is noted here that dialogic approaches to education are all based on the assumption that teacher and learner interact with each other. From a theoretical point of view, this interaction can be represented as an action pair: communicative action and communicative reaction. This is what Weigand (2010, 129) calls the minimal communicative action game, which is the most basic form of dialogic interaction.

In technology enabled environments dialogue can be successfully achieved through a diversity of channels – from telephony and radio to an almost overwhelming array of options facilitated by social media. While the affordances of social media are said to characterise so-called *Web 2.0* (Rambe 2012) the scene for engagement in networked communications was already set prior to the invention of the Web with numerous electronic mail discussion lists and Internet-based bulletin boards facilitating asynchronous text-based communications (Hart and Mason 1999). Looking beyond the current dominance of social media, however, a number of opportunities for innovation in technology supported learning environments arise – but these are discussed later in this chapter.

Dialogic inquiry

Probing the role of dialogue in learning from perhaps a deeper theoretical perspective Wells (1999, 2000) introduces the term *dialogic inquiry*, to highlight the central role that language has in meaning-making and learning. Drawing on the work of Bahktin (1981), Vygotsky (1978) and Halliday (1993), Wells presents an inter-disciplinary social constructivist theory of learning in which "linguistic discourse [mediates] […] communicating and knowing right across the curriculum" (1999, 119). In doing so he also highlights the dialectic relationship between the individual and society that can be adequately addressed within a "community of inquiry" in which both teachers and students develop their understanding and knowledge (Wells 2000, 63). For Wells, this is made possible because language is learned by a child in interactions with his or her immediate community; in other words, because language is embedded in social activity it is naturally geared for dialogue, and "collaborative meaning making" (2000, 267). In a similar vein,Weigand's Mixed Game Model (2010, 72, 272) states that meaning is negotiated between the dialogue partners. Taking meaning making as a necessary condition for the construction and co-construction of knowledge, it is obvious that learning is, to a significant extent, a dialogic activity.

Theory is, of course, always conceptual and likely to stimulate debate and further discourse – because concepts and their associated terms have meanings and meaning is typically contextual. For example, Wegerif (2008) suggests that "superficial resemblances between the ideas of Bakhtin and those of Vygotsky have led to *dialogic* being conflated with *dialectic*" (Wegerif 2008, 357 [*my emphasis*]) while Renshaw (2010, 1) puts an alternative case by highlighting the value arising from the intersection of these discourses. This is not the place to resolve such issues apart from noting that it is common for terminology found in one discipline or discourse to be appropriated by another and when inter-disciplinary or cross-disciplinary discourse is pursued both collisions and confluence of meaning also occur. As such, no discipline or discourse ever really *owns* a term because natural language evolves. For example, in the Australian Macquarie Dictionary (2011) there are over eighty separate definitions for the common word "open": such as 'not shut, to disclose, an unobstructed space, to render accessible to knowledge, to cut or break into, to begin, to uncover' … etc. This common word has been used in recent decades by diverse communities of practice enjoying the benefits of the Internet but for different purposes, and with different meanings: *open learning* (independent, inquiry-based, and self-determined learning); *open systems* (systems with interfaces that enable interoperability); *open source* (shared intellectual input into the development of software with specific but royalty-free licensing requirements); *open access* (freely available academic research); and, *open educational resources* (content, digital tools, and standards developed for free public access and use) (Dewey 1916; Gasser 1991; Kelly et al. 2007; Leeson and Mason 2007). On this latter term, mathematically speaking, with over eighty differences in meaning for *open*, nine for *resource*, and with even only one for *educational* that would give in the order over 720 possibilities! But of course, human beings are able to parse semantics very efficiently enabling shared meanings (or assumed shared meanings) to be readily established in the course of dialogue. In short, natural language allows for or accommodates nuance of meaning and dialogue could not take place effectively without this intrinsic capability. Such flexibility of semantic function has also led to linguistic terms like 'semantic prosody' to be coined to describe the way certain words can be used to add further connotation in meaning (Sinclair 1991, 70–75; Hunston 2007).

Practice is somewhat more grounded than theory and recent literature reporting on the application of dialogic inquiry within the classroom suggests that while this interactive approach can demonstrably lead to greater student engagement, implementing it within systems that default to monologic (invitation-response-feedback) pedagogic practice is not easily achieved (Lyle 2008; Warwick et al. 2011). Success stories also exist and in reporting on teacher participation in professional learning communities Nelson and Slavit (2007, 23) show that "dialogic inquiry grounded in classroom-based data is a key element in teachers' professional growth."

Importantly for the underlying theme of this chapter, Wells' conceptualisation of dialogic inquiry also raises issues concerning sense making and the construction of knowledge:

> If, as teachers and teacher educators, we hope to bring about significant improvements in the way in which the practice of education is enacted in school classrooms, an important first step [...] is to attempt to clarify our own understanding of what is involved in the construction and reconstruction of knowledge.
>
> (Wells 1999, 53)

This chapter is in part a response to this call; it also makes use of other conceptual constructs in order to point to the opportunities that can arise in the conceiving how dialogic inquiry might effectively be enabled in technology supported learning environments. The following discussion therefore introduces other key theoretical constructs of this chapter: *sense-making* and the notion of *question primitives*. Doing so involves the presentation of a number of models and the exposition of an epistemological approach adopted from the broad discourse on Knowledge Management (KM). As both an academic discourse and an organisational intervention KM is, after all, focused on *knowledge* – its creation and curation. This is also true of some branches of philosophical tradition (such as epistemology and gnoseology), which is where this discussion now turns in order to situate a key facet of knowledge and knowing – *knowing-why* – and its connection to *learning-why*. Why? In short, it is because among its numerous functions, the word *why* often serves as a trigger for both dialogue and inquiry.

Philosophical considerations

Epistemology, ontology and paradigm

As a branch of philosophy epistemology is concerned with such things as the nature, origins, components, and limitations of human knowledge – and it addresses questions such as *what is knowable* and *what is reality*. As such, it represents an open discourse that is investigative in character. Likewise, *ontology* is also a branch or philosophy but it is focused on the nature of being and experience; and, unlike epistemology, it is a term that has been appropriated by Computer Science to refer to a "formal, explicit specification of a shared conceptualization" (Gruber 1993) that functions as a relational, semantic taxonomy and is typically constrained to be domain specific. Ontologies are used in computer systems for the purpose of enabling semantic interoperability, enabling the discovery, aggregation, and exchange of content that is semantically related. However, both philosophical terms are also routinely used within educational and social research when framing methodologies and in declaring conceptual paradigms, as *positivist, critical, interpretive*, or as *naturalistic inquiry* (Patton 1990; Dash 1993). While much research can be classified according to these terms in practice much educational and social research adopts a mixed methods approach, often drawing from more than one paradigm with the aim of triangulating or validating findings. It could be argued, then, that much of this current discussion draws from critical, interpretive and naturalistic inquiry paradigms.

Changing paradigms

The emergence and development of the technology enabled global information infrastructure over the last few decades represents nothing less than a profound re-configuration of social, economic, and technological structures with networks driving both innovation and disruption (Benkler 2006). Such context therefore demands global perspective in grappling with what the dynamics and trends are.

It invites inter-disciplinary thinking with many commentators either observing or arguing for "paradigm shifts" in the disciplinary discourses that prevail. As a prelude to this Bruner (1990, 4) observed that as part of the "cognitive revolution" and emergence of constructivist thinking, there was a shift taking place from the "*construction* of meaning" to "*processing* of information". More recently, Wierzbicki and Nakamori identify a change in paradigms from the *principle of reduction* to the *principle of emergence* as coincident with the beginnings of a "new informational knowledge civilization era" from around 1980 that they forecast will likely last around 120 years (Wierzbicki and Nakamori 2006, 1–13). In their book focused on knowledge creation they argue that:

> At the end of the 20th Century, together with the emergence of knowledge-based economy, the economic demand resulted in the need of a better understanding of creative processes, of micro-theories of knowledge and technology creation … we speak about a new scientific revolution that concentrates on the understanding of detailed mechanisms of creative processes, needed today and tomorrow for knowledge economy and informational society.
> (Wierzbicki and Nakamori 2006, 6)

How does this manifest in the education sector? In 2013 within the Graduate Programs at the University of British Columbia, for example, a subject called *Creating Technology Enhanced Learning Environments* is offered and described as follows:

> Paradigm shifts in education have influenced significant change in learning environments. This course is an inquiry into learning environments (past, present, and future) and explores the learning theories, software, hardware, and instructional strategies that support them. (University of British Columbia 2013)

In fact, it is commonplace within the broad discourse associated with digital learning to find *changing paradigms* being referred to. An example is the emergence of the so-called 'flipped classroom' – a term that has caught on in recent years to describe the removal of instructional lectures from the classroom, with students instead being asked to make use of Internet based content at home focused on a particular topic prior to engaging in discussion and problem solving activities in the classroom (Tucker 2012). The assumption here is that in many cases students can discover content equally as informative as what an instructor might initially provide. But the innovation goes deeper in that it also promotes inquiry-based learning followed by dialogue and collaborative activity. This may represent a paradigm shift in terms of practice but it is also consistent with a social constructivist approach to teaching and learning.

Becoming to know

The work of Jakubik (2011) on the "knowledge creation paradigm" within the broader Knowledge Management discourse represents an important contribution beyond the discourse community for which it is targeted. Jakubik presents a "becoming epistemology" and a "becoming to know framework" with a conceptualisation at its core that emphasises a virtuous cycle (or spiral) involving learning, knowing, and becoming (see Figure 2). As an epistemology, it moves beyond propositional statements toward a theory of actualisation.

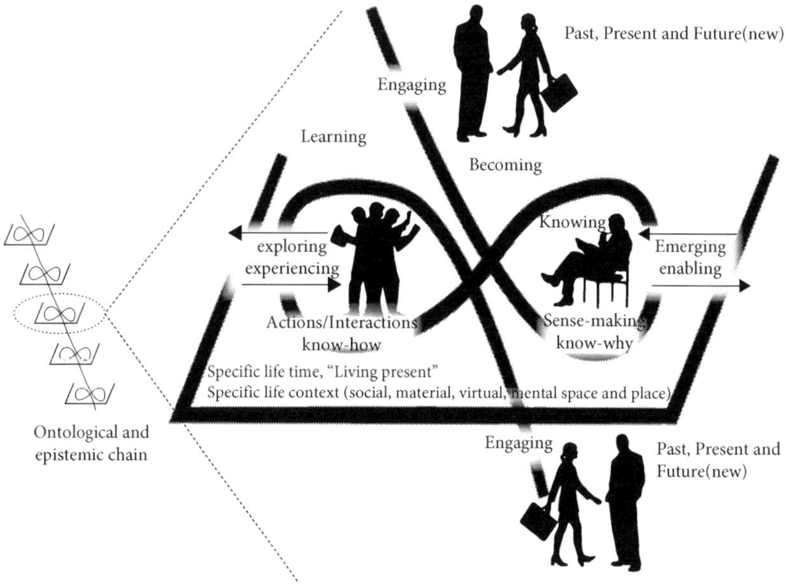

Figure 2. Becoming to Know. Adapted from Jakubik (2011, 381)

For Jakubik:

> Becoming … is viewed not only as evolution, change, a dynamic and emerging process, but as a dialectic and iterative process of continuous experiencing, learning and sense making. "Becoming epistemology" is both an engagement (actions and interactions) with the real world in a living present and making sense of the experience. It is a movement or flow from the past toward the future through the living present. Because both reality and humans evolve (i.e. are being changed) and because the learner (subject) and what it is to learn (object) are in unity, there is a dynamic and dialectic interplay between learning and knowing … "becoming epistemology" is a synthesis of learning and knowing […]. (Jakubik 2011, 392)

Key to Jakubik's framework is *engagement*, a shared context for knowledge creation where activities such as dialogue are instrumental. In explaining the semantics embedded in her conceptualisation Jakubik makes use of the philosophical term *phronesis*, a term associated with the application of wisdom in clearly identifying *ends* and discerning the best *means* to achieve them. This term is described by Nonaka et al., the originators of Knowledge Management as a distinct discourse, as a "forgotten kind of knowledge ... practical wisdom" (Nonaka and Takeuchi 2011, 58). In Jakubik's conceptual framework it is certainly not forgotten, as it has a key function in connecting *know-why* and *sense-making* with *know-how* (see Figure 2).

So why is *know-why* important here? For Jakubik (2011, 389) becoming has a teleological dimension, one of three primary explanatory functions of *why*-questioning as outlined by Evered's (2005) "typology of explicative models":

Causal: (*Why E? Because C* (C = cause));
Teleological: (*Why E? In order to P* (P = Purpose)); and
Gestaltic: (*Why E? For these reasons, R* (R = Reasons))

There are other reasons why *know-why* is important and to elucidate further the discussion now turns to what distinguishes *explanation* from *information* and the implications this has for technology supported learning environments.

Questions and Inquiry

Questions initiated by *who, what, when, where, why* and *how* belong to a set sometimes referred to as the journalists' questions (Urquhart and McIver 2005, 82). Why this label? For the simple reason that answers to these questions help create or frame a story. More importantly, without answers to *who, what, when,* or *where* – the most basic facets of factual information – there is no news and nothing to report. As it happens, these four key questions also comprise the core semantics of all metadata schemas – that is, schemas used particularly by librarians to identify, organise and classify information for structured purposes of information retrieval and resource discovery, particularly on the Internet (Mason 2009). Together, responses to these four basic questions also define the core aspects of provenance and the *aboutness* of content – in other words, the descriptive dimension of content. Whether the *what* is a description of the content, a keyword, kind of resource, or even weighting information about the number of hyperlinks associated with it, this still refers to the aboutness of content. For these reasons the four basic questions have been described as the "primitives of information retrieval" (Mason 2008, 547) or as the "kernel" of Dublin Core metadata (Kunze 2001). However, when answers to questions of *who, what, when,* and *where* are supplemented with answers to *how* and *why* then storytelling takes place and information is accompanied by explanation or elaboration – whether it is hypothetical, rhetorical, truthful, or otherwise (see Figure 3).

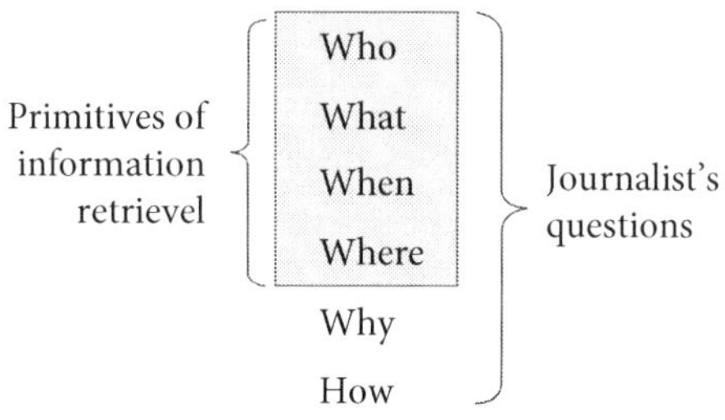

Figure 3. Question Primitives of Information and Explanation

At this point it seems natural to ask the question why *why* and *how* not part of the core set of primitives for information retrieval, when in conversation they can certainly elicit information as a response. Put simply, the main reason is that the semantics of *why* and *how* as standalone terms do not carry sufficient context to map clearly to factual information and are either ambiguous (*why* having causal, teleological, or gestaltic implications) or relate to procedural knowledge, as with *how* (Mason 2009; Verberne 2010). In the case of a *why*-question, what is typically expected in response is either some kind of rationale or plausible explanation – as such, the response just needs to satisfy the conventions of dialogue which are often concerned with achieving a sense of *shared meaning*. In this function *why*-questioning is an act of inquiry that seeks to make sense or understand – information is not its core concern. Because of this search engines do not currently respond effectively to *why*-questions, as contextual information is difficult to infer from a single *why*-question. This presents a challenge for designers of tools that might help learners interact directly with explanatory content and suggests that a dialogic approach might guide such development.

In terms of teaching practice that puts student questioning and inquiry at the forefront of learning, Rothstein and Santana (2011) outline the Question Formulation Technique, an approach to collaborative learning in which divergent thinking (through opening the mind to new possibilities), convergent thinking (involving synthesis, analysis and meaning making), and metacognition (reflection upon these processes) are all brought together in a structured sequence (Rothstein and Santana 2011, 16–20). In this technique students are encouraged to ask their own questions and in class activity learn to classify different question types and to appreciate the difference between open and closed questions. After many years of applying this technique results show:

> Students who learn the difference between closed- and open-ended questions climb a sharp learning curve in a very small amount of time. We have seen in many settings that it is a transformative moment when the student discovers and truly understands this one important lesson: *the construction and phrasing of a question shapes the kind of information you can expect to receive.*
>
> (Rothstein and Santana 2011, 74)

Questioning not only drives dialogue it is also an important aspect of learning and a powerful tool when it is the student who constructs questions for further inquiry. When these questions touch upon the need for explanation or elaboration – that is, something more than information – then *sense-making* is stimulated. Likewise, storytelling invokes sense-making beyond the communication of factual information. And one reason why storytelling is a powerful means of knowledge preservation and sharing, as is evidenced by pre-literate Indigenous cultures, is that it situates information within a context broader than that described by *who, what, when,* and *where*; it connects with experience, an *epistemology of becoming,* and the necessity to continually make sense of the world.

Sense-making

Among the many cognitive activities that can take place while learning *making sense of things,* or *sense-making,* is integral to comprehension and the development of understanding. Whether this act is interpretive or reflective it can also be understood as conducive to the creation of knowledge (Weed 2003, 143). While it is not necessarily a component of all learning or knowledge creation, as in the case of rote learning, it plays a particularly important role during inquiry, taking place at any time from initiation to culmination of an inquiry, or during reflection once inquiry has ceased.

Sense-Making can also be seen as terminology with high utility as it has been used as a formal methodology in recent years in academic discourses such as Communications (Dervin 1998), and a key term within Management (Weick 1995), Complexity (Snowden 2002), and Information Systems (Sharma 2010). There are differences in approach and detail but essentially:

> The concept of sensemaking is well named because, literally, it means the making of sense. Active agents construct sensible, sensable … events … They 'structure the unknown' … How they construct what they construct, why, and with what effects are the central questions for people interested in sensemaking … [importantly] Sensemaking is grounded in both individual and social activity.
>
> (Weick 1995, 4–6)

Whether it takes place as a single cognitive act or a series of cognitive acts, *sense-making* involves more than eliciting *meaning* from communication or content and the construction of knowledge based upon that meaning. Sense-making also involves *comprehension* and *understanding,* both essential components of learning and achieving these may require abstraction and/or construction of models that express relationships and processes (Bloom 1956; Anderson and Krathwohl 2001; Krathwohl 2002). To make sense of things is to find or perceive a certain coherence in things; a pattern of relations, causes and effects; to *understand why* actions or events have taken place; or, to discern natural phenomena or social conventions. For Wells, however, there is an added dimension when sense-making takes place within dialogic inquiry: "[I]t is by attempting to make sense with and for others, that we make sense for ourselves" (Wells 2000, 57).

Importantly, sense-making may also invoke "sense un-making" because constructing knowledge may involve the dismantling of a former conceptualisation (Dervin 1999, 729); or, it may also represent conditions of *stasis,* where plateaus of understanding function, inquiry pauses, and conceptualisation of the world has sufficient coherence. Thus, for most people, the concept of gravity can be readily understood in the way Newton understood it – it makes sense as a *law* of the natural world, and apples do predictably fall from trees. However, it is also the case that for fewer numbers of people the sophisticated conceptualisations of physicists like Einstein and Hawking can be readily understood. While it may make sense to accept the judgement of the scientific community actually understanding the science is another thing altogether. Thus, while scientific method and thought may point to deeper, discoverable truths, grounded in evidence, scientific discourse also contains many competing theoretical models that both describe and explain the way things are. To be useful, then, theories and models just need to be plausible in order to make sense. If something makes sense, then sufficient understanding is enabled allowing new concepts and knowledge to be created. A metaphor for this process can be found in standards development, in which a standard can be understood as a stable document representing consensus from a community of practice. Standards are only ever developed to completion when two conditions are met – they are fit for purpose; and, they have gained sufficient consensus for adoption. In other words, they make sense in having utility for a defined constituency and a specific purpose.

The question now emerges as to how to best make sense of the *why dimension – asking, learning, understanding, knowing,* and *explaining why* – so that components within technical specifications such as data models, information models, and ontologies can be created to inform development of digital technologies to support learning. One approach is to consider existing models.

Knowledge modeling

The use of models and frameworks to represent conceptual domains and enable the development of shared conceptualisations are proven devices to stimulate sense-making. Whether expressed as a simple taxonomy or classification, a table, an entity-relationship model, computational code representing rules for interactions within a domain, or as a complex data model for an IT specification, knowledge modelling takes place within many discourses and communities of practice – including Anthropology (Wilkins 2013, 5), Educational Theory (Bloom 1956; Krathwohl 2002), and Knowledge Management (Nonaka et al. 1995; Snowden 2002). Take for example the *wisdom pyramid* as depicted in Figure 4.

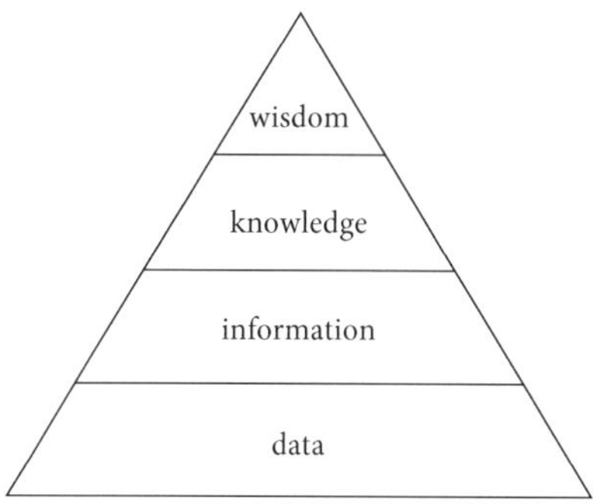

Figure 4. Data-Information-Knowledge-Wisdom (DIKW) Pyramid

The wisdom pyramid (also known as the DIKW pyramid) depicts a simple hierarchical relationship between data, information, knowledge and wisdom. As such, it can readily make sense and has utility when conveying that the higher conceptual entities within it are supported by those beneath. It also implicitly involves a progression from no context (data) to the development of meaning, understanding, and insight. Combined with syntax and semantics, data becomes information; as information is contextualised and interpreted it becomes knowledge; and as knowledge is tempered with experience it can become wisdom.

Despite the simplicity of the DIKW model it has attracted much attention and debate. Detailed study of the literature reveals a broad use of semantics, with the conceptual boundaries between *knowledge* and *information* where most divergence exists (Cleveland 1982; Adler 1986; Zeleny 1987; Ackoff 1989; Hey 2004) and variance in where to situate concepts like *understanding*. For example, Zeleny (1987, 60) represents the hierarchy as a progression from "know-nothing" (data) to "know-why" (wisdom) while Ackoff (2009) represents a progression of deepening understanding from *relations* (data into information) to *patterns* (information into knowledge) to *principles* (knowledge into wisdom). Others have probed this broad usage and identified insufficient treatment of wisdom (Rowley 2007) or provided critiques (Mason 2003, 2009; Frické 2009; Sharma 2010) that point to inadequacy of the model to inform ICT systems development, because it is not an accurate representation for all contexts and rendering knowledge into data where possible is also a value-chain that is commonly pursued. Following this, it can be argued that the cliché of the *knowledge age* describing our times has already morphed into the *data age*, because data is now seen as the higher value entity in which knowledge is perceived more as latent.

Probably the biggest weakness of the wisdom hierarchy as an adequate model of knowledge is that it lacks explicit representation of movement or dynamics as does the epistemological framework of Jakubik shown in Figure 2. In the conceptual modelling of Snowden (2002, 110) knowledge is far more complex because it is "both a thing and a flow". This same point is taken up by Dervin (1998, 36), a prominent exponent of "Sense Making methodology", when she conceptualizes "knowledge and information as a verb". *Verbing* concepts to account for the dynamics of learning can be also seen in Krathwohl's (2002) revision of Bloom's taxonomy of educational objectives, shown in Table 1, in which each term is reworked into active tense in the same sense of *becoming*. It is also notable in Krathwohl's revision that *knowledge* as a key term has been removed, partly due to the fact that in Bloom's usage factual knowledge (*knowing-that*) is not a complete representation of knowledge. For Krathwohl, knowledge can be classified into four kinds: factual, conceptual, procedural, and metacognitive (Krathwohl 2002, 214).

Table 1. Bloom's Taxonomy – original and revised

Higher order thinking

Bloom's Original Taxonomy (1956)	Revised taxonomy (Krathwohl 2002)
Evaluation	Creating
Synthesis	Evaluating
Analysis	Analyzing
Application	Applying
Comprehension	Understanding
Knowledge	Remembering

Lower order thinking

Bloom's taxonomy has made sense to educators for over fifty years. It continues to do so – particularly in its revised form and when grounded within discipline-specific subject matter – as teachers endeavour to teach in ways that develop higher order thinking skills. But, again, just like a standard, it is a model that has utility within a defined scope of application and it is not intended to mean that all cognitive activity associated with learning must begin with remembering factual information in order to understand it or that teaching factual knowledge is a prerequisite to enabling any creative knowledge construction. It is, however, not immediately clear where *why dimension* might be situated within the taxonomy although *explaining* can be an aspect of understanding, *asking* an aspect of analysing, and *knowing* an aspect of evaluating. From an inquiry-based learning perspective, it is also arguable that such taxonomies are at odds with representations such as the Inquiry Cycle (Figure 1) in which inquiry does not necessarily depend upon subject knowledge to proceed. Such dissonance does not render either approach as wrong but it points to limitations in the application of these models. So, what other representations might be of use?

The use of spirals to represent interactions of tacit and explicit dimensions of knowledge has been used following Polyani's (1967) work within the philosophy of science highlighting the tacit dimension in which he famously stated "we can know more than we can tell". Much of the discourse on knowledge management initiated by Nonaka and Takeuchi in 1995 draws upon Polyani in proposing a dynamic model that represents the organisational knowledge lifecycle as interactions of tacit and explicit knowledge throughout four ongoing processes involving socialisation, externalisation, combination, and internalisation known as the "SECI model". Within this model dialogue plays a key role in the externalisation of tacit knowledge as aspects of it become explicit. This approach to modelling is common within the KM literature and is also present in Jakubik's epistemological framework. Moreover, it aligns well with Wells' treatment of dialogic inquiry:

> The understanding attained through knowledge building dialogue at the end of one cycle provides the basis for *making sense* of further experience and information in the next. This is one of the senses in which there is a *spiral of knowing* over successive engagements with the object of the activity which the knowing serves to mediate. (Wells 2000, 70 [*my emphasis*])

Because this chapter has been concerned with inquiry, questions of how to harmonise these and other approaches to knowledge modelling are left lingering – although a synthesis relevant to inquiry is proposed in Figure 5, where a relationship between reflective and dialogic activity is depicted within processes of asking, learning, understanding, knowing, and explaining why. While reflection has not been dealt with in any detail within this chapter and dealt with elsewhere (Mason 2012) Figure 5 is intended to emphasise its relationship to dialogue, with reason connecting both. In some ways, as already argued, such models are adequate in whatever context they make sense; while the lingering questions are also questions that need to be pursued further if new ICT tools are to be developed from rigorously produced conceptualisation and modelling.

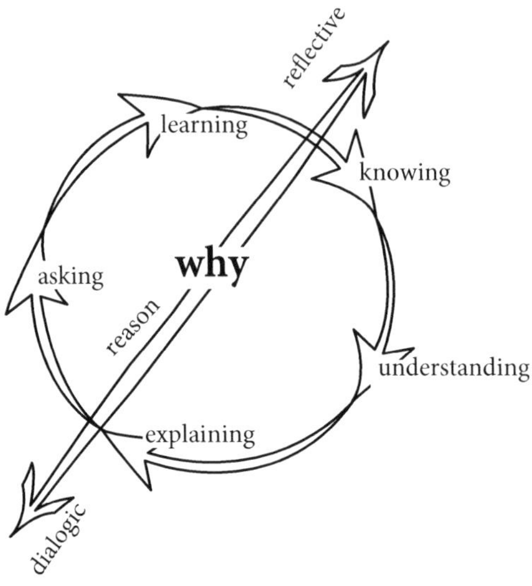

Figure 5. The *Why Dimension* of Inquiry

Tools for sense-making – Tools for inquiry

In technology supported learning environments sense-making is stimulated by many things: text, symbols, graphics, animations, video, navigational design, questions, and engagement or dialogue with others. In recent commentary that reaches a large constituency of educational professionals (the annual *Horizon Report* published by the New Media Consortium), sense-making has been appropriated as an important term within the discourse on e-learning:

> The abundance of resources and relationships made easily accessible via the Internet is increasingly challenging us to revisit our roles as educators in sense-making, coaching, and credentialing. (Johnson et al. 2010, 3)

Part of this challenge involves development of critical thinking skills in this context of abundant information resources and networked opportunities for social and professional engagement. But is also invokes a call for the development of inquiry skills (Kuhlthau et al. 2007) and use of dialogue in the development of reasoning skills (Ravenscroft 2007, 2011). In order to maximise the advantage of the richly networked environment of the Internet skills are required beyond point-and-click searching or browsing the vast information spaces and socially connecting with others; skills that require discernment, engagement, reasoning, dialogue and inquiry.

So, what will the tools be within technology supported environments that might stimulate this? In sum, the tools useful for sense-making will need to interoperate well with the tools of inquiry. Existing tools include social media and collaborative workspaces such as wikis that promote reflective writing and social engagement; they also include intelligent tutoring environments that utilise discourse technologies (Gholson et al. 2012; Graesser 2011) and application-specific games (Ravenscroft 2007). Dialogue is part and parcel of such tools; however, these tools can also be seen as in the early stages of development in that they do not provide explicit or sophisticated support for dialogic inquiry initiated by *why*-questioning – or any other explicit support for the *why dimension*.

A number of promising frontiers useful for supporting the *why dimension* of inquiry – and, in particular, dialogic inquiry – are already emerging. These include automated question-generation, a field that has arisen out of the intelligent tutoring community, and is focused on building systems that can create questions appropriate for any content and enable students to be scaffolded in the construction of well-formed questions. Thus, Graesser et al., observe, that in traditional classroom settings:

> Most teachers, tutors, and student peers do not ask a high density of deep questions … so students have a limited exposure to high-quality inquiry. There are a few role models in school environments through which students can learn good question asking and answering skills vicariously. This situation presents a golden opportunity for turning to technology to help fill this gap.
>
> (Graesser et al. 2010, 125)

Conclusion

Through focusing on dialogic inquiry and how it manifests in technology supported learning this chapter has introduced the *why dimension* as a construct that represents dialogic and reflective inquiry across a continuum of activities. A variety of sense-making models have also been introduced which highlight the role of the *why dimension* in contexts that involve both learning and knowing. Specifically, Figure 2 highlights *knowing-why* within a 'becoming to know' epistemological framework; Figure 3 distinguishes between information and explanation; and, Figure 5 represents a set of key activities of the *why dimension* – *asking, learning, understanding, knowing,* and *explaining why*.

Within any learning context the *why dimension* represents activities that are either foundational or integral to inquiry – and therefore this construct can be seen to function as a sense-making model that might also inform the design of technology supported learning. There are limits to what models can express, however, and while they are important to sense-making their utility is defined by context. Reasoning, reflection, and dialogue are all activities associated with dialogic inquiry and these activities provide the context for consideration of how the *why dimension* in technology supported learning environments may be supported.

While there exists an abundance of digital technology that can be harnessed for purposes of inquiry and learning it is the mainstream *search* tools that maintain a dominant role due to their high utility. But, as powerful as they are for purposes of data mining, information seeking, and enriching social networks, they remain limited in their capacity for sustaining inquiry that needs to probe deeper into reasoning, problem solving, and interacting with *explanatory* content. Whether it is through the agency of social media, intelligent tutoring, or some other innovation in digital technology, technology support of a dialogic approach to inquiry holds much promise.

References

Ackoff, Russell. 1989. "From Data to Wisdom." *Journal of Applied Systems Analysis* 16: 3–9.

Ackoff, Russell, L. Herbert J. Addison, and Andrew Carey. 2010. *Systems Thinking for Curious Managers: With 40 New Management F-Laws*. Axminster, UK: Triarchy Press Limited.

Adler, Mortimer J. 1986. *A Guidebook to Learning: for a Lifelong Pursuit of Wisdom*. New York: Macmillan.

Anderson, Lorin, and David Krathwohl (eds). 2001. *A Taxonomy for Learning, Teaching, and Assessing: A Revision of Bloom's Taxonomy of Educational Objectives*. New York: Longman.

Bahktin, Mikhail. 1981. *The Dialogic Imagination – Four Essays*. ed. by Michael Holquist, Trans. by Caryl Emerson, and Michael Holquist. Austin, Texas: University of Texas Press.

Benkler, Yochai. 2006. *The Wealth of Networks: How Social Production Transforms Markets*. New Haven, USA: Yale University Press.

Berge, Zane L., and Lin A. Muilenburg (eds). 2013. *Handbook of Mobile Learning*. United Kingdom: Routledge.

Bloom, Benjamin (ed.). 1956. *Taxonomy of Educational Objectives – Handbook 1: Cognitive Domain*. Reproduced 1984. New York: Longman.

Bruck, Peter A., and Madanmohan Rao (eds). 2013. *Global Mobile: Applications and Innovations for the Worldwide Mobile Ecosystem*. Medford, NJ: Information Technology Today, Inc.

Bruner, Jerome. 1966. *Toward a Theory of Instruction*. Cambridge, MA: Harvard University Press.

Bruner, Jerome. 1990. *Acts of Meaning. The Jerusalem-Harvard Lectures*. Cambridge, MA: Harvard University Press.

Casey, Leo, and Bertram C. Bruce. 2011. "The Practice Profile of Inquiry: Connecting Digital Literacy and Pedagogy." *E-Learning and Digital Media* 8 (1): 76–85. DOI: 10.2304/elea.2011.8.1.76

Cleveland, Harlan. 1982. "Information as a Resource." *The Futurist* 16 (6): 34–39.

Dash, Nirod. 1993. "Research Paradigms in Education: Towards a Resolution". *Journal of Indian Education* 19 (2): 1–6.

Dervin, Brenda. 1999. "On studying Information Seeking Methodologically: the Implications of Connecting Metatheory to Method". *Information Processing & Management* 35 (6): 727–750. DOI: 10.1016/S0306-4573(99)00023-0

Dervin, Brenda. 1998. "Sense-Making Theory and Practice: An Overview of User Interests in Knowledge Seeking and Use". *Journal of Knowledge Management* 2 (2): 36–46. DOI: 10.1108/13673279810249369

Dewey, John. 1966. *Democracy and Education: an Introduction to the Philosophy of Education* (originally published 1916). New York: The Free Press.

Evered, Roger. 2005. "A Typology of Explicative Models." In *Foundations for Inquiry: Choices and Tradeoffs in the Organizational Sciences*, ed. by Craig Lundberg, and Cheri Young, 198–202. Stanford, CA: Stanford Business Books.

Frické, Martin. 2009. "The Knowledge Pyramid: A Critique of the DIKW Hierarchy." *Journal of Information Science* 35 (2): 131–142. DOI: 10.1177/0165551508094050

Gasser, Les. 1991. "Social Conceptions of Knowledge and Action: DAI Foundations and Open Systems Semantics." *Artificial Intelligence* 47 (1–3): 107–138. DOI: 10.1016/0004-3702(91)90052-L

Gholson, Barry, Amy Witherspoon, Brent Morgan, Joshua K. Brittingham, Robert Coles, Arthur C. Graesser, Jeremiah Sullins, and Scotty D. Craig. 2012. "Exploring the Deep-Level Reasoning Questions Effect during Vicarious Learning among Eighth to Eleventh Graders in the Domains of Computer Literacy and Newtonian Physics." *Instructional Science* 37 (5): 487–49. DOI: 10.1007/s11251-008-9069-2

Graesser, Arthur C. 2011. "Learning, Thinking, and Emoting with Discourse Technologies." *American Psychologist* 66 (8): 746–757. Accessed June 24, 2013. DOI: 10.1037/a0024974

Graesser, Arthur, Yasuhiro Ozuru, and Jeremiah Sullins. 2010. "What is a Good Question?" In *Bringing Reading Research to Life*, ed. by Margaret McKeown, and Linda Kucan, 125–126. New York: The Guilford Press.

Griffin, Patrick, Barry McGaw, and Esther Care. (Eds.). 2012. *Assessment and Teaching of 21st Century Skills*. London: Springer.

Gruber, Thomas R. 1993. "A Translation Approach to Portable Ontology Specification." *Knowledge Acquisition* 5 (2): 199–220. DOI: 10.1006/knac.1993.1008

Guthrie, William K. C. 1989. "Socrates". In *The Oxford Companion to the Mind*, ed. by Richard Gregory, 723. New York, NY: Oxford University Press.

Halliday, Michael A. K. 1993. "Towards a Language-Based Theory of Learning". *Linguistics and Education* 5: 93–116. DOI: 10.1016/0898-5898(93)90026-7

Hart, Graeme, and Jon Mason. 1999. "Computer-Facilitated Communications in Transition". In *Virtual Instruction – Issues and Insights from an International Perspective*, ed. by Carine Feynten, and Joyce Nutta, 147–171. Colorado: Libraries Unlimited, Inc.

Hey, Jonathan. 2004. *The Data, Information, Knowledge*, Wisdom Chain: The Metaphorical link. Intergovernmental Oceanographic Commission (UNESCO).

Hunston, Susan. 2007. "Semantic Prosody Revisited." *International Journal of Corpus Linguistics* 12 (2): 249–268. DOI: 10.1075/ijcl.12.2.09hun

Jakubik, Maria. 2011. "Becoming to Know. Shifting the Knowledge Creation Paradigm". *Journal of Knowledge Management* 15 (3): 374–402. DOI: 10.1108/13673271111137394

Johnson, Larry, Alan Levine, Rachel Smith, and S. Stone. 2010. *The 2010 Horizon Report*. Austin, Texas: The New Media Consortium.

Kelly, Brian, Scott Wilson, and Randy Metcalfe. 2007. "Openness in Higher Education: Open Source, Open Standards, Open Access." *Proceedings ELPUB2007 Conference on Electronic Publishing*, 161–174. Accessed June 2013. http://elpub.scix.net/data/works/att/140_elpub2007.content.pdf.

Kelly, Patricia. 2008. *Towards Globo Sapiens: Transforming Learners in Higher Education*. Educational Futures: Rethinking Theory and Practice. Rotterdam: Sense Publishers.

Krathwohl, David R. 2002. "A Revision of Bloom's Taxonomy: An Overview". *Theory into Practice* 41 (4): 212–218. DOI: 10.1207/s15430421tip4104_2

Kuhlthau, Carol C. 2009. "Guided Inquiry: Learning in the 21st Century." *Proceedings, 38th Annual Conference incorporating the 13th International Forum on Research in School Librarianship*. Abano Terme (Padua), Italy: International Association of School Librarianship.

Kuhlthau, Carol C. 2004. *Seeking Meaning: A Process Approach to Library and Information Services*. London: Libraries Unlimited.

Kuhlthau, Carol C., Leslie Maniotes, and Ann Caspari. 2007. *Guided Inquiry: Learning in the 21st Century*. Westport, CT: Libraries Unlimited.

Kunze, John. 2001. "A Metadata Kernel for Electronic Permanence." In *Proceedings of the International Conference on Dublin Core and Metadata Applications DC-2001*, 177–184. Tokyo, Japan: National Institute of Informatics.

Leeson, Jerry, and Jon Mason. 2007. "The Open Agenda and Organisational Alignment." *Supplementary Proceedings, the 15th International Conference on Computers in Education* 1: 189–194. Accessed June 2013. http://www.intercog.net/publications/20071105_ICCE_Leeson_Mason.pdf.

Lipscomb, Lindsay, Janet Swanson, and Anne West. 2004. "Scaffolding". In *Emerging Perspectives on Learning, Teaching and Technology. The Global Text Project*, ed. by Michael Orey, 226–238. Zurich, Switzerland: Jacobs Foundation. Accessed June 2013. http://textbookequity.com/oct/Textbooks/Orey_Emergin_Perspectives_Learning.pdf.

Lyle, Sue. 2008. "Dialogic Teaching: Discussing Theoretical Contexts and Reviewing Evidence from Classroom Practice". *Language and Education* 22 (3): 222–240. DOI: 10.1080/09500780802152499

Mandinach, Ellen B., and Sharnell S. Jackson. 2012. *Transforming Teaching and Learning through Data-Driven Decision Making – Classroom Insights from Educational Psychology*. Thousand Oaks, CA: Corwin.

Mason, Jon. 2012. "Scaffolding Reflective Inquiry – Enabling Why-Questioning while e-Learning." *Research and Practice in Technology Enhanced Learning* 7 (3): 175–198.

Mason, Jon. 2009. "Knowledge Management and Dublin Core." *Proceedings, International Conference on Dublin Core and Metadata Applications*, Seoul, Korea, 41–50.

Mason, Jon. 2008. "A Model for Sense-Making: Exploring Why in the Context of Learning and Knowing". *Proceedings of the 16th International Conference on Computers in Education (ICCE2008)*, 545–549. Taipei, Taiwan: Asia-Pacific Society for Computers in Education.

Mason, Jon, Don Norris, and Paul Lefrere. 2003. "An Expeditionary Approach to E-Knowledge." *Proceedings of EduCause in Australasia*. Adelaide, 137–143.

Nelson, Tamara, and David Slavit. 2007. "Collaborative Inquiry among Science and Mathematics Teachers in the USA: Professional Learning Experiences through Cross-Grade, Cross-Discipline Dialogue". *Journal of In-Service Education* 33 (1): 23–39. DOI: 10.1080/13674580601157620

Nonaka, Ikujiro, and Hirotaka Takeuchi. 2011. "The Big Idea: The Wise Leader". *Harvard Business Review* 89 (5): 58–67.

Nonaka, Ikujiro, and Hirotaka Takeuchi. 1995. *The Knowledge Creating Company: How Japanese Companies Create the Dynamics of Innovation*. New York: Oxford University Press.

Patton, Michael Q. 1990. *Qualitative Evaluation and Research Methods*. 2nd edn. Newbury Park, CA: Sage.

Paul, Richard, and Linda Elder. 2007. "Critical Thinking: The Art of Socratic Questioning, Part I". *Journal of Developmental Education*. 31 (1): 36–37.

Paul, Richard. 1990. *Critical Thinking: What Every Person Needs to Survive in a Rapidly Changing World*. Rohnert Park, CA: Center for Critical Thinking and Moral Critique.

Polanyi, Michael. 1967. *The Tacit Dimension*. New York: Anchor Books.

Rambe, Patient. 2012. "Constructive Disruptions for Effective Collaborative Learning: Navigating the Affordances of Social Media for Meaningful Engagement". *The Electronic Journal of e-Learning* 10 (1): 132–146.

Ravenscroft, Andrew. 2011. "Dialogue and Connectivism: A New Approach to Understanding and Promoting Dialogue-Rich Networked Learning." *The International Review of Research in Open and Distance Learning* 12 (3). Accessed June 2013. http://www.irrodl.org/index.php/irrodl/article/view/934/1676.

Ravenscroft, Andrew. 2007. "Promoting Thinking and Conceptual Change with Digital Dialogue Games." *Journal of Computer Assisted Learning* 23 (6): 453–465. DOI: 10.1111/j.1365-2729.2007.00232.x

Renshaw, Peter D. 2010. "Dialogic Learning Teaching and Instruction". In *Dialogic Learning: Shifting Perspectives to Learning, Instruction, and Teaching*, ed. by Jos van den Linden, and Peter Renshaw, 1–15. The Netherlands: Kluwer Academic Publishers.

Rothstein, Dan, and Luz Santana. 2011. *Make Just One Change: Teach Students to Ask Their Own Questions*. Cambridge, MA: Harvard Education Press.

Rowley, Jennifer. 2007. "The Wisdom Hierarchy: Representations of the DIKW Hierarchy." *Journal of Information Science* 33 (2): 163–180. DOI: 10.1177/0165551506070706

Sharma, Nikhil. 2010. *Sensemaking Handoffs: Why? How? and When?* Doctoral Thesis, University of Michigan.

Sinclair, John M. 1991. *Corpus, Concordance, Collocation*. Oxford: Oxford University Press.

Snowden, Dave. 2002. "Complex Acts of Knowing: Paradox and Descriptive Self-Awareness". *Journal of Knowledge Management* 6 (20): 100–111. DOI: 10.1108/13673270210424639

Stumpf, Samuel E. 1983. *Philosophy: History and Problems*. New York, NY: McGraw-Hill.

Teo, Yiong Hwee. 2003. *Assessing Critical Thinking Through Scaffolded Asynchronous Online Discussion*. Singapore: Nanyang Technological University.

Tokuhama-Espinosa, Tracey. 2011. *Mind, Brain, and Education Science: A Comprehensive Guide to the New Brain*. New York: W.W. Norton.

Tomioka, S. 2009. "Why Questions, Presuppositions, and Intervention Effects". *Journal of East Asian Linguistics* 18 (4): 253–271. DOI: 10.1007/s10831-009-9053-0

Tucker, Bill. 2012. "The Flipped Classroom: Online instruction at home frees class time for learning." *Education Next* 12 (1). Accessed June 2013. http://educationnext.org/files/ednext_20121_BTucker.pdf

Urquhart, Vicki, and Monette McIver. 2005. *Teaching Writing in the Content Areas*. Alexandria, VA: Association for Supervision and Curriculum Development Publications.

Verberne, Suzanne. 2010. *In Search of the Why: Developing a System for Answering Why-Questions*. Nijmegen, The Netherlands: Radboud Universiteit.

Vygotsky, Lev S. 1978. *Mind in Society: The Development of Higher Psychological Processes*. Cambridge, MA: Harvard University Press.

Warwick, Paul, Sara Hennessy, and Neil Mercer. 2011. "Promoting Teacher and School Development through Co-Enquiry: Developing Interactive Whiteboard Use in a 'Dialogic Classroom'." *Teachers and Teaching* 17 (3): 303–324. DOI: 10.1080/13540602.2011.554704
Wegerif, Rupert. 2008. "Dialogic or Dialectic? The Significance of Ontological Assumptions in Research on Educational Dialogue". *British Educational Research Journal* 34 (3): 347–361. DOI: 10.1080/01411920701532228
Wells, Gordon. 1999. *Dialogic Inquiry: Towards a Sociocultural Practice and Theory of Education*. Cambridge, England: Cambridge University Press. DOI: 10.1017/CBO9780511605895
Wells, Gordon. 2000. "Dialogic Inquiry in Education: Building on the Legacy of Vygotsky". In *Vygotskian Perspectives on Literacy Research*, ed. by Carol Lee, and Peter Smagorinsky, 51–85. New York: Cambridge University Press.
Weed, Laura. 2003. *The Structure of Thinking – A Process-Oriented Account of Mind*. Exeter, UK: Imprint Academic.
Wells, Gordon. 1999. *Dialogic Inquiry: Towards a Sociocultural Practice and Theory of Education*. New York: Cambridge University Press. DOI: 10.1017/CBO9780511605895
Weick, Karl E. 1995. *Sensemaking in Organizations – Foundations for Organizational Science*. Thousand Oaks, CA: Sage Publications.
Weigand, Edda. 2010. *Dialogue: The Mixed Game*. Amsterdam: John Benjamins. DOI: 10.1075/ds.10
Wierzbicki, Andrzej, and Yoshiteru Nakamori. 2006. *Creative Space, Models of Creative Processes for the Knowledge Civilization Age* (Studies in Computational Intelligence 10). The Netherlands: Springer.
Wilkins, Andrew. 2013. "Shades of Freire: Exorcising the Spectre Haunting Pedagogy." *Journal of Pedagogy* 4 (1): 5–10. DOI: 10.2478/jped-2013-0001
Williams, Roy, Regina Karousou, and Jenny Mackness. 2011. "Emergent Learning and Learning Ecologies in Web 2.0." *The International Review of Research in Open and Distance Learning* 12 (3). Accessed June 24, 2013. http://www.irrodl.org/index.php/irrodl/article/view/883/1686.
Wood, David, Jerome Bruner, and Gail Ross. 1976. "The Role of Tutoring in Problem Solving". *Journal of Psychology and Psychiatry* 17 (2): 89–100. DOI: 10.1111/j.1469-7610.1976.tb00381.x
Zeleny, Milan. 1987. "Management Support Systems: Towards Integrated Knowledge Management." *Human Systems Management* 7 (1): 59–70.

Author's address

Jon Mason
Charles Darwin University & Queensland University of Technology
PO BOX 115
PARAP NT 0804
Australia
jon.mason@cslld.edu.au
jon@intercog.net

PART II

Learner-centered pedagogy

Building knowledge and constructing meaning in dialogic learning communities

Dialogue-oriented analysis of constructivist teaching and learning within a UK company

Robert M. Foster
The Research Institute for Information and Language Processing – Wolverhampton University

Within the UK company featured in this article, the use of Multiple Choice Questions (MCQs) has increased significantly in recent years (Foster 2013). Meta-cognitive analysis (Degrave 1996) forms part of ongoing research into the MCQ-Creation process operated by the organisation. The measurable assessments and learning outcomes from these investigations show that the internal dialogue (Hermens 1992) that occurs during MCQ-Creation facilitates constructivist learning at both individual (Mynard 2011) and corporate (Kirby 2011) levels. The recommendation is that the quality of corporate assessment and learning would be improved if the company held regular MCQ-Creation workshops. In addition to generating corporate knowledge in a usable MCQ format, MCQ-Creation workshops would also improve the overall corporate internal dialogue.

1. Introduction

The motivation for this research is a dramatic increase in the usage of Multiple Choice Questions (MCQs) within the host company. A recent survey provides clear evidence for the sharp increase in MCQ usage over the past decade and selected diagrams and tables from the survey are used to illustrate this increase within the company as a whole. Then some more focused presentations of the figures are used to show how MCQ usage levels vary depending upon the domain being tested and the assessment context in which the MCQs are used.

The creation of the MCQs is carried out by staff members, as opposed to relying upon MCQs produced outside the company. This MCQ-Creation process regularly prompts dialogue at a corporate level concerning the company's rules and procedures. This dialogue leads to re-constructions of the policy documents i.e. 'learning' at a corporate level (Kirby 2011).

The MCQs are intended to ensure that staff members have acquired the knowledge they need in order to discharge their responsibilities efficiently and safely. However, after working through the MCQ routines in formative, summative and refresher assessment contexts, candidates often also provide feedback concerning their struggle to select the correct response. The feedback contained in the incorrect responses together with their explanations of struggles to identify the correct response, provide crucially important exchanges in what becomes another dialogue about the company's policy documents. If these learners change their own internal representation of the company rules and procedures as a consequence of using the MCQs then this represents an internal learning dialogue. This is 'learning' at an individual level (Mynard 2011) that has occurred as a consequence of the prompting of MCQs.

Also, if those people who are most affected by approved documents that contain out-dated or impractical rules and procedures, have struggled to give the correct response to an MCQ after revising from these documents, then this is a signal to the policy writers that changes to the approved documents might be required. This is another instance of learning at a corporate level (Kirby 2011) in which the MCQs have prompted a dialogue that guides re-constructions of the company's policy documents.

Therefore, the suggestion within this article is that the creation and answering of MCQs within this corporate environment is a form of internal dialogue (Hermens 1992) that occurs at both individual (Mynard 2011) and corporate (Kirby 2011) levels. The foundation for exploring this idea is provided in the form of a new model for analyzing a 'constructivist learning dialogue' that is suitable for application within a variety of assessment contexts. The description includes the allocation of different categories of staff within the company to roles within the model. Application of the model is illustrated by applying a model of how MCQ-Creation operates within the host company in the context of a case study. Analysis of the currently applied methods for MCQ-Creation and its associated constructivist learning dialogue, revealed a series of other products that have arisen from what has developed into a conscious (meta-cognitive) constructivist learning dialogue.

The products from the dialogue include a new methodology Construed Antonym Realisation Exercise Generation (CAREGen) for MCQ-Creation and two new measures for its evaluation. The CAREGen methodology includes some steps that ensure that complete control is retained by the people engaged in MCQ-Creation.

The recommendation is that the company as a whole, and many staff as individuals, would benefit greatly from learning the skills of MCQ-Creation and thereby examining the constructivist learning dialogue which is perpetually operating within the company. It is therefore proposed that MCQ-Creation workshops should be undertaken by all staff involved in writing company rules and procedures. It is also noted that CAREGen includes some steps which might be completed automatically using software tools. Further consideration of this idea is provided in the Recommendations and Conclusions sections.

2. Context

2.1 Background

Under the UK Health and Safety at work, etc. Act 1974 (HASWA), participants in work activities have a Duty of Care for the health and safety of themselves and their colleagues. The Act specifically requires UK companies to provide information, instruction, training and supervision to ensure the health and safety at work of their employees:

> 2. (1) It shall be the duty of every employer to ensure, so far as is reasonably practicable, the health, safety and welfare at work of all his employees.
> (2) Without prejudice to the generality of an employer's duty under the preceding subsection, the matters to which that duty extends include in particular:
> (A)… (B) … (C) the provision of such information, instruction, training and supervision as is necessary to ensure, so far as is reasonably practicable, the health and safety at work of his employees; (D)… (E)….
>
> Health and Safety at Work, etc. Act 1974 – Section 2

In the 1990s, the host company introduced systems of training and assessment that use Multiple Choice Questions (MCQs) as part of their response to these legal requirements and sequences of MCQ test items are now used regularly within the company, as part of the process for helping managers of safety and training to meet their Duty of Care under HASWA. A recent survey of MCQ usage within the host company demonstrates that the use of Multiple Choice Questions (MCQs) has increased significantly in recent years (Foster 2013). The survey used a new measure of MCQ usage which is referred to as 'KACE' (Knowledge Acquisition Confirmation Events) (Foster 2012b). The KACE count shows the total number of correct responses to MCQs that have been registered by the host company's MCQ delivery system within the specified year. So for example, the KACE count of 32,890 for 2008 shows that on 32,890 separate occasions in the year 2008, users of the company's MCQ delivery system selected a correct response to a MCQ that was presented to them in either a refresher, summative or formative assessment context. Using a count of KACEs, Figure 1 and the accompanying Table 1, illustrates the dramatic rise in MCQ usage between 2008 and 2012. The authors explain that KACE figures are available for the years from 1998, but that the numbers are fairly stable for the years before 2008.

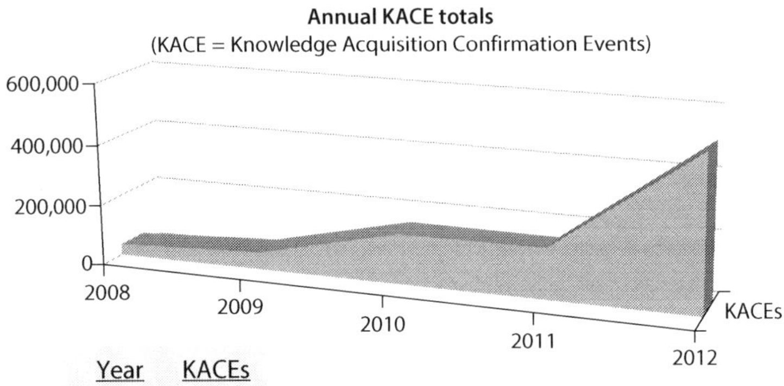

Year	KACEs
2008	**32,890**
2009	**53,655**
2010	**162,680**
2011	**164,031**
2012	**511,062**

Note: 1 × KACE = 1 × correct response to a MCQ test item covering a fact related to the specified sub-domain by a staff member

Figure 1 and Table 1. KACE totals between 2008 and 2012

Figure 2 and the accompanying Table 2, provides a comparison of the proportions of KACEs that occurred in formative, summative and refresher assessment contexts during 2012. These figures are examined in more detail in Section 4.

Assessment type 2012 KACE totals

Assessment type	KACEs
Formative	**7,800**
Summative	**22,149**
Refresher	**481,653**

Note: 1 × KACE = 1 × correct response to a MCQ test item covering a fact related to the specified sub-domain by a staff member

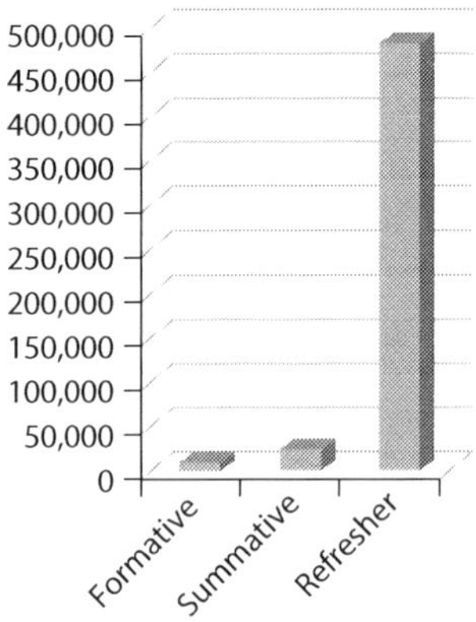

Figure 2 and Table 2. 2012 KACE counts categorized by assessment type

In 2012, only a small number of MCQs were used in formative and summative assessment contexts. The majority of MCQ usage is within the context of knowledge refresher assessments.

Table 3 shows how MCQ use has expanded into new content sub-domains since 2008.

Table 3. KACE counts in 2008, 2010 and 2012 by Content Sub-domain

Content sub-domain	2008 KACEs	2010 KACEs	2012 KACEs
Chainsaws	0	0	28,840
Heavy Plant	7,620	25,380	31,380
Operational Safety	0	47,480	271,685
Safety Health and Environment	25,270	55,920	104,160
Specific Risk	0	31,500	45.588
Apprentice Training	0	2,400	29,949

2.2 A model for a constructivist learning dialogue

This section uses the metaphor and terminology of a 'dialogue' to define a model for analysing constructivist learning within the featured company. First we define the roles of staff who are involved with learning and then there is a description of motivations and contexts for each of the defined roles. The roles in a constructivist learning dialogue during MCQ-Creation might reasonably be defined as is shown in Table 4.

Table 4. Roles within a constructivist learning dialogue focused around MCQ-Creation

Role	Description
<Learner>	A <Learner> is linked to the company through the relationship of 'Employee'
<Advisor>	A <Advisor> is linked to the company through the relationship of 'Technical specialist' or 'Internal Consultant' (this group would include those people who write documents that define the company's Rules, Procedures and Policies)
<Stakeholder>	A <Stakeholder> is linked to the company through the relationship of 'Shareholder', 'Director' or 'Manager'
<Guardian>	A <Guardian> is linked to the company through a relationship of 'Legislator' or 'External Consultant' (this group would include Governments, Unions, Professional bodies who define the rules within which the company must operate)

The motivations of the identified roles within a constructivist learning dialogue that is focused around MCQ-Creation, might reasonably be defined as is shown in Table 5.

Table 5. Motivations of roles within a constructivist learning dialogue focused around MCQ-Creation

Role	**Seeks a balance between …**
<Learner>	a. aspiration towards higher levels of authorisation/ responsibility b. limits in their ability for cognitive and experiential learning within time constraints
<Advisor>	a. aspiration towards higher levels of knowledge and understanding within <Learner>s b. Intrinsic Human limitations of <Learner>s reinforced by stated limiting requirements from <Guardian>s
<Stakeholder>	a. aspiration towards higher levels of profits and dividends in response to new opportunities within the environment b. limits in the organisation's ability for communication of Policy changes in both the cognitive and psychomotor learning domains (Bloom 1956)
<Guardian>	a. impose an absolute requirement for 'No accidents' (see HASWA 1974) b. provide guidance to help organisations to achieve this requirement

The case study that follows illustrates how the host company uses MCQs. The case study provides the background that is used in later sections to describe the outputs from the company's constructivist learning dialogue. After the case study description, the above terminology will be applied to the MCQ-Creation process.

2.3 Case study: MCQs for trade test knowledge check on high voltage cable jointing skills

On completion of their training which can take up to three years, apprentices at the host company must demonstrate that they have achieved a sufficient level of the knowledge and skills for effective conduct of their trade (Overhead Lines, Cable-Jointing, Substation-Fitting). In addition to monitoring progress of apprentices through their formal training courses, the company's progress monitoring system also ensures that a sufficient breadth of experience has been achieved by new recruits before they are put forward for their trade test and then become fully qualified crafts-persons. The trade test includes a knowledge check. These knowledge checks are carried out using MCQs. The MCQ test items used within trade-test knowledge-checks are provided in a NON interactive mode that does NOT deliver immediate feedback.

The trade-test knowledge-checks use two different formats of MCQ test item:

a. Traditional 4-option Multiple Choice (4MC) test items and
b. Multiple Alternative Choice (MAC)-formatted MCQ test items.

Meta-cognitive analysis (Degrave 1996) forms part of the ongoing research into the MCQ-Creation process operated by the organisation, which was started to investigate ways of improving the effectiveness of MCQ usage and in particular to find ways of improving MCQ-Creation efficiency. The MCQ Knowledge check in preparation for the Jointing trade test provides the context for our investigations into constructivist learning dialogues operating during MCQ-Creation at the company. The case study provides tangible illustrations of how the dialogues produce beneficial results, but it also demonstrates how the process of initial specification by managers and stakeholders, followed by developments and evaluations by subject experts and the responses from learners as they use the MCQs, can be viewed as exchanges within a constructivist learning dialogue. This is described in more detail in the next section.

3. Investigations of Manual MCQ-Creation using the constructivist learning dialogue model

Having defined a terminology for describing the roles and motivations that might be imagined to exist within the constructivist learning dialogue of a company, we can now use this terminology to define the constructivist learning dialogue. Analysis was made of the MCQ-Creation process as it occurred in several activities within the company which aimed to produce, disseminate and maintain the company's rules and procedures. This analysis produced many different representations of the MCQ-Creation processes. One shared outcome from all investigations was the identification of Formative (Crooks 2001), Summative (Glickman et al. 2009) and Refresher (Foster 2012b) assessment contexts:

a. Formative: Promote construction of knowledge in the mind of <Learner>
b. Summative: Confirm successful knowledge transfer from <Advisor> to <Learner>
c. Refresher: Refresh <Learner> knowledge after changes have occurred in the <Learner> cognitive state (eg due to the passage of time) or after <Advisor>s have pointed out to <Stakeholder>s (and possibly <Guardian>s) that changes have occurred in the company's operating and legislative environment.

In addition to these contrasting assessment contexts, the detail of the MCQ-Creation process can be expressed as follows using the terminology of the constructivist learning dialogue model applied to MCQ-Creation which was defined earlier:

Table 6. Steps within the MCQ-Creation process expressed using the terminology of constructivist learning dialogue focused around MCQ-Creation

Step	Description
STEP 1	<Guardian> highlights the need for a change in policy following a change in the company's operating or legislative environment
STEP 2	<Stakeholder> appoints a relevantly trained <Advisor> to write or amend the appropriate approved documents
STEP 3	<Advisor> identifies the groups of <Learner>s who will be required to interpret and implement the amended rules and procedures
STEP 4	<Advisor> amends the documents, ensuring they comply with the requirements of all relevant <Guardian>s
STEP 5	<Stakeholder> approves the documents as providing a good definition of the company's rules and procedures
STEP 6	<Stakeholder> decides how to present the amended policy to <Learner>s. The choices available to <Stakeholder> are: (6a) Send the documents directly to <Learner> (6b) Organise face to face launch sessions and induction and refresher training courses between <Advisor> and <Learner>s. (6c) Multiple Choice Question (MCQ) test routines that present the approved documents to <Learner>s.
STEP 7 (only possible after STEP 6c)	Feedback is created either during evaluation of MCQs by <Advisor> or by <Learner>s when the MCQ is actually in use. If <Stakeholder selects (6a) or (6b) then the 'dialogue' descends into a one-way 'dissemination' of knowledge from <Stakeholder> to <Learner> with some initial modifiying inputs from <Advisor> and/or <Guardian>). However, if <Stakeholder> selects (6c) then perhaps they have identified the benefit of using MCQs as the introduction of a feedback loop into the dialogue with every response selection that is made.
STEP 8	Revisions and updated versions of the approved documents can be produced by <Advisor>s in response to feedback from <Learner>s Of course, changes can be imposed from outside by the relevant <Stakeholder>s and <Guardian>s by returning to STEP 1. However, if MCQs have been introduced into the dialogue then <Learner>s can also provide feedback.
STEP 9	<Learner> feedback can be captured in many forms, including written reports from <Advisor>s during annual 'field checks' and refresher training courses and through analysis of <Learner> responses to Multiple Choice Question (MCQ) test routines.

The use of MCQ test items has been well received and a rapid expansion of the library of MCQ test items is underway. This provides a tempting possibility for supporting the auditing work of the <Advisor> by prompting thousands of highly focused opportunities for feedback exchanges between <Learner> and <Stakeholder> about the company's policies. In addition to the description in STEP 1 of the approved documents as 'corporate knowledge', the approved documents described above can also be accurately described as a 'social construction', since several distinct roles are clearly involved in their formulation and revision. Therefore the dialogue described above can be referred to as a constructivist learning dialogue.

In the next section the component concepts of a new MCQ-Creation methodology are described which have emerged from the meta-cognitive analysis of this company's MCQ-Creation processes. One of the appendices to this chapter also provides an outline of a MCQ-Creation workshop which has been designed to facilitate constructivist teaching and learning of this new MCQ-Creation methodology.

4. Products from constructivist learning dialogue

There have been a number of discoveries made through the ongoing constructivist learning dialogue about MCQ-Creation within the host company. These include, but are not limited to:

a. Two new evaluations measures for comparing the efficacy of MCQ-Creation methodologies (Foster 2012b)
b. Controlled Specific Learning Objectives (CSLO) and Controlled Rhetorical Structure Theory (CRST) (Foster 2009) – The 'CRST-compliant CSLO' structure of specific learning objectives was specified and refined through the constructivist learning dialogue that developed during examination of existing MCQ-Creation methods. The specification draws from the concepts of controlled language, to unite Robert Mager's theory of Specific Learning Objectives (Mager 1975) with Mann and Thompson's Rhetorical Structure Theory (Mann et al. 1988) and also influenced by the theories of Benjamin Bloom (Bloom 1956) and the work of Norman Gronlund (Gronlund 2009).
c. The Multiple Alternative Choice (MAC) MCQ format (Foster 2010a) – This format became the preferred MCQ format following the conclusive results from the evaluation.

d. The method of Causal Relation Explication, Addition and Manipulation (CREAM) for suggesting MCQ stem questions (Foster 2010b) – When applying standard MCQ-Creation methods to the 'TAR induction' case study, a particular system for categorising causal coherence relations (Sanders et al. 1993) was particularly helpful in producing well-formed MCQ stems.

However, the CAREGen methodology for MCQ-Creation (Foster 2012a) is the principal output from this dialogue. The CAREGen methodology for MCQ-Creation is described in the next section and instances from the case study are used to illustrate its application.

4.1 The CAREGen methodology for MCQ-Creation

The CAREGen methodology for MCQ-Creation emerged after comparisons were made between the manual processes of MCQ-Creation that currently operate within the company and other proposed methodologies for MCQ generation that are described in the literature (Brown et al. 2005; Mitkov and Ha 2003, 2006; Tsumori and Kaijiri 2007). The specification of changes to the existing system that arose from this investigation were different to the specifications of any other available systems, and so the CAREGen methodology was developed to incorporate the improvements that had been identified.

The CAREGen methodology for MCQ-Creation includes a step in which there is a narrowing of the range of construal operations offered to those answering MAC test items so as to reduce the required cognitive level within the cognitive domain of Bloom's Taxonomy (Bloom 1956) for learners to deliver a correct response. More specifically, the Construed Antonym Realisation Exercise (CARE) Generation methodology allows designers to identify the salient features within potentially very complex Antonym ranges (Paradis 2010) and rationalise them into relatively simple domain-specific and construal-specific Complementarities (Cruse and Togia 1995), which can be traced back to exact phrases within the source documents. The item design processes can then identify alternative construal operations (Croft and Cruse 2004) that might be applied by readers, and prompt decisions about whether each of the construal operations is either erroneous or correct in the context of the specified CSLO (Foster 2009). All 'correct' construal operations that a learner might apply to the stem are associated with the 'correct' response option and all incorrect construal operations are associated with the 'incorrect' response option. These elements are then presented within the framework of a Multiple Alternate Choice (MAC) test item.

A summary of the steps of the CAREGen methodology is presented below:

Table 7. Summary of steps within the CAREGen MCQ-Creation methodology

Step	Description
STEP 1	Define Objective of the MCQ routine in a CSLO
STEP 2	Identify the most appropriate source documents
STEP 3	Explicate (and if necessary Add) Coherence Relations for sentences that meet certain criteria and then re-work them into CRST-compliant CSLOs
STEP 4	Extract candidate antonym pairs for each of the identified sentences
STEP 5	Apply construal operations in the context of identified antonym pairs
STEP 6	Generate MAC test items by inserting generated components into a template.

There follows an Illustrative example in which the methodology is applied to the case study defined earlier.

4.2 Applying CAREGen to create MCQs in the HV Cable Jointing domain

The knowledge required for high voltage cable-jointing is a domain with a rich variety of illustrative work situations and domain specific entities, relationships and boundaries. Members of the target audience are likely to use a combination of the full range of learning styles as they interpret the documented rules for this domain. The quoted examples demonstrate how reader mis-construal of written instructions can sometimes be anticipated. The examples also show the power of MAC formatted MCQ test items when they are used to explicate different construal operations that might be applied by different readers to the same source sentence.

4.2.1 *Step 1 – Define Objective of the MCQ routine in a CSLO*

The first step in the application of the CAREGen methodology is to define the objective of the test routine. For example the CSLO (Controlled Specific Learning Objective) (Foster 2009) for the cable jointing case study is to: "Identify candidates who can correctly recognize LV general jointing procedures for live and dead working (ST:CA1C)".

4.2.2 *Step 2 – Identify the most appropriate source documents*

The second step is to use the CSLOs to identify appropriate source documents. It might seem that the above CSLO makes this easy because the identifier for a single source document is included. However there is a good chance that this document refers to further subsidiary documents and it is important that those documents are also identified and added to the source document collection. For the purposes of this case study the source document will be regarded as just the single document referred to in the CSLO. "Sentences contained within a date-specific version of ST:CA1C 'Relating to General Requirements Low Voltage Jointing".

4.2.3 *Step 3 – Explicate (and if necessary Add) Coherence Relations for sentences that meet the selection criteria and then re-work them into CRST-compliant CSLOs*

The third step is to apply the Explication and Addition components of the CREAM method (Foster 2010b) to sentences which contain:

a. lexemes that have some semantic relationship to the CSLO
b. lexemes that indicate coherence relations that can be reliably manipulated into MAC stems
c. textual patterns which indicate implicit or incomplete coherence.

The illustrative example was generated following the identification (within the document whose reference number is quoted in the CSLO) of the lexeme 'if' and 'do not' but missing the lexeme 'then'. These features indicate that the sentence can probably be manipulated into a MAC but first the implicit 'then' needs to be positioned correctly.

> If the flame is accidentally extinguished do not attempt to relight the gas and do not allow any naked flame near, until the accumulated gas has been dispersed by opening ventilators, tent flaps or doors. ST:CA1C – General Requirement 1

Before this sentence could be put forward to the next step, the 'Condition' Relation had to be Explicated by adding 'then', and the sentence did not make sense without also 'Explicating' using a lexeme from the title of the section from which it was taken. The result of the 'Explication' action taken in step 3 of the CARE creation process was:

> If the flame of a gas torch is accidentally extinguished then do not attempt to relight the gas and do not allow any naked flame near, until the accumulated gas has been dispersed by opening ventilators, tent flaps or doors.
> ST:CA1C – General Requirement 1 (modified)

4.2.4 *Step 4 – Extract candidate antonym pairs for each of the identified sentences*

The fourth step is to identify lexical items within the list of extracted sentences that co-locate within syntactic patterns that have been previously identified as likely to co-locate with 'opposite' word pairs (Cruse and Togia 1995). Complementarities are awarded the highest scores while increasingly complex and ambiguous antonyms are awarded progressively lower scores. Complementarities and Antonyms are relations between construal operations, not between lexical items (Croft and Cruse 2004 – Chapter 7).

4.2.5 *Step 5 – Apply construal operations in the context of identified antonym pairs*

The fifth step of the CARE Generation methodology gives more detailed guidance about the Manipulation step than is specified in CREAM (Foster 2010b). An attempt is made to perceive each of the sentences from the source document through as many of the construal operations (Croft and Cruse 2004 – Chapter 3) as are sensible. Each of the identified antonym pairs is then applied to form an AC item set. One of the created MAC test items includes the result of applying a spacio-temporal mis-construal to the source sentence:

> The use of the disposable plastic gloves provided should eliminate any contact, but if it occurs, the affected area should be washed immediately with plenty of soap and water. ST:CA1C – General Requirement 37

… in the context of the antonym pair: "Correct action vs NOT the correct action"

4.2.6 *Step 6 – Generate AC item sets by inserting generated components into a MAC template*

The CARE creation process concludes by using the 'correct' and 'incorrect' statements and associated antonym pairs to generate AC item sets. AC item sets which use the same antonym pair are grouped together in order to produce MAC test items ready for evaluation. The MAC test item that resulted from the illustrative example process application in this section is provided below:

What action should be taken if the flame of a gas torch is accidentally extinguished?

This is Company Policy This is NOT Company Policy	Immediately try to relight the gas with any available flame source
This is Company Policy This is NOT Company Policy	Leave the work site immediately and do not stop to gather personal belongings
This is Company Policy This is NOT Company Policy	Open vertilators, tent flaps or doors
This is Company Policy This is NOT Company Policy	Turn off the gas supply

Figure 3. Example of a Multiple Alternative Choice (MAC) formatted MCQ

Many other products have emerged from the meta-cognitive analysis of the constructivist learning dialogue surrounding MCQ-Creation, but the CAREGen methodology is the one which has been most actively developed.

5. Recommendations

There were several instances during the examination of MCQ creation methodologies when the dialogues between the subject experts revealed divergent thought processes concerning the appropriate interpretation of the selected rules and procedures. One recommendation of this research is that MCQ-Creation workshops should be arranged for all staff who are involved in writing approved documents that define the company's rules and procedures. The MCQ-Creation workshops would provide a platform for discussion about possible divergence from policy and to either prompt clarification of the rules or to produce MCQs that can bring the debatable points to the attention of everyone who might be affected and then emphasize which is the correct response.

The workshops should include practical application of the CAREGen methodology for MCQ-Creation. They should also cover evaluation of MCQ-Creation methodologies so that staff can carry out their own investigations into the relative effectiveness of MCQs. This will also allow them to appreciate the problems encountered by people who must work from the documents they create. The MCQ-Creation workshops might also include exercises involving the application of Computational Linguistics and statistical Natural Language Processing (NLP) software to the approved documents in an effort to achieve equivalent outputs to those generated by manual application of the methodology. The number of investigations into these possibilities is likely to increase in the coming years.

6. Conclusions

MCQs are becoming increasingly important in the effective communication of corporate knowledge, rules and procedures. The manual process of MCQ-Creation has been analysed by viewing the process as part of a constructivist learning dialogue that surrounds the management of approved documents. First a system of labels was proposed for the roles that typically operate when MCQ-Creation is carried out manually. Then the proposed labels were used to describe the existing manual process of MCQ-Creation as it is currently carried out within the host company.

A summary list of the products from this constructivist dialogue was then provided. This included the specification of two new evaluation measures for MCQ-Creation methodologies (Foster 2012b) which developed following analysis of current evaluation methods and MCQ response analysis. In addition to the two new evaluation measures, other useful products from the dialogue were identified including evidence supporting the use of MAC formatted MCQs, a method for specifying the objectives to be addressed by generated MCQs and a more formal presentation of the manual steps being applied when creating MCQs. These products, alongside the MCQs themselves, provide strong evidence that the internal dialogue (Hermens 1992) prompted by MCQ-Creation, facilitates constuctivist learning at both individual (Mynard 2011) and corporate (Kirby 2011) levels. The recommendations stated that running MCQ-Creation workshops which include practical application of the steps of the CAREGen methodology, for staff within the company who are involved in creating approved documents would improve the constructivist learning dialogue within the company.

References

Bloom, Benjamin Samuel. 1956. *Taxonomy of Educational Objectives: Book 1 Cognitive Domain.* New York: Longmans, Green.

Brown, Jonathan.C., Gwen A. Frishkoff, and Maxine Eskenazi. 2005. "Automatic Question Generation for Vocabulary Assessment Processing". In *Proceedings of Human Language Technology Conference and Conference on Empricial Methods in Natural Language Processing (HLT/EMNLP)*, 819–826. Vancouver: Association for Computational Linguistics.

Butler, Andrew C., and Henry L. Roediger III. 2008. "Feedback Enhances the Positive Effects and Reduces the Negative Effects of Multiple-Choice Testing." *Memory and Cognition* 36 (3): 604–616. DOI: 10.3758/MC.36.3.604

Croft, William, and Alan Cruse. 2004. *Cognitive Linguistics.* Cambridge: Cambridge University Press. DOI: 10.1017/CBO9780511803864

Crooks, Terry. 2001. "The Validity of Formative Assessments." Paper Presented to the *British Educational Research Association Annual Conference*, University of Leeds. http://www.leeds.ac.uk/educol/documents/00001862.htm. (last date of access 17 Sept. 2013).

Cruse, D. Alan, and Joan P. Togia. 1995. "Towards a Cognitive Model of Antonymy." *Lexicology* 1: 113–141.

De Grave, Willem S., Henny P.A. Bodshuizen, and Henk G. Schmidt. 1996. "Problem-Based Learning – Cognitive and Metacognitive Processes during Problem Analysis" *Instructional Science* 24 (5): 321–341. DOI: 10.1007/BF00118111

Foster, Robert Michael. 2013. "Improve MCQ-Creation Skills to Support Corporate Learning" In *Proceedings of Ireland International Conference on Education*, Dublin, 2013, 38–41.

Foster, Robert Michael. 2012a. "Using a New MCQ Generation Methodology (CAREGen) in the UK Electricity Distribution Industry." *Infonomics Society, UK – International Journal of Digital Society (IJDS)* 3 (1): 643–651.

Foster, Robert Michael. 2012b. "Evaluating an Application of the CAREGen MCQ Creation Methodology." In *Proceedings of London International Conference on Education*, London, 630–634.

Foster, Robert Michael. 2011. "Creating a High Voltage Cable-Jointing knowledge check using the CARE generation methodology." *Proceedings of London International Conference on Education*, London, 208–214.

Foster, Robert Michael. 2010a. "Multiple Alternative Choice Test Items (MACs) Deliver more Comprehensive Assessment Information than Traditional 4-option MC Test Items." *Proceedings of London International Conference on Education*, London, 26–29.

Foster, Robert Michael. 2010b. "Automatic Generation of Multiple Alternate Choice (MAC) Test Item Stems by Applying Causal Relation Explication, Addition and Manipulation (CREAM) to Pre-processed Source Documents." *Proceedings of the London International Conference on Education 2010*, London.

Foster, Robert Michael. 2009. "Improving the Output from Software that Generates Multiple Choice Question (MCQ) Test Items Automatically using Controlled Rhetorical Structure Theory." *Borovets, Bulgaria. Proceedings of Student Conference RANLP 2009*, 29–34.

Glickman, Carl D., Stephen P. Gordon, and Jovita M. Ross-Gordon. 2009. *Supervision and Instructional Leadership: A Developmental Approach*." Boston, MA: Allyn and Bacon.

Gronlund, Norman Edward, and Susan M. Brookhart. 2009. *Gronlund's Writing Instructional Objectives*. Upper Saddle River N.J.: Pearson/Merrill Prentice Hall.

Hermans, Hubert J. M., Harry J. G. Kempen, and Rens J. P. Van Loon. 1992. "The Dialogical Self: Beyond Individualism and Rationalism." *American Psychologist* 47: 23–33. DOI: 10.1037/0003-066X.47.1.23

Kirby, Elizabeth A. 2011. "A Conceptual Model for Critical Incident Analysis." *The Journal of the Academy for Critical Incident Analysis* 1 (1). http://jcia.aciajj.org/volume-1-no-1/a-conceptual-model-for-critical-incident-analysis. (last date of access 17 Sept. 2013).

Mynard, Jo. 2011. "The Role of the Learning Advisor in Promoting Autonomy." *Learner Autonomy in Language Learning*. http://ailarenla.org/lall. (last date of access 17 Sept. 2013).

Mager, Robert Frank. 1975. *Preparing Instructional Objectives*. 2nd edn. Belmont, CA: Lake Publishing Co.

Mann, William C., and Sandra Annear Thompson. 1988. "Rhetorical Structure Theory: Toward a Functional Theory of Text Organization." *Interdisciplinary Journal for the Study of Discourse* 8 (3): 243–281.

Mitkov, Ruslan, and Le An Ha. 2003. "Computer-Aided Generation of Multiple-Choice Tests." In *Proceedings of HLT-NAACL 2003. Workshop on Building Educational Applications Using Natural Language Processing*, Edmonton, Canada, 17–22.

Mitkov, Ruslan, Le An Ha, and Nikiforos Karamanis. 2006. "A Computer-Aided Environment for Generating Multiple-Choice Test Items." *Cambridge Journals – Natural Language Engineering* 12 (2): 177–194. DOI: 10.1017/S1351324906004177

Paradis, Carita. 2010. "Good, Better and Superb Antonyms: A Conceptual Construal Approach." *The Annual of Texts by Foreign Guest Professors*, 385–402. Prague: Faculty of Arts, Charles University.

Sanders, Ted J. M., Wilbert P. M. Spooren, and Leo G. M. Noordman. 1993. "Coherence Relations in a Cognitive Theory of Discourse Representation." *Cognitive Linguistics* 8: 93–133. DOI: 10.1515/cogl.1993.4.2.93

Shin'ichi, Tsumori, and Kenji Kaijiri. 2007. "System Design for Automatic Generation of Multiple-Choice Questions Adapted to Students' Understanding." In *8th International Conference on Information Technology Based Higher Education and Training*, Kumamoto, JAPAN, 541–546.

Author's address

Robert Michael Foster
The Research Institute for Information and Language Processing
University of Wolverhampton,
Wulfruna Street, Wolverhampton, WV1 1LY,
The Research Institute for Information and Language Processing
R.M.Foster@wlv.ac.uk
www.rmfoster.co.uk

Appendix

MCQ-Creation Methodologies Workshop
(20 November 2012, London, United Kingdom)
… in conjunction with LONDON INTERNATIONAL CONFERENCE on EDUCATION 2012
"At MCQ-Creation we discuss empirical studies of MCQ creation methodologies and then suggest improvements."

Background
The specific objectives of assessment authorities and the languages of learner populations are continually changing. This implies that assessment tools, which are used to confirm accurate transfer of knowledge to learners within a domain of discourse, must also change.

The MCQ-Creation Workshop brings together educationalists from industry, governmental examining bodies, universities and schools to examine the merits and pitfalls in traditional processes for creating Multiple Choice Question (MCQ) test items. The output from the workshop will be proposals for new (or adapted) MCQ creation methodologies that are appropriate to the domains defined by the presenters.

MCQ-Creation Workshop – Call for Papers
Presenters at MCQ-Creation will give an overview of their domain of discourse (ie the context of their assessments) and will describe how they have either
described and evaluated an established formal method for MCQ test item creation as applied within their domain of discourse.
or
described and evaluated a demonstrably **NEW** MCQ test item creation methodology within their domain of discourse.

MCQ-Creation Workshop – Submissions Process
All those whose title/abstract has been accepted by the committee are invited to give a presentation to the MCQ-Creation Workshop session. If the title/abstract was submitted BEFORE the submissions deadline (15 September) then this will be included in the programme for the main LICE conference along with the notes supporting the keynote address. However, if the title/abstract was submitted AFTER the submissions deadline and has been accepted by the comittee then the presentation at the workshop will still be welcome, but the title/abstract will not be included in the main conference proceedings.

All presenters at the MCQ-Creation workshop (including those whose title/abstract was received after the submissions deadline) are invited to submit a 4–8 page paper describing their MCQ-Creation methodology evaluation activities before 30 January 2012. Successful papers will be included in the MCQ-Creation Workshop electronic proceedings, published on this page. http://www.testcentres.co.uk/MCQ-Creation

MCQ-Creation Workshop – Important dates
Online Proceedings Submissions deadline: 30 January 2012
Online Proceedings Submissions deadline: 20 February 2012

MCQ-Creation Workshop – Submission Requirements
All papers must be submitted in.pdf format. For format requirements please refer to the main LICE website at http://www.liceducation.org/

Each submission will be reviewed by the Workshop Committee, who have experience in both academia and industry. The final decisions will be made based on these reviews. Email pdf versions of your paper attached to an emails sent to:
MCQ-Creation@testcentres.co.uk

Welcome to the first MCQ Creation Methodologies Workshop in conjunction with the LICE (London International Conference on Education). I look forward to hearing your ideas … and sharing some of mine of course!

Best Wishes
Bob Foster

http://www.testcentres.co.uk/MCQ-Creation

Programme

Welcome and introductions

Aims of MCQ-Creation workshop. Repeat Call for papers

Introduce My Domain (Summary of recent research)

Unit 1 – Lecture 1: Defining domains
EXERCISE 1: Describe YOUR domain

Unit 1 – Lecture 2: What should be tested / measured?
EXERCISE 2: What will you test / measure in YOUR domain?

Unit 1 – Lecture 3: Validity
Unit 1 – Lecture 4: How do we measure achievement?
EXERCISE 3: What are the available types of MCQ?

Unit 2 – Lecture 1: The MCQ Creation Process
EXERCISE 4: Important components of the MCQ-Creation

Unit 2 – Lecture 2: The MCQ Creation Guidelines
EXERCISE 5: Important Guidelines for your domain

Case Studies:
- **High Voltage Cable Jointing**
- **Heavy Plant Lifting**
- **Apprentice Progress Monitoring**

EXERCISE 6: What have you learned?

http://www.testcentres.co.uk/MCQ-Creation

Exploring the opportunities of social media to build knowledge in learner-centered Indigenous learning spaces

Henk Huijser and Jurg Bronnimann
Batchelor Institute of Indigenous Tertiary Education, Australia

This chapter explores the opportunities online learning environments offer to address issues related to Indigenous pedagogy and Indigenous approaches to teaching and learning, with a specific focus on social and mobile media. Social media tools have created many opportunities for social approaches to teaching and learning, and specifically to developing Indigenous learning communities, and overall much more explicitly learner-centered approaches. In this chapter we argue that social media are well suited to address the learning needs of Indigenous students in Australia, and at the same time we use Batchelor Institute of Indigenous Tertiary Education, and its 'both-ways' philosophy, as a case study to explore some of the opportunities and potential barriers that social media present within learner-centered pedagogy.

1. Introduction

Globally, the impact of new technologies on higher education is profound and accelerating. However, this is not just a one way street or something that is externally imposed, but rather something that higher education institutions themselves are deeply engaged in as well. Indeed, many changes and new applications are in fact driven by higher education institutions themselves (Johnson et al. 2013; Cope and Kalantzis 2009). This accelerated development of online learning environments and tools on the one hand creates major opportunities, while on the other hand it creates new potential barriers that need to be taken into account. For example, for those who are well connected, the information stream is almost endless, and higher education opportunities abound, many of which are even free to access. This includes for example the currently exploding MOOCs universe (Massive Open Online Courses), increasing availability of open access course materials (Johnson et al. 2013), and initiatives such as The University of the People and Melbourne Free University. This in turn leads some to argue that higher education has never been more accessible or affordable (Usher 2009). However, to be able to exploit the opportunities afforded in online, and increasingly mobile, environments requires access to both the technology itself, and to the skills needed to get the most out of what is available and to adapt the information to your own particular needs, and the needs of your community. As Deakin Crick notes, "knowledge and its manifestations are no longer 'out there', to be acquired from the centre, mastered and applied" (2007, 135). She goes on to argue that "the key skills needed are the speedy and confident handling of technically and culturally changing and overflowing data and its reformulation to meet new and specific demands of the networked society" (2007, 136). Again, this draws attention to the importance of access to both the network and the skills to utilise this network to your advantage, and this is crucial from an Indigenous perspective, although not necessarily for the most obvious reasons.

In a discussion about potential barriers for Indigenous communities in the Northern Territory of Australia, Nadarajah (2012) makes a useful distinction between two categories of challenges: one, access to reliable infrastructure; and two, knowledge about how to use that infrastructure. "The need for knowledge is agreed but how that knowledge is best taught and best learned is the challenge" (Loban, quoted in Nadarajah 2012, 6). While the first challenge will steadily improve, especially as the National Broadband Network is being rolled out across Australia, in this chapter we specifically focus on the opportunities that online learning technologies, and social media in particular, provide to slot into, and perhaps even drive, learner-centred pedagogies that are relevant to Indigenous learners. The broad framework for such a pedagogy already exists at Batchelor Institute of Indigenous Tertiary Education, based on what has been termed a 'both-ways' philosophy (Ober and Bat 2007a, 2007b; Bat, Kilgariff and Doe forthcoming). The importance of relationships is central to that framework, which is largely imagined in face-to-face contexts. Online learning technologies, and social media in particular, provide opportunities to build such relationships in an online environment, thereby providing a way to address low access and participation rates (Bradley et al. 2008; Behrendt et al. 2012).

2. 'Both-ways' philosophy at Batchelor Institute

Batchelor Institute of Indigenous Tertiary Education has played a vital role in higher education for Aboriginal and Torres Strait Islander people in providing them a unique place of knowledge and skills where they can undertake a journey of learning for empowerment and advancement, while strengthening identity (Batchelor Institute 2007, 2). To this end Batchelor Institute has developed what they have termed a 'both-ways' philosophy as an integral part of student learning journeys. The 'both-ways' philosophy is characterised by three key principles and forms the foundation of all learning and teaching at Batchelor Institute:

- A shared learning journey
- Student/community centred
- Strengthens Indigenous identity

In its simplest representation, the 'both-ways' is a philosophy of education that "brings together Indigenous Australian traditions of knowledge and Western academic disciplinary positions and cultural contexts, and embraces values of respect, tolerance and diversity" (Batchelor Institute Strategic Plan 2012–2014, 6). The 'both-ways' philosophy is founded on the metaphor of Ganma used by Marika (1999), and based on Yolngu culture of North East Arnhem Land in Australia's Northern Territory. The Ganma process occurs in a space where fresh water (Yolngu knowledge) and salt water (non-Aboriginal knowledge) come together in a briny lagoon. This lagoon is "a nutrient-rich environment in which some plant and animal life lives that is not found elsewhere. So too with both-ways – there is no need to compromise either epistemological position, but rather a new space can come into being that supports the creation of new understandings and knowledge" (Bat et al. forthcoming). Batchelor Institute acknowledges that this is the metaphor that has formed the basis of the development of the both-ways philosophy (Ober and Bat 2007a).

Indigenous Australians who come from strong traditional backgrounds have different concepts of time, ways of questioning, and protocols, but also come from highly diverse cultures (Winch and Hayward 1999). A true 'both ways' approach ensures that these differing ways of making sense of the world, the western way, and culturally variant Indigenous ways must all be accepted as valid, equal alternatives. Moreover, the true spirit and productive potential of a 'both ways' approach is thus ultimately to allow for the potential to arrive at what Bhabha (1994) has called a 'third space', where new knowledge and understanding is created that is neither one nor the other. This is a hybrid space, which is reflected in the briny Ganma lagoon.

Although this sounds good in theory, transferring this philosophy into a coherent and consistent learning and teaching approach is not a straightforward process. For a start, there are many different ways of interpreting concepts like 'shared learning journey' and 'student/community centred', and different teachers have different ideas about what that looks like in a classroom or any other place of learning. For this reason, Batchelor Institute has embarked on the development of a learning and teaching framework that is grounded in 'both-ways' philosophy, but it is envisaged that, once agreed upon, it will offer teachers a series of practical steps that will ensure that 'both-ways' is the underlying philosophy. Again, this is by no means a straightforward process, and the expectation is that in many ways it will mean fundamental changes in teachers' approaches to learning and teaching at Batchelor Institute in order to incorporate what Nakata (2007) calls a discernible "Indigenous voice" in the production of knowledge. Therefore, to be successful, a whole-of-institution approach to its implementation is needed, which will consist of professional development, but more importantly will include a strategy for learning places and spaces that fits with such a framework, including online learning spaces.

3. A learning framework grounded in 'both-ways' philosophy

Following the principles of the 'both-ways' philosophy, for learning to be relevant and successful for Indigenous students it needs to happen within a specific context of a community of learners or practitioners (Lave and Wenger 2003). With the student at the centre of the learning experience these learning communities will encourage and will allow the construction of new knowledge built on the learners' prior knowledge, ideas and concepts (Ganma metaphor) and leading them to a deeper understanding. In practice, this means that time needs to be allowed for upfront to develop relationships and to create a context which is culturally safe and therefore conducive to knowledge sharing (Ober and Bat 2007b). For example, after an initial welcome to country, an activity can be scheduled whereby students draw on metaphors that have meaning for them to share some of the prior knowledge they bring into the learning space. Deeper awareness will be demonstrated in that the learners will take on new responsibilities as they acquire new skills (Bransford, Vrown, and Cocking 2003). In the context of this chapter this could include the confident and competent use of social media. However, to allow what could be coined as 'contextual learning' to occur, there needs to be a common understanding and agreement that Indigenous ways of knowing and learning differ significantly from Western knowledge. Western knowledge is divided into domains or disciplines (Cochran et al. 2008) whereas Aboriginal ways of knowing and being are holistic, non-linear, visual kinaesthetic, social and contextualised (Yunkaporta 2007). Despite the often dichotomous portrayal of the two pedagogies – spontaneous versus structured, repetitive versus inquiring, and so on (Hughes 1987), this is not to say that they are incompatible, but rather that the focus should be on their commonalities, or as Battiste (2002) suggests, "focusing on similarities between the two systems of knowledge rather than on their differences may be a more useful place to start."

Drawing inspiration from the 'both-ways' philosophy and trying to find a solution on how to better engage with Aboriginal learning processes, while at the same time involving educators in a dialogue of the commonalities between Indigenous and non-Indigenous pedagogies, Yunkaporta (2009) developed the 'eight-way framework of Aboriginal Pedagogy', which is visually represented in Figure 1.

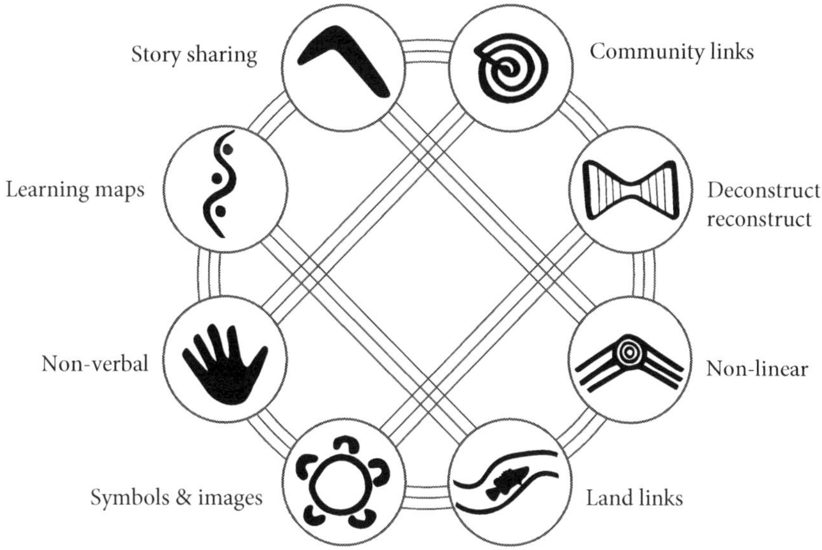

Figure 1. 8-ways Aboriginal Pedagogy Framework (Yunkaporta 2009)

What follows is a brief description of the eight interconnected concepts that underlie this framework:

Story sharing: The key principle in the framework, according to Yunkaporta, is the sharing of stories. It is through 'yarning' that Indigenous people transmit knowledge, learn about the world and keep their strong connection to Country. As the word 'to yarn' implies, it is not a monologic activity but a shared dialogue between teacher and learner. Furthermore, 'yarning' is not time-bound, and cannot be captured in pre-determined time. In other words, 'yarning' is fluid and develops according to a set of circumstances that cannot be captured in terms of pre-determined outcomes; rather, the amount of knowledge that is shared at any one time is context-bound and indeterminate from the outset.

Deconstruct-reconstruct: The initial learning process focuses on the whole rather than the parts. Concepts are modelled first by a more knowledgeable individual – an elder of the community – before the learner tries it independently. In that sense, it is much closer to a Confucian style of learning than to western, individualised and compartmentalised ways of learning.

Non-linear: As highlighted previously, Indigenous pedagogy is not sequential but new knowledge is built by making connections with and building on existing knowledge. There is a lot of repetition and re-iteration of perceptions and ideas which ultimately lead to deeper understanding. Again, this has major implications for the way time is organised around learning, as learning can take place any time and any place…or not. Regardless however, learning takes place over time, and when pre-determined outcomes will be achieved cannot be clearly pinpointed from the outset. This aligns very nicely with social media, as social media allow for non-linear and fluid communication and therefore potentially learning. Cope and Kalantzis (2009) call this 'ubiquitous learning', and 'new learning' (Kalantizis and Cope 2008), and it means that learning does not only increasingly happen anywhere, anytime, but also that it is characterised by continuous feedback by peers, rather than formal and linear, with the feedback coming only from the teacher as the privileged source of knowledge.

Land-links: Aboriginal pedagogies are intimately linked to the living landscape, to Country. For Indigenous people the learning is about making connection to the land. All knowledge is ultimately linked to Country. Social media, and mobile media in particular, create opportunities to maintain this connection to Country from wherever you are. Indeed, in a New Zealand context, *Facebook* has been called 'the new marae' (Maori meeting house).

Community links: The Indigenous way of learning is very much group orientated and is closely connected to real life contexts. Learning is also about helping the community. This is intimately linked to the importance of caring for Country as outlined above, reinforcing the holistic nature of the 8 ways framework.

Non-verbal: In the Indigenous context learning happens far more by doing and by the use of body language and silence. This is not to say there is a limited language capacity, but rather Indigenous learners test knowledge through experience, reflection and practical application. An example of a practical application is a painting, which in Indigenous contexts is not always simply an individual work of art in the western sense, but more often a medium through which to convey knowledge about country (Martin 2007). Mobile technologies provide opportunities here as well, as they allow for the visual capture of actions that can then be shared via social media like *YouTube*, potentially without spoken or written language if deemed appropriate. This in turn potentially removes the western emphasis on the written word, opening up the possibility of learning in non-verbal visual digital learning spaces.

Learning maps: Learning happens mainly through the use of visual aids, such as drawing diagrams and images. The images serve as a reference point for the learner. Social media are inherently *multi*media and lend themselves perfectly to the electronic sharing of learning maps.

Symbols and images: Symbols and metaphors are used to understand concepts and content. "Knowledge is coded in symbols, signs, images and metaphors and is therefore a tool for learning and memorising complex knowledge" (Yunkaporta and

Kirby 2011). In Indigenous contexts, there are often strict protocols around what knowledge can be shared, and whom it can be shared with. However, many social media platforms (e.g. *Vimeo*, *YouTube* and even *Facebook*) allow for choice in their settings in terms of whom content gets shared with.

Applying the 8 ways learning framework in Indigenous contexts has many advantages as it allows for more contextualised learning, it is reflective and self-directed and probably most importantly it is meaningful and relevant to Indigenous students, and hence highly motivating. Recognising and respecting different ways of knowing and the importance of building community relationships are essential ingredients in a community of learning. It will create the trust that is necessary especially where diverse ways of knowing (western and Indigenous) engage in cognitive interactions. The development of the 8 ways Aboriginal pedagogy framework has paved the way to move beyond the binary oppositions (Yunkaporta 2009) of western and Indigenous knowledges and thus create new opportunities in teaching and learning, one of which we argue in this paper is the use of social media in Indigenous contexts. Yunkaporta's 8 ways framework is a holistic framework which draws its strength from the sum of its parts, much like Indigenous knowledges themselves. Social media present opportunities to develop learning spaces in which such holistic approaches to learning can thrive.

4. Social media, relationships and learner-centredness

Digitial technologies in general, and social media in particular, have huge potential to overcome the 'tyranny of distance', and with specific reference to Indigenous contexts in Australia, the 'tyranny of remoteness'. Even though remote communities are increasingly becoming 'connected', "currently online learning is not available for most remote living Indigenous people in the Northern Territory (NT)" (Vodic et al. 2012, 34). This means that for many Indigenous people in remote communities, learning still follows a well-trodden path of (mostly) non-Indigenous trainers and teachers flying in and out to 'deliver' self-contained learning modules largely in isolation, without necessarily being linked together, nor necessarily being linked to a local context. In other words, despite all good intentions, this is essentially a 'tick-box' kind of approach where the emphasis is on the teacher being able to sign off on the delivery being achieved, or the learning being 'delivered on time'. Whether it has been 'received' is of course an entirely different question. It is thus very much a teacher-centred approach, which is driven by administrative convenience, rather than self-identified or co-constructed Indigenous learning needs. This in turn creates the ongoing risk of what Plater (2013, 157) calls 'over-functioning': "many non-Aboriginal and Torres Strait Islander educators have, in their approach to providing teaching and learning support for Aboriginal and Torres Strait Islander students, tended towards over-functioning, or rescuing and co-dependency". In other words, this teacher-centred approach generally, and almost inevitably, forces Indigenous learners into 'deficit' mode, from which they need to be 'rescued'.

While this is very far removed from the learning and teaching framework – centred around 'both ways' principles – that Batchelor Institute is trying to implement, it is still the reality in many remote Indigenous learning contexts. The rhetoric follows the ideal scenario in which the importance of community engagement and the centrality of relationship building is repeatedly emphasised. Indeed, in the case of Batchelor Institute's learning and teaching framework, 'relationships' has literally been positioned at the heart of 'everything we do'. There are good reasons for this, as the importance of relationships is frequently cited in the research literature as the crucial prerequisite for successful learning in Indigenous contexts (Perso 2012). However, developing relationships takes time, and it is precisely this time factor that often jars with the 'audit driven' efficiency of 'flying in-flying out' delivery. To really make an impact and force a shift towards more learner-centred approaches, and by extension more community-driven and relevant approaches, would require structural changes to the way learning and teaching is organised in Indigenous contexts (or *for* Indigenous contexts), or perhaps a series of new technologies that can help to forge a paradigm shift in this respect. We would argue that social media, in combination with mobile technologies, indeed have the potential to upset the *status quo* and create a situation where relationship building can take centre stage on an ongoing basis. Ultimately, this would then lead to much more learner-centred approaches with the power to match the rhetoric, and it would apply to all levels of tertiary education, including postgraduate education. In the latter case for example, Trudgett (2011) has argued for the need to involve Indigenous community elders in the supervision process, but this is not always easy to achieve. However, social and mobile media have the potential to make this much more common, and thereby significantly improve the learning experience for Indigenous postgraduate students (Stanton 2013).

As Heron points out (cited in Nadarajah 2012, 6), "for the first time we have the opportunity to do away with the 'remote'. Indigenous communities no longer have to be isolated – they can be connected. Limitations of time and space no longer need to apply". In other words, while teachers may still 'fly in and fly out', there are now increasing opportunities to maintain and develop relationships on an ongoing basis over time. Interestingly, if teachers learn how to leverage existing social media use, it would in many ways be learner-centred already, because Indigenous people in general, and particularly young Indigenous people appear to have taken to social media use, and technology in general, in a big way (Stanton 2013). So when Vidic et al. (2012, 37, our emphasis) recommend that "technical and educational support must be made available within communities (*particularly around the time of training delivery*) to support people in their efforts to access online education", they do have a point, but at the same time they miss the key point, which is that new technologies (and social media in particular) have the potential to blur the boundaries between formal learning and the ongoing social context in which such learning should be situated. Thus, the adage '*particularly around the time of training delivery*' becomes almost irrelevant as the support should be there on an ongoing basis, and not just as it relates to online education per se but rather as it relates to education in a social context. *Existing* social media use should be the driving force in this process, rather than social media use designed by educators; only then will it be relevant and authentic, and thus have the power to develop ongoing engagement with learning that matters at a community level. As a caution, this is *not* about 'kow-towing to students' whims' or about 'pleasing' students, but rather about situating learning in appropriate and relevant contexts, and most importantly, at an appropriate level for those students. This is the part that would make it highly learner-centred.

5. Exploring the potential of social media – the what and the how

In their report about social media use in higher education, Moran, Seaman and Tinti-Kane (2011, 4) identify the key element and key potential of social media: "for the first time, the world faces a medium [sic] that is by its very nature non-centralized, meaning that in both form and content, it is user created, user controlled, flexible, democratic, and both very transparent and very not so." It is not difficult to see the potential links here to learner-centred approaches and to Indigenous approaches to learning. Moran et al. (2011, 4) go on to argue that social media's most distinctive aspect lies in its "potential to transform from a way of pushing content outward to a way of inviting conversation, of exchanging information, and of invoking unparalleled individual, industry, societal, and even global change". The slight hyperbole notwithstanding, they do make an important point about the fact that social media are inherently social and you could therefore argue that they are thus by their very nature learner-centred, rather than teacher-centred. The 'democratic' element is further elaborated on by Selwyn (2011, 1), who notes that "social media use is often described in terms of collaboration, conviviality and creativity. Social media applications are seen to be open rather than closed, bottom-up rather than top-down." He also makes a specific link to learning, or what he calls a 'new culture of learning', "i.e. learning that is based around principles of collective exploration, play and innovation rather than individualised instruction" (2011, 3). All of this points towards major potential for more relevant and learner-centred pedagogical approaches in Indigenous contexts, but questions remain at this stage around how to capitalise on that potential. Table 1 provides some initial first steps in developing ways to draw on existing social media use for Indigenous learning contexts.

Table 1. Characteristics of Social Media vs Traditional Teaching Approaches

Social Media for Learning	Traditional teaching approaches
Social	Individual performance & achievement
Group work/ Group discussion	Individual performance & opinion
Oral communication	Written communication
Multi-modal/ multi-media	Focus on the written word/ traditional literacy
Just-in-time, applied social knowledge creation	Read / write – individual knowledge acquisition

Specifically important for Indigenous contexts is the collectivist approach to learning and knowledge, rather than the individualist approach that is fundamental to western, and teacher-centred, approaches to learning. As a word of caution, we are very much talking about broad characteristics and we therefore always need to be vigilant in preventing this from turning into a set of rigid, essentialist 'rules' (Trudgett 2011). Culture is fluid and forever changing, and in the case of Indigenous cultures in Australia, there is a huge diversity that has to be taken into account. However, this is part of the point we are making here: that social media allow us to start the learning process from where Indigenous students are at, and allow us to draw on existing knowledge, rather than simply imposing a knowledge set on them, because *we* (as in western educators) have decided that is what they should know. In the case of language in particular, leveraging social media use potentially allows us to shift the emphasis away from written communication in English, which creates huge barriers to learning in many Indigenous contexts where English literacy levels are low. As noted above, social media are also inherently *multi*media, and this creates opportunities to learn in context and learn by using media that students are comfortable with, and that are culturally appropriate. This is not to say that traditional literacy in English is not important, but rather that the timing can be more flexible, and that learning can take place before literacy in English has been achieved, if indeed the latter is deemed to be a relevant and desirable outcome in the particular context in which the learning is to take place.

As we have discussed and outlined the relevance of Yunkaporta's (2009) '8 Ways' framework above, Table 2 identifies potential social media tools that may be aligned with some of these eight ways. These are *potential* tools, and the eight ways listed in the left hand column are by no means restricted to, or limited by, the tools listed in the right hand column. However, those tools are currently the most widely known and used, and may currnelty be the most appropriate.

Table 2. Aligning '8 Ways' with Social Media Tools

"8 Ways"	Social Media Tools (& Mobile Tools)
Story Sharing	Collaborate, MS Lync, Skype, YouTube, Vimeo
Community Links	Collaborate, MS Lync, Skype, Facebook, Twitter
Deconstruct/ Reconstruct	Discussion forums, Chatrooms
Non-Linear	a-synchronous discussion forums, Facebook, Twitter, YouTube, Flicker
Land Links	Facebook, YouTube, Flicker, Vimeo
Symbols & Images	Facebook, YouTube, Flicker, Vimeo
Non-Verbal	YouTube, Flicker, Vimeo
Learning Maps	Collaborate, a-synchronous discussion forums

As becomes clear in Table 2, there is an increasing array of social media tools that can potentially be leveraged for learning in Indigenous contexts, and indeed for learner-centred approaches to learning that respect and value Indigenous knowledges and Indigenous ways of learning. In terms of their use, we are only beginning to scratch the surface, even if social media use in higher education is apparently increasing rapidly (Moran et al. 2011). For example, in explaining their use of *Facebook*, Jenkins et al. (2012, 66) hope to achieve two main goals: firstly to improve the effectiveness of communications to their cohort of students, and secondly to energise communications among the student cohort. These are still relatively modest goals, and ones that are echoed by some 'early adopters' at Batchelor Institute. The additional advantage in Batchelor Institute's case is that *Facebook* provides a continuous communication tool. In other words, while students change their phones and sim cards on a regular basis, there *Facebook* account is often the only stable space for teachers to get in touch with them. Although this is a promising start, and it is learner-centred in the sense that we meet students 'where they are at', there are many new ways and social media tools that are waiting to be explored to achieve more effective learning outcomes in Indigenous contexts.

6. Conclusion

If this all sounds highly idealistic, then that is quite deliberately so. In a context where the statistics about educational outcomes for Indigenous students continue to be depressing (Bradley et al. 2008; Trudgett 2011), the potential of social media and other new technologies warrants a certain level of optimism, especially as there appears to be a high uptake of such technologies in Indigenous communities. However, there are some cautions to take into account. As Selwyn (2011, 5) notes, "it is unhelpfully idealistic to imagine social media as providing a level playing field for all", and he identifies ongoing 'digital inequalities' that are "especially pronounced in terms of socio-economic status, social class, race, gender, geography, age and educational background". While these are all relevant in Indigenous contexts, they are factors that have been integral to Indigenous disadvantage for a very long time. The idealism in this paper stems from a strong sense that social media have the potential to put the power of tools for learning in the hands of the learner, rather than learning being defined by non-Indigenous teachers and imposed from the top down. The latter teacher-centred approach has done Indigenous learners very few favours, and we have argued here that social and mobile media have the potential to shift the balance towards much more learner-centred and culturally relevant approaches to learning and teaching in Indigenous contexts.

References

Bat, Melodie, Claire Kilgariff, and Tina Doe. 2013 (forthcoming). "Indigenous Tertiary Education – We're all Learning: Both-ways Pedagogy in the Northern Territory of Australia". *Higher Education Research & Development.*

Batchelor Institute of Indigenous Tertiary Education. 2012. *Strategic Plan 2012–2014.* http://www.batchelor.edu.au/biite/wp-content/uploads/2012/08/Strategic-Plan_V4.7-web.pdf.

Batchelor Institute of Indigenous Tertiary Education. 2007. *Strategic Plan: The Decade That Counts 2007–2016 – Creating the Future Together.* Batchelor: Batchelor Institute.

Battiste, Marie. 2002. *Indigenous Knowledge and Pedagogy in First Nations Education: A Literature Review with Recommendations.* Ottawa: National Working Group on Education and the Minister of Indian Affairs, Indian and Northern Affairs Canada.

Behrendt, Larissa, Steve Larkin, Robert Griew, and Patricia Kelly. 2012. *Review of Higher Education Access and Outcomes for Aboriginal and Torres Strait Islander People: Final Report.* Canberra: Australian Government.

Bhabha, Homi K. 1994. *The Location of Culture.* London and New York: Routledge.

Bradley, Denise, Peter Noonan, Helen Nugent, and Bill Scales. 2008. *Review of Australian Higher Education.* http://www.deewr.gov.au/HigherEducation/Review/Pages/ReviewofAustralianHigherEducationReport.aspx.

Bransford, John D., Ann L. Brown, and Rodney R. Cocking (eds). 2003. *How People Learn: Brain, Mind, Experience, and School* (Expanded Edition). Washington D.C.: National Academy Press.

Cochran, Patricia A. L., Catherine A. Marshall, Carmen Garcia-Downing, Elizabeth Kendall, Doris Cook, Laurie McCubbin, and Reva Mariah S. Gover. 2008. "Indigenous Ways of Knowing: Implications for Participatory Research and Community". *American Journal of Public Health* 98 (1): 22–27. DOI: 10.2105/AJPH.2006.093641

Cope, Bill, and Mary Kalantzis. 2009. *Ubiquitous Learning.* Chicago: University of Illinois Press.

Deakin Crick, Ruth. 2007. "Learning How to Learn: The Dynamic Assessment of Learning Power". *The Curriculum Journal* 18 (2): 135–153. DOI: 10.1080/09585170701445947

Hughes, Paul. 1987. "Aboriginal Culture and Learning Styles – A Challenge for Academics in Higher Education Institutions". In *The Second Frank Archibald Memorial Lecture.* Armidale: New South Wales.

Jenkins, Greg, Kenneth Lyons, Ruth S. Bridgstock, and Lauren Carr. 2012. "Like Our Page – Using Facebook to Support First Year Students in their Transition to Higher Education: A Practice Report". *The International Journal of the First Year in Higher Education* 3 (2): 65–72. DOI: 10.5204/intjfyhe.v3i2.131

Johnson, Larry, Samantha Adams, Malcolm Cummins, Victoria Estrada, Alex Freeman, and Holly Ludgate. 2013. *NMC Horizon Report: 2013 Higher Education Edition*. Austin, Texas: The New Media Consortium.

Kalantzis, Mary, and Bill Cope. 2008. *New Learning: Elements of a Science of Education*. Cambridge: Cambridge University Press. DOI: 10.1017/CBO9780511811951

Lave, Jean, and Etienne Wenger. 2003. *Situated Learning: Legitimate Peripheral Participation*. Cambridge: Cambridge University Press.

Marika, Raymattja. 1999. "Milthun Latju Wanga Romgu Yolgnu: Valuing Knowledge in the Education System". *Ngoonjook: A Journal of Australian Indigenous Issues* 16: 23–39.

Martin, Karen. 2007. "The Intersection of Aboriginal Knowledges, Aboriginal Literacies and New Learning Pedagogies for Aboriginal students". In *Multiliteracies and Diversity in Education: New Pedagogies for Expanding Landscapes*, ed. by Annah Healy, 58–61. Melbourne: Oxford University Press.

Moran, Mike, Jeff Seaman, and Hester Tinti-Kane. 2011. *Teaching, Learning, and Sharing: How Today's Higher Education Faculty Use Social Media*. Boston, MA: Pearson Learning Solutions.

Nadarajah, Hujjat. 2012. "A Passion for Connection: Heron Loban". *Our Place* 43: 5–6.

Nakata, Martin. 2007. *Disciplining the Savages: Savaging the Disciplines*. Canberra: Aboriginal Studies Press.

Ober, Robyn, and Melodie Bat. 2007a. "Paper 1: Both-Ways: The Philosophy". *Ngoonjook: A Journal of Australian Indigenous Issues* 31: 64–86.

Ober, Robyn, and Melodie Bat. 2007b. "Paper 2: Both-Ways: Philosophy to Practice". *Ngoonjook: A Journal of Australian Indigenous Issues* 32: 56–79.

Perso, Thelma. 2012. *Cultural Responsiveness and School Education, with Particular Focus on Australia's First Peoples: A Review and Synthesis of the Literature*. Darwin: Menzies School of Health.

Plater, Suzanne. 2012. "'For the Life of Me, I Can't See Why Those Students Were Let Go on So Long': Educating the Educators, Aboriginal and Torres Strait Islander-Style". *The Australian Journal of Indigenous Education* 41 (2): 156–161. DOI: 10.1017/jie.2012.24

Selwyn, Neil. 2011. "Social Media in Higher Education". *The Europa World of Learning*. http://www.worldoflearning.com.

Stanton, Sue. 2013. "Elders Panel". *Indigenous Knowledges in a Changing World: Charles Darwin Symposium 2013*, Charles Darwin University, Darwin, 21–22 April.

Trudgett, Michelle. 2011. "Western Places, Academic Spaces and Indigenous Faces: Supervising Indigenous Australian Postgraduate Students". *Teaching in Higher Education* 16 (4): 389–399. DOI: 10.1080/13562517.2011.560376

Usher, Alex. 2009. "Ten Years Back and Ten Years Forward: Developments and Trends in Higher Education in the Europe Region". *UNESCO Forum on Higher Education in the Europe Region: Access, Value, Quality and Competitiveness*. Bucharest.

Vodic, Alex, Kate Senior, Brett Dwyer, and Penny Szybiak. 2012. *A Remote Chance? Widening Participation of Remote Indigenous Students in the Northern Territory via ICT-Enabled Learning*. Darwin: Charles Darwin University.

Winch, Joan, and Ken Hayward. 1999. "'Doing it Our Way': Can Cultural Traditions Survive in Universities?" *New Doctor* Summer: 25–27.

Yunkaporta, Tyson. 2009. *Aboriginal Pedagogy at the Cultural Interface*. Professional Doctorate, Thesis. Townsville: James Cook University.

Yunkaporta, Tyson, and Melissa Kirby. 2011. "Yarning Up Indigenous Pedagogies: A Dialogue about Eight Aboriginal Ways of Learning". In *Two Way Teaching and Learning: Toward Culturally Reflective and Relevant Education*, ed. by Hannah Rachel Bell, Gina Milgate, and Nola Purdie, 205–214. Camberwell Victoria: ACER Press.

Authors' addresses

Henk Huijser, PhD
Senior Lecturer, Flexible Learning and Innovation
Division of Higher Education and Research
Batchelor Institute of Indigenous Tertiary Education
Corner Nurndina Street & Kirra Crescent, Batchelor, NT 0845
Phone: +61 8 89397140
henk.huijser@batchelor.edu.au
http://henkhuijser.webs.com

Jurg Bronnimann, PhD
Head of School, Higher Education
Division of Higher Education and Research
Batchelor Institute of Indigenous Tertiary Education
Corner Nurndina Street & Kirra Crescent, Batchelor, NT 0845
Phone: +61 8 89397328
jurg.bronnimann@batchelor.edu.au

Teams construct knowledge during project-driven social interactions

A facet of the CYBER Kids method

Yiannis Laouris
Cyprus Neuroscience and Technology Institute

The educational model of the twentieth century has become obsolete partly because we did not pay enough attention to facilitating interaction and collaboration between learners and partly because it has been rendered irrelevant to real life. The replacement of the teacher-centered paradigm with the child-centered paradigm is not a sufficient condition for promoting collaboration, and it does not, by itself, encourage more interactions between individual learners. Interactions require structured methodologies, and collaboration requires a purpose. In this chapter, we highlight how a project-driven construction of knowledge is achieved when (1) projects are socially relevant, (2) projects are carried out as group activities, (3) technology serves to create the learning space, and (4) structured methodologies facilitate meaningful, well-organized interactions between the members of the project team.

Introduction

The exponential growth of data and knowledge, in connection with the emergence of powerful personal computing and wide access to the Internet-which – together render students more independent of their teachers-necessitates major reforms of our educational paradigms. This chapter argues that in addition to a strong educationally and socially relevant vision, three practical aspects should be key considerations in designing future educational paradigms. First, the role reversal between educators and learners is a necessity imposed by developments related to both the exponential expansion of knowledge and the earlier exposure of children to the worlds of adults. Second, lesson plans and curricula can no longer focus on abstract knowledge; instead, they have to become embedded within educationally and socially relevant projects. Therefore, the design of appropriate team projects assumes a central role in the process of developing curricula. Third, the design of successful and meaningful lesson plans requires a new formula: a *learning object* (Gerard 1967; Polsani 2003) specification that will enable the creative, meaningful, and constructive integration of educational, psychological, social, economic, national, and other objectives.

The educational model of the twentieth century has become obsolete partly because we did not pay enough attention to facilitating interaction and collaboration between learners and partly because it has been rendered irrelevant to real life. The replacement of the teacher-centered paradigm with the child-centered paradigm is not a sufficient condition for promoting collaboration, and it does not, by itself, encourage more interactions between individual learners. Interactions require structured methodologies, and collaboration requires a purpose. In this chapter, we show how a project-driven construction of knowledge is achieved when (1) projects are socially relevant, (2) projects are carried out as group activities, (3) technology serves to create the learning space, and (4) structured methodologies and learning-object specifications facilitate meaningful, well-organized interactions between the members of the project team.

The following section expands on the requirements for a transition from teacher-centered to child-centered educational paradigms and describes how Information Technologies (IT) can support this process. Subsequent sections will elaborate on how the CYBER Kids methodology, developed by the authors and implemented in several countries, satisfies the above requirements. The chapter concludes with a discussion of how a project-oriented, problem-solving approach satisfies practically all the requirements for key competencies for employability and lifelong learning posed by the Organization for Economic Co-operation and Development (OECD 2005a, 2005b), the European Reference Framework (European Parliament and Council 2006), and the European Growth Strategy (European Commission 2010).

The rise of child-centered educational paradigms

The transition from teacher-centered to child-centered educational paradigms is neither a technological fashion nor an expression of postmodernism. On the contrary, it is the only sensible response to social, economic, and political developments that have occurred over the past few decades independent of any educational context. One could list a number of factors that created the necessity for the transition to child-centered paradigms.

The top elements of such a list would likely include the following: (1) the fact that children now enter the adult world at a younger age and are allowed, or sometimes even expected, to become independent and responsible for their own learning and protection much earlier (Punch 2003) and (2) the exponential expansion of knowledge (as mentioned above), which alone renders it practically impossible to maintain the teacher-to-student model for "transferring" knowledge. Many other factors have also played significant roles. For example, the development of the Internet, which facilitates direct access to worldwide knowledge bases, has empowered students to such a degree that it is very difficult for even the most knowledgeable teachers to defend their roles as "experts." Furthermore, the growth of the middle class, in connection with its financial strengthening, has brought concepts of democratization and equal rights into the educational arena. An increasing number of children today are raised by educated parents who teach them to expect and even demand their rights. Moreover, the continuing bombardment of young people with new ideas, innovative products, attractive services, and novel forms of social interaction causes twenty-first century children to broaden their interests and become more demanding. Their expectations rise to levels that traditional teachers can no longer meet. For these and many other reasons, the transition from teacher-centered to child-centered educational paradigms is not merely necessary, but indeed the only option available to us. The question, therefore, is no longer about comparing, or arguing for the superiority of, the benefits of a child-centered educational paradigm, but how to design the best possible environments and methodologies to maximize the benefits of its implementation. This chapter makes the case that the project-oriented, problem-solving approach is ideal for achieving meaningful role reversal.

Designing engaging "projects"

What is the difference between projects assigned to a class by the teacher and projects envisioned and formulated by the class itself? The answer is simple: a huge difference. The first distinguishing aspect is *trouble* because assignments are mostly perceived as schooling obligations. A project envisioned and implemented by children can be very *gratifying* because, being self-initiated, it reinforces a sense of ownership (Glass 1978; Morrow 1989). Another distinguishing aspect is the fact that student-initiated projects encourage and cultivate creativity and imagination in the initial phases of project envisioning and definition. But probably the most important facet is that it promotes role reversal, thus rendering students responsible for their own learning. Students *own the problem* and turn to their teachers for advice and help.

The challenge of role reversal

The greatest challenge for the twenty-first century educator is how to reconcile the fact that he or she has to teach a curriculum imposed by the government while simultaneously being expected to allow students to choose their own subjects and thus become responsible for their own learning. For example, let us assume a school curriculum requires an educator to teach a math class, and the expected outcomes for students include grasping both the logic and usefulness of quadratic equations. Moreover, students are expected to become capable of solving relevant problems. Can the teacher just do that and refuse, for example, the students' wishes to play sports or have a geography lesson instead? Should he or she remain firm in teaching quadratic equations, or will we grant him or her the freedom to deviate from the school program and teach geography or something else instead? Can the teacher take the students to the courtyard and work with them on a team sports project? Indeed, modern curricula, especially in elementary schools, offer teachers such freedoms. In this chapter, however, we will not investigate the pros and cons of that approach, which has its own merits and challenges (e.g., how to stay on track with what is being taught and what the kids learn). These apparently trivial dilemmas for the twentieth-century educator offer no simple answers for the twenty-first-century teacher.

In this section, we will show how twenty-first-century educators can engage students in appealing self-initiated projects that are also aligned with school curricula. The trick is to structure our educational approach in reverse order. As mentioned above, the crown of every lesson plan should be to render learners capable of solving problems relevant to the educational content. In the above example, the challenge for the educator is to develop a field project that engages children with quadratic equations. For example, the trajectory of rocks thrown in the air follows a quadratic equation. Playing war games with pressured water also introduces learners to the trajectory of water. In short, the aim should be to achieve the desired learning outcome by selecting projects appropriate for the particular context. However, such projects are not usually born from the blue sky. On the contrary, projects usually emerge in response to a problem, a challenge, or a child's desire. Identifying problems that are both interesting to the child and relevant to the curriculum is, therefore, the primary requirement for developing a good project. Once an appropriate problem is identified (either by the educator alone or through discussion with the learners), the next task of the educator is to guide the group discussion to highlight various aspects of the problem and create a challenge that could be tackled by designing creative activities. Inspiration from the Socratic Method (*vide infra*) could prove quite helpful in this respect.

In summary, the approach described here significantly reduces the task of the educator to that of simulating a situation using one of several possible paradigms. The educator can provoke responses to a proposed problem by asking, for example, "Does anyone know what kind of equation we need to describe the path of a thrown rock?" Alternately, he or she could throw an object toward a student and ask the others to describe the shape of the trajectory. Within such a discussion, one could draw attention to the challenge of mathematically describing the path. Going to the yard and using an *experiment* to show the parabolic projectile trajectory of thrown objects or pressured water will leave students amazed and speechless. The challenge of this illustrative example is how to embed the content domain targeted by the curriculum within a project that learners will be excited to take upon themselves.

The CYBER Kids experiment

Almost a decade before the turn of the century, we launched an island-wide experimental educational project (CYBER Institutes 1990) that became widely known as CYBER Kids.[1] Our vision was to "re-define the *methods, tools* and *purpose* of education in light of relevant social change." Our method was partly inspired by the way the Socratic circle operates. A Socratic circle is a method or process (Wikipedia 2013) to help students understand the meaning of a difficult text by creating a dialectic in class. Participants try to gain a deeper understanding of the complex ideas in the text through thoughtful dialogue rather than by memorizing information. It is not a debate. The goal is to have participants work together to construct shared meanings, not for one student or group to "win" the argument. These Socratic ideas have been adapted to apply to projects rather than texts. While a Socratic circle text is a tangible document that can generate thought-provoking discussion, a CYBER Kids project identifies a complex challenge that would benefit from discussion, which in turn inspires appropriate activities and projects that lead to improved understanding of the question at hand. Within this context, the key characteristics of a good project include the following:

1. *Inspiring context and contemporary values.* Projects create enthusiasm and energy in a team context when inspiring ideas surround them and when contemporary values are included, challenged, and/or considered. For example,

1. Through the business model of franchising, the chain of learning centers expanded between 1991 and 1999 in seven countries. In Cyprus alone, almost 15% of children and 10% of adults attended classes.

the emerging globalization of virtually everything can be a source for many inspiring and innovative projects that could provoke discussions regarding values and contemporary global challenges, such as those related to the Millennium Development Goals (United Nations 2000).

2. *Challenging complexity*. Projects should not be straightforward, and they should not be easy to complete. They should be rich both in ideas and complexity. There should be many ways to approach and complete them.
3. *Relevance to students' interests and school curriculum*. Although this requirement is not easy to satisfy, it is imperative that educators always strive to align their activities with both the school curriculum and their students' interests. If we must prioritize, however, the student should come first.
4. *Ambiguity*. Just as Socrates provoked critical thinking using cases that could be considered from a variety of perspectives, including those that were mutually exclusive, a good project should stimulate students to develop different ways of approaching the challenge. This process will both kindle creativity and encourage them to engage in and practice debating and negotiation. They not only have to deliberate as a team and collectively develop a plan, but must also sometimes compromise on an approach that satisfies most of their requirements and desires.

In addition to these characteristics, which to some extent align with the Socratic circle process, a good CYBER Kids project provokes discussion on how to resolve the challenge and mobilizes students to work enthusiastically toward a solution. This encourages them to use the essential tools and/or acquire the necessary knowledge much faster than they would have without such motivation. We have witnessed situations that could be called extraordinary.[2]

Designing powerful projects – The Knowledge Packet concept

We proposed a model for designing constructivist problem-solving-based lesson plans and projects (CYBER Institutes 1993) using a simple template structure. The 1994 version of the Knowledge Packet is shown in Table 1.

2. In one case in 1994, six 12–13-year-old students were taken for a three-day vacation to a small seaside hotel. During their retreat, they were challenged to discuss the processes related to the operation of the resort and maybe develop software for its needs. To make things worse, they had no other language available except a new one (they were familiar with HyperCard, but they had SuperCard with them, a language that was similar but with more commands). Because of the situational motivation and inspiration, and also because children generally have no way of judging whether a certain task is ambitious or not, they managed to complete a professional package during that weekend.

Table 1. Key features coded within a typical 1994 version of the Knowledge Packet™

	Element	Description
1	Title/coding	Title of the unit/lesson plan and digital code
2	Language	Language(s) in which it is available (curriculum is made available in all countries that use the methodology)
3	Content domain/subdomain	For example, physics/trajectories
4	Level identifier or target groups	Age or educational level; for CYBER Kids, this indicates the instructional levels (minors A/B/C, juniors A/B, seniors A/B/C)
5	Duration	How long the creator anticipates it will take for implementation of the complete activities
6	Prerequisite Knowledge Packets™	If they exist
7	Specific know-how and knowledge	Actual know-how and knowledge that is supposed to be transferred to the learner
8	Lesson plan	Detailed instructions for the educator on how to approach, present, and monitor the process
9	Tools required	Software or other IT tools needed to implement the tasks; besides the name of the software, the specific technical feature to be used is also included (e.g., Word-learn to use the mail merge tool)
10	Mental development	Mental abilities targeted; in line with CYBER Kids research and classification scheme of mental abilities that are expected to be acquired and/or developed
11	Real-life applications	Specific ideas on how this activity links to real-life situations and to societal problems and challenges
12	Social value	Social value and importance of the specific knowledge
13	Keywords	Keywords or tags (or *metadata*) used for searching
14	Author	Individual who has developed the unit
15	Date	Date created and uploaded
16	Owner	Legal owner of the unit
17	Users	Keeps track of who is using this unit

To accommodate their novel structure, we proposed a new learning-object standard, which in some respects is analogous to today's LOMS (learning object metadata standard) and IEEE LOM standards (IMS Global Learning Consortium Inc. 2001) but in many ways also different. We coined the term Knowledge Packet™ to describe the intermingling and superposition of different descriptors, dimensions, and educational objectives and targets within a single *educational object*. A comparison between IEEE/LOMS and Knowledge Packets™ (Laouris 2005) reveals that the CYBER Kids specification emphasizes: (1) linking to society using extracurricular activities, (2) activities that require team collaboration, and (3) mental development. The requirement we imposed to link educational activities in school to the outside world was considered a great innovation in the early 1990s. Today, it is not simply relevant but obligatory that schools open their doors (not necessarily voluntarily) to the outside world. The approach used in the 1990s to engage learners with the outside world and to link the educational process with the real society is documented in a later section in the form of best practices (see *Linking to society: examples of activities*). The only third-party learning-object specification that comes close to the Knowledge Packet™ specification is the standard that was proposed and adopted by the Canadian government (E-learning Sub-group 2004). Experiences based on the application of Knowledge Packets™ have been published (Laouris and Eteokleous 2005a), and some work has been done more recently toward the application of the Knowledge Packet™ specification in the emerging field of mobile learning (Laouris and Eteokleous 2005b). It was argued that without a well-defined set of pedagogical- and human-centered tools, our net-centric economy poses significant challenges for reforming our educational systems. The authors also alarm about the dangers that accompany unwise use of new technologies. With the rapid development of cloud-based learning resources, the need for educationally relevant metadata in learning objects is becoming an absolutely essential requirement for designing modern educational materials and a necessary condition for portability, extensibility, and reusability (Laouris and Eteokleous 2005c)."

The structure of a typical lesson plan

All curriculum units (i.e., lesson plans) follow a well-defined structure that satisfies the Knowledge Packet™ standard. In the unit illustrated in Fig. 1, the instructor is expected to teach object-oriented programming. However, the technological aspect of the process remains hidden in the background. The technical content usually appears as a subtitle. The aspects of educational value and linking to society appear as priority elements because the whole curriculum is constructed around these aspects. The computer skills targeted by the unit are embedded in the process. The class may begin with a discussion about the complexity of keeping track of mathematical calculations and how calculators sometimes come in handy. Most important is that the learners appreciate value of the specific tool (a calculator in this case) in everyday life. In this example, students may be challenged with a contemporary problem that requires complex calculations. Then they can be encouraged to design and program their own problem-specific calculators to solve the problem. This process stimulates their creativity in parallel with their ability to understand the problem, develop the relevant algorithms, and code each button to perform the required operations. By associating code with a button, the code *moves* together with wherever the button is copied. In other words, its properties are inherited in all copies of that button. In this way, without even realizing it or talking about it, young students (in this case, a nine-year-old) are introduced to the basics of object-oriented programming.

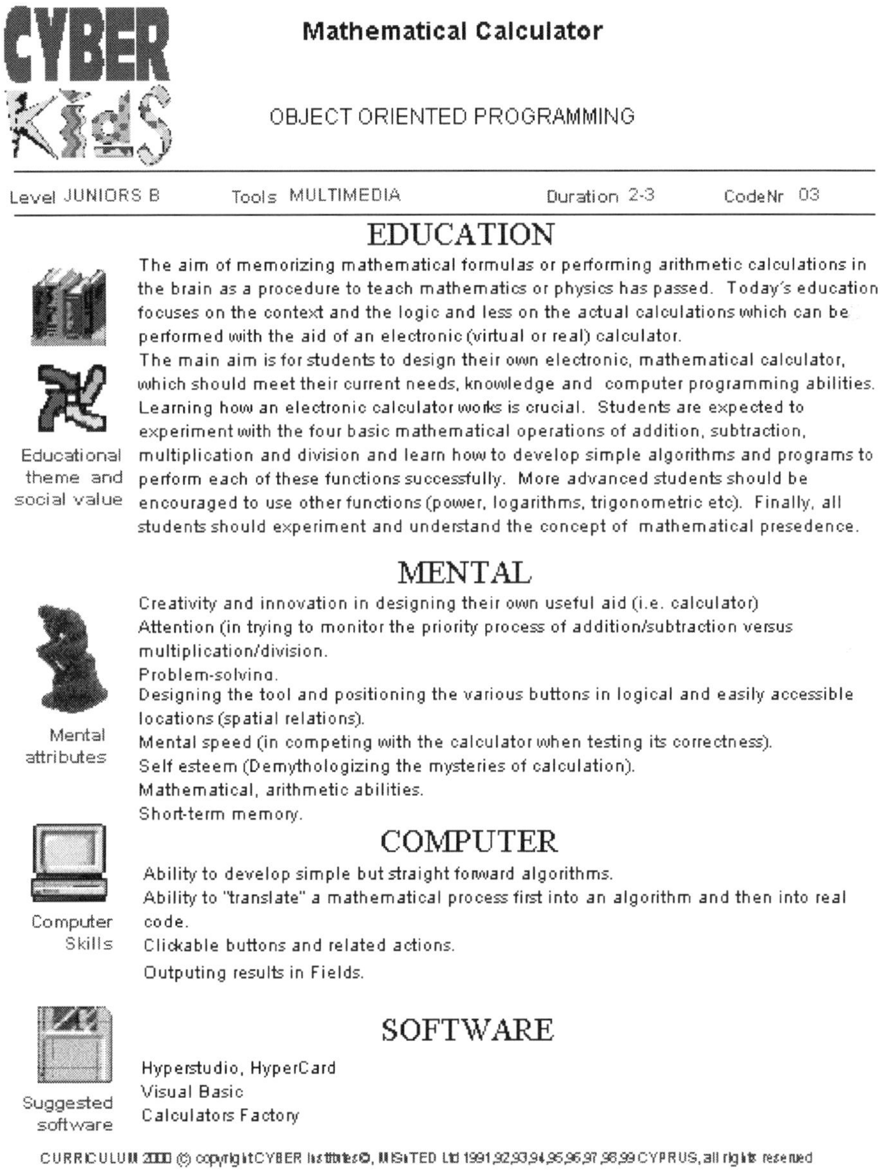

CYBER Kids

Mathematical Calculator

OBJECT ORIENTED PROGRAMMING

Level JUNIORS B   Tools MULTIMEDIA   Duration 2-3   CodeNr 03

EDUCATION

Educational theme and social value

The aim of memorizing mathematical formulas or performing arithmetic calculations in the brain as a procedure to teach mathematics or physics has passed. Today's education focuses on the context and the logic and less on the actual calculations which can be performed with the aid of an electronic (virtual or real) calculator.
The main aim is for students to design their own electronic, mathematical calculator, which should meet their current needs, knowledge and computer programming abilities. Learning how an electronic calculator works is crucial. Students are expected to experiment with the four basic mathematical operations of addition, subtraction, multiplication and division and learn how to develop simple algorithms and programs to perform each of these functions successfully. More advanced students should be encouraged to use other functions (power, logarithms, trigonometric etc). Finally, all students should experiment and understand the concept of mathematical presedence.

MENTAL

Mental attributes

Creativity and innovation in designing their own useful aid (i.e. calculator)
Attention (in trying to monitor the priority process of addition/subtraction versus multiplication/division.
Problem-solving.
Designing the tool and positioning the various buttons in logical and easily accessible locations (spatial relations).
Mental speed (in competing with the calculator when testing its correctness).
Self esteem (Demythologizing the mysteries of calculation).
Mathematical, arithmetic abilities.
Short-term memory.

COMPUTER

Computer Skills

Ability to develop simple but straight forward algorithms.
Ability to "translate" a mathematical process first into an algorithm and then into real code.
Clickable buttons and related actions.
Outputing results in Fields.

SOFTWARE

Suggested software

Hyperstudio, HyperCard
Visual Basic
Calculators Factory

Figure 1. First page of a typical curriculum unit first developed in 1991. The actual lesson plan and proposals for relevant extracurricular activities are not shown here since they appear in subsequent pages of this extract.

Linking to society: Examples of activities

This section presents examples of best practices used by CYBER Kids as extracurricular activities that aim to link classroom learning to real life. Certain activities might be less relevant to the reader's context, but they are nevertheless presented, as they were originally implemented, in the hope that they might inspire interested readers to design alternatives.

- *Linking to the world of professions.* Senior CYBER Kids groups (those with about four years of attendance; usually aged 10–13) had planned and scheduled visits to professional environments such as publishing houses, research institutions, and business and accounting enterprises. Their purpose was to meet, talk, and interact with professionals and correct possible misconceptions they might have had about particular professions, reflect on their own interests and talents, exercise their communication skills, and train their ability to extract the information they wanted and use it for their projects.
- *Students as creators of advanced multimedia projects.* In almost all cases, out-of-class endeavors were combined with the development of some project (usually multimedia based) related to the needs and operations of the places they visited. More often than not, student projects reached high levels of excellence. For example, they developed complete programs for touch-screen kiosks, hotels, and video stores. Following a competition in 1996 among our most talented children in graphic design, we adopted a more lively, colorful, and technically manageable logo (see http://www.cyber-kids.net) revised by one of the students.
- *Engaging them in research.* Within the framework of special agreements, students collaborated on research activities and performed joint presentations with college students in addition to completing internships and apprenticeships with research organizations (e.g., the Cyprus Neuroscience and Technology Institute; www.cnti.org.cy) and academic institutions. Their interaction with senior scientists acquainted them with the attitudes, styles, and working habits of hardworking, forward-thinking people. It also familiarized them with the world of science and research, thus breaking the stereotypes and misconceptions many people may have about these communities.
- *Presenting their innovative ideas in public forums.* Students were encouraged to come up with innovative ideas and inventions and present them in national or international schools and industrial innovation competitions. The brainstorming sessions that precede the process and the activities related to documenting an idea and preparing it for presentation stimulate creativity and develop problem-solving skills. Participating in forums lead by representatives from

local and government authorities, industry, and financial bodies boosted their self-esteem and confidence. For examples, see the Innovation-Technology-Social Progress Fair (CNTI 1993).

- *Camping, sports, museum visits, exploration expeditions.* Taking young children on various expeditions is a great way to combine physical and cognitive exercise. A few times a year, we organized mass events in which students from different educational centers and different geographical locations participated. During such events, teams worked on well-specified projects that involved data collection (recordings, videotaping, interviews, data collection through questionnaires etc.) and the subsequent development of multimedia projects. It is important in such activities that the lab (tools such as computers, cameras, recorders, and notebooks) travels with the students. This contributes not only to situated learning, but also toward preparing children to expect technology to accompany them wherever they go rather than having to visit geographically fixed sites to use it.
- *Contributions to art and culture.* Computers are great tools for nurturing imagination and creativity. Indeed, we have argued that a child's first experience with IT determines his or her lifelong relationship with it. If, for example, the first encounter involves playing simple video games without any educational value, the child will always look at the machine as an entertainment box. However, if the first interaction involves painting a picture or creating a story, then the child will always see the computer as a companion that helps him or her *create.* For this reason, at least once a year students were encouraged to submit artistic creations to art competitions and exhibitions. Such endeavors cultivate not only creativity but also understanding and appreciation of the value of art and culture. For examples, visit the Electronic Art Fairs page (CYBER Kids 1994).
- *Interacting with video games not as players but as evaluators.* Video games have become an inevitable aspect of children's lives. Prohibiting them will not work. In our educational centers, we allowed students to play video games after completing projects during their sessions, but also at any other time (outside of regular classes) that they wished. The games were chosen by the researchers to comply with certain age and complexity standards. Students were assigned small research projects that asked them to evaluate the games for characteristics such as the degree of interactivity, fun, engagement, educational value, learned skills, and so forth. Engaging them as researchers and evaluators helped them develop a critical perspective on video games while also drilling certain skills. We observed that students who attended our classes for more than a year were less attracted to simplistic video games that demand low cognitive effort and more attracted to constructive and demanding games or programming environments.

- *Participating in leadership, debate, conflict resolution, and other communication-related workshops.* The rise of organized civil society offers unique opportunities for young people to come into contact with humanistic values and democratic principles situated within real-world contexts and within the communities of civil activists. In the case of Cyprus, we have encouraged students to collaborate with peace initiatives and civil society organizations. For example, our students participated in youth workshops designed to develop their skills in communication, negotiation, leadership, and conflict resolution. At the same time, we asked our students to support civil initiatives through their own projects, thus provoking them to develop creative projects and assume responsibility for transforming the world around them. This kind of involvement helped them apply and sharpen their skills during the implementation phases of their own team projects. For example, they learned how to negotiate the division of labor among themselves, debate the specifics of their joint projects, and collaborate to present them to their peers and compete for excellence as a team.
- *Social volunteer work.* In Cyprus, our students were encouraged to come up with ideas and/or plans of action to support children with special needs or other children who might be disadvantaged. Such initiatives are most efficient when taken shortly before Christmas or in parallel with national events or fund-raising campaigns. The active participation of learners and their tangible contributions develop their social responsibility and deepen their ethical norms.

Discussion

The CYBER Kids experiment was performed on the island of Cyprus on a relatively large scale during the last decade of the twentieth century.[3] More than two decades later, the conceptual framework, the philosophy, and the vision for a new approach to education have become even more relevant. This is because technology has really taken off. At the time CYBER Kids was being implemented, there were no mobile phones and no Internet (except for Macintosh-based Internet, which was what we were using), and *Windows was just beginning to make its appearance.* Moreover, computer penetration in households (in Cyprus) was less than 5% (CYSTAT 1995).

3. For "fifteen-year-after" reflections, the interested reader may refer to a 2005 conference paper (Laouris and Anastasiou 2005).

The discussion below concentrates on the burning need for a vision-driven complete reform of the educational system and specifies two requirements: (1) the technical requirement for developing and adopting a functional specification for the design and development of future curricula and (2) a philosophical requirement for making real-world linkage an obligatory, not optional, feature of any educational process.

Vision-driven educational reforms

When our group launched CYBER Kids, we claimed that the educational system was about to become obsolete. We argued that no remedy could save it, not because it was badly designed, but because it had become so irrelevant to the needs and wishes of the new generation that only a complete bottom-up redesign would make sense. This is why we used such strong statements in our vision statement: "Our vision is to redefine the purpose, methods, and tools of education in light of relevant social change." It's fascinating that about twenty years later, Sugata Mitra (Mitra 2013) makes international news: "It's quite fashionable to say that the education system is broken – it's not broken, it's wonderfully constructed. It's just that we don't need it any more. It's outdated." We proposed a complete bottom-up redesign of the educational system more than 20 years ago (Laouris 1998). Today, we assert that not only the educational system but also the system of governance and many other systems require complete reinvention (Future Worlds Center 2011; Global Agoras 2008; Laouris et al. 2014; Laouris 2008; Papandreou 2013; Petridou et al. 2012).

Requirement for educationally relevant learning objects

The Knowledge Packet™ can be considered a forerunner learning object (LO) conglomerate that features numerous dimensions to accommodate and superimpose diverse requirements. It facilitates portability, reusability, and extensibility because it is standardized. It provides a scaffold for educators to extend or enrich our LOs, adapt their own existing lesson plans to meet the new standard, or develop their own new LOs. The Knowledge Packet™ allows an educator to develop a lesson plan that addresses a plethora of requirements simultaneously. It poses both constraints and opportunities. On the one hand, it is extremely difficult to design a one- or two-hour-long lesson that would sufficiently address all the requirements, which include mastering the relevant knowledge of the specific domain; facilitating mental, psychological, and social development; acquiring skills; and stimulating creativity, innovation, and entrepreneurship. On the other hand, it is a scaffold that supports the talented and enthusiastic educator in developing and practicing the skills that he or she wants his or her students to develop: being creative, innovative, enthusiastic, engaging, relevant, and interesting with regard to their concerns.

Designing small or large collaborative projects

The decision about how big or difficult a good project should be could be a matter of argument. If we consult Vygotsky's concept of "zones of proximal development," we could use his rule of thumb that an ideal project is one that is more difficult than a student can handle alone but not so difficult that it can't be managed with the support of peers or teachers (Vygotsky 1987). The features of collaboration may vary with different age groups. If classes include children of different ages, then it is desirable to facilitate situations in which older children mentor younger ones. This type of peer support is highly beneficial for both groups. Younger kids learn easier and faster when they receive knowledge or know-how from their older peers (also siblings) because the language used is closer to theirs and because they exhibit less inhibition and more interest. For the older one, helping a younger child is a confidence-boosting endeavor and an opportunity to externalize knowledge, which is known to be a powerful means of knowledge consolidation (Nonaka 1994). The benefits of formal and informal peer-to-peer education are well documented (Liu and Yang 2012; Ondrejka 2008).

Linking education to the needs of the real world

Schooling is a rather recent invention in our world (Collins, Brown, and Newman 1990; Laouris and Eteokleous 2005; Laouris et al. 2010). While the separation between school and the outside world has served its purpose for many centuries, the time has come for a new system. Building on our 1992 prediction that in the next twenty to thirty years education would incrementally move out of the classroom, we included in our educational scheme strong extracurricular dimensions. There is a distinctive difference between formal classroom education and education that is situated in a socially relevant environment. The formal classroom paradigm provides the learner with a third-person perspective: he or she "sees" the world and is expected to derive wisdom and knowledge through the eyes of others (i.e., the educator's). On the contrary, taking students out of the classroom and placing them in context allows them to see the world with their own eyes. This develops a first-person perspective and helps them build up their own points of view. Using recording instruments (digital cameras, voice and sound recorders, etc.) and technology for later digitization and processing (scanners, audio and video editors, etc.) equips them with enormous capabilities and opens astonishing possibilities. As we advocated in the 1990s, computer technology – as the first human construction that amplifies mental rather than physical abilities (Laouris 1992) – significantly expands a learner's perspective to go far beyond a superficial understanding of the issue at hand and consider it within the relevant real-world context. In other words, new technologies equip them with "eyes" and "ears" to experience the world from multiple perspectives. Not available in the 1990s, but widely available today, are additional technologies such as GPS, Proximity sensor, Motion sensor/accelerometer, Ambient Light sensor, Moisture sensor, Gyroscope, Google Maps, Google Earth, and many others that allow them to use "senses" well beyond those available to ordinary people. Imagine, for example, how the *Umwelt* (we borrow the term *Umwelt* from German, which in philosophy and cognitive science refers to "the world") would look like if we could experience it from the perspective of an ant or an alien on a spaceship.[4] Each of us lives in his or her own environment and develops his or her own understanding of the world. This is because each individual is subject to different physical, biological, cognitive, and cultural constraints. Technology provides transducers (i.e., machines that can record signals from the world that the normal human cannot, like zooming capability or mobile telephone communication across the globe) that can not only break such constraints, but when working in teams and within a well-defined context contribute toward constructing a joined cognitive and mutually acceptable model of the world. Learning becomes more experiential, and thus constructivist and less bound to the classroom. One could almost compare it to an adventure game experience. Moreover, the zooming in and out of our observations of the world inevitably cultivates values such as appreciation and acceptance of whatever is unknown or different. The multiple activities envisioned and implemented by learners that take place within wider societal contexts serve the higher aim of designing socially responsible educational paradigms.

At roughly the same time as we were first introducing in our island-wide experiment what we called the *extracurricular*[5] *dimension*, other researchers experimented with practically the same concept, for which they coined the term

4. This is also the case when projects include aspects that are outside of everyday life experiences-like, say, a project about snakes. Talking about and doing a project about snakes not only familiarizes a child with the unknown, but also extends his or her worldview by breaking the limits of what we usually regard as within the boundaries of everyday life. This approach, which is naturally embedded in fairy tales (and this is the main reason they are so important in the lives of children), has been a key requirement in the design of lesson plans for minors (ages 5–8).

5. It sounds, to say the least, out of place after this discussion to talk about authentic learning as being *extracurricular*!

situated cognition (Cognition and Technology Group at Vanderbilt 1993). The extracurricular components of our curricula turned out to fit better with the *cognitive apprenticeship* term introduced by Collins (Brown, Collins, and Duguid 1989; Collins 1988; Collins, Brown, and Newman 1990). Also, Jean Lave (1988) is credited with starting the situated cognition movement, although the concept is not really new when one considers that John Dewey (1974) and Lev Vygotsky (1962, 1987) both advocated similar approaches. Dewey viewed education as a process of living, not of preparation for the future, and Vygotsky proposed constructivism to explain how knowledge is constructed when new information comes into contact with existing knowledge developed from real-life experiences. Herrington and Oliver (2000) more recently attempted to systematize the features they considered instrumental for the successful design and implementation of extracurricular (i.e., situated) learning (see Table 2).

Table 2. Key features instrumental for the successful design and implementation of situated learning. Reprinted from Herrington and Oliver (2000)

#	Requirement
1	Provide authentic context that reflects the way the knowledge will be used in real life.
2	Provide authentic activities.
3	Provide access to expert performances and the modeling of processes.
4	Provide multiple roles and perspectives.
5	Support the collaborative construction of knowledge.
6	Provide coaching and scaffolding at critical times.
7	Promote reflection to enable abstractions to be formed.
8	Promote articulation to enable tacit knowledge to be made explicit.
9	Provide for integrated assessment of learning within the tasks.

Herrington and Oliver offer "support[ing] the collaborative construction of knowledge" as one of their nine requirements. However, they, like many others, do not center their attention on collaboration. In contrast, the CYBER Kids approach promotes collaboration as a key ingredient of extracurricular (or situated) learning.

Conclusions

The experiences derived from the CYBER Kids experiment have important implications for education with regard to the skills and competencies of both teachers and graduates, especially in relation to the latter's self-esteem, happiness, and employability. The Organization for Economic Co-operation and Development (OECD 2005a, 2005b) has defined *competency* as "more than just knowledge and skills; it is the ability to apply skills in a specific context to meet complex demands" (Jayaram 2012, 3). This is in complete alignment with the concept of taking students out of the classroom and engaging them in real-life situations. Also, practically all requirements proposed by the Results for Development Institute (Pegg et al. 2012) are satisfied by our project-oriented, problem-solving, situated approach. For example, business and customer awareness, with a basic understanding of the key drivers for business success, can only be acquired when students truly interact with businesses, as they do through envisioning, designing, and implementing their projects.

The development of language and communication skills, which is underscored as a key competence by the European Commission, is also a skill that develops when children discuss their ideas, negotiate their solutions, and present their works to real people in organizations or in forums such as art shows (CYBER Kids 1994), innovation competitions, or fairs (CNTI 1993). The recommendations of the European Parliament and the Council of December 18, 2006, regarding key competencies for lifelong learning that became a European Reference Framework (European Parliament and Council 2006) are listed in Table 3 (Key Competencies for All 2010).

Table 3. The recommendations of the European Parliament and the Council of December 18, 2006, on key competencies for lifelong learning

#	Key Competence
1	Communication in the mother tongue
2	Communication in foreign languages
3	Mathematical competence and basic competencies in science and technology
4	Digital competence
5	Learning to learn
6	Social and civic competencies
7	Sense of initiative and entrepreneurship
8	Cultural awareness and expression

Practically all competences envisioned and demanded by the European Parliament and the Council in 2006 can be satisfied through project-driven curricula that encourage peer-to-peer and student-to-real-world social interactions. The methods and approaches proposed and implemented by us and other researchers almost two decades earlier offer solid scientific grounding to support the design of contemporary educationally and socially relevant curricula. Basic IT skills, including familiarity with word processing, spreadsheets, file management, and Internet search engines, have been identified by the European Parliament and the Council as key competences. The project-oriented, problem-solving CYBER Kids approach, similar to other situated learning approaches, does not focus on teaching word processing, spreadsheets, etc., but embeds such skills within real-life projects. Children must learn to use computers not as an end, but as tools to help them design and implement challenging real-life group projects (thus supporting key competencies 1, 2, and 6). As they engage with IT, they benefit not only by sharpening their digital skills (key competence 4) and scientific thinking (key competence 3), but also from the balanced development of their mental abilities (key competence 5). The engagement of learners in real-life projects that demand teamwork cultivates collaboration and interaction, again supporting the development of their communication and social skills (key competencies 1, 2, and 6) and their understanding of and respect for personal, national, and cultural differences (key competence 8).

Underpinning all the competencies proposed by the European Parliament and the Council, the key foundation must be a positive attitude-a can-do approach, a readiness to participate and contribute, openness to new ideas, and a drive to make these things happen. Again, this is the natural consequence of a role-reversal, student-initiated, project-based approach (key competence 7). Furthermore, what both employers and universities frequently mention-entrepreneurship, innovative thinking, creativity, collaboration, and risk taking-are skills that can only be acquired when students face authentic challenges and are given incentives and freedoms to develop their own collaborative and innovative solutions.

The greatest implication of the work described in this chapter is that the educator's role has changed: he or she is now the inspirer, architect, negotiator, mentor, and facilitator. He or she no longer owns either exclusivity to knowledge or experience. True knowledge is constructed in collaboration with his or her students using real-life problems. Hand in hand with modern IT and other emerging technologies, the educator supports students to learn to use IT as their personal brain amplifier (Laouris 1992) and as a tool that allow them to collaborate.

Acknowledgments

Those who truly believed in and embraced the CYBER dream, with special mention of my wife Joulietta Kalli-Laouri, my daughter Romina, and my partners George Vakanas, Maria Symeonides, Dinos Georgiades, Harry Anastasiou, and Evros Alexandrou. Dedicated to the instructors, the parents, and more importantly the thousands of students who embraced the methodology and to whom the future belongs.

References

Brown, John Seely, Allan Collins, and Paul Duguid. 1989. "Situated Cognition and the Culture of Learning." *Educational Researcher* 18 (1): 32–42. DOI: 10.3102/0013189X018001032

CNTI. 1993. "Innovation-Technology-Social Progress Fair." *Futureworlds.eu*. http://futureworlds.eu/wiki/Innovation-Technology-Social_Progress_Fair. (last date of access August 10 2013).

Cognition and Technology Group at Vanderbilt. 1993. "Toward Integrated Curricula: Possibilities from Anchored Instruction." In *Cognitive Science Foundations of Instruction*, ed. by Mitchell Rabinowitz, 33–55. Hillsdale, NJ: Lawrence Erlbaum.

Collins, Alan, John Seely Brown, and Susan Newman. 1990. "Cognitive Apprenticeship: Teaching the Crafts of Reading, Writing, and Mathematics." In *Knowing, Learning, and Instruction: Essays in Honor of Robert Glaser*, ed. by Lauren B. Resnick, 453–494. Hillsdale, NJ: Lawrence Erlbaum.

Collins, Allan. 1988. *Cognitive Apprenticeship and Instructional Technology: Technical Report*. Cambridge, MA: BBN Labs Inc.

CYBER Institutes. 1990. "Nation-wide Experiment: Introduction of IT in the Lives of Children." *cyber-kids.net*. http://www.cyberkids.net/Nationwide_experiment:_Introduction_of_IT_in_the_lives_of_children. (last date of access 20 Sept. 2012).

CYBER Institutes. 1993. "The Knowledge Packet Innovation." *Cyber-kids.net*. http://www.cyber-kids.net/The Knowledge Packet Innovation. (last date of access 5 Sept. 2013).

CYBER Kids. 1994. "CYBER Kids Electronic Art Fairs." *Futureworlds.eu*. Futureworlds.eu/wiki/Electronic_Art_Fair. (last date of access 27 July 2013).

CYSTAT. 1995. "Information Society." *Mof.gov.cy*. http://www.mof.gov.cy/mof/cystat/statistics.nsf/science_technology_93main_en/science_technology_93main_en?OpenForm&sub=3&sel=1. (last date of access 19 Sept. 2013).

Dewey, John. 1974. "Science as Subject-Matter and as Method." In *John Dewey on Education: Selected Writings*, ed. by R. D. Archambault. Chicago: University of Chicago Press.

E-learning Sub-group. 2004. "Guidelines for the Government of Canada Education (GCed) Met Application Profile." *cio-dpi.gc.ca*. http://www.cio-dpi.gc.ca/im-gi/mwg-gtm/emssml/docs/2004/gced/gced00_e.asp. (last date of access 5 September 2012).

European Commission. 2010. "Europe 2020 Growth Strategy." *Europa.eu*. http://ec.europa.eu/europe2020/index_en.htm. (last date of access 1 August 2013).

European Parliament, and Council. 2006. "Key Competences for Lifelong Learning." *Europa.eu*. http://europa.eu/legislation_summaries/education_training_youth/lifelong_learning/c11090_en.htm. (last date of access 3 March 2011).

Future Worlds Center. 2011. "Using Democratic Dialogue to Reinvent Democracy." *Futureworlds.eu*. http://www.futureworlds.eu/wiki/Using_democratic_dialogue_to_reinvent_democracy. (last date of access 11 October 2012).

Gerard, Ralph W. 1967. "Shaping the Mind: Computers in Education." In *Applied Science and Technological Progress: A Report to the Committee on Science and Astronautics*, 207–228. US House of Representatives: National Academy of Sciences.

Glass, Vicki. 1978. *Emerging Literacy: From Research to Practice*. Lethbridge, AL: University of Alberta.

Global Agoras. 2008. "Anticipating the Challenges to the Obama Vision of Bottom-up Democracy." *Institute for 21st Century Agoras*. http://obamavision.wikispaces.com/ (last date of access accessed July 30, 2013).

Herrington, Jan, and Ron Oliver. 2000. "An Instructional Design Framework for Authentic Learning Environments." *Educational Technology Research and Development* 48 (3): 23–48. DOI: 10.1007/BF02319856

IMS Global Learning Consortium Inc. 2001. "Learning Resource Meta-data Specification." *imsglobal.org*. http://www.imsglobal.org/metadata/. (last date of access 11 July 2013).

Jayaram, Shubha. 2012. *Skills for Employability: The Need for 21st Century Skills*. Washington, DC: Results for Development Institute.

Key Competencies for All. 2010. "Online Employment Toolkit Handbook for Facilitators and Trainers." http://www.keycompetences.eu/wordpress/wp-content/uploads/2011/09/Handbook-Facilitators-final-ENG-redux.pdf. (last date of access 22 June 2013)

Laouris, Yiannis. 1992. *Computer: The First Human Construction That Amplifies Mental Abilities Rather Than Physical*. Cyberkids Talks Series, Nicosia CY: Cyberkids Press.

Laouris, Yiannis. 2005. "Educationally Relevant Meta-data in Learning Objects: Necessary Condition for Re-usability." In *Proc. 8th Cost 276 Workshop: Information and Knowledge Management for 61 Integrated Media Communication*, Trondheim, May 26–28, 2005, 61–65.

Laouris, Yiannis, and Harry Anastasiou. 2005. "Experiences from a Nation Wide Experiment Introducing IT in Lives of Children; Fifteen Years After." In *Proc. 4th World Conference on Mobile Learning*, Cape Town, South Africa, mLearn 2005; 25–28 October.

Laouris, Yiannis, Kevin M.C. Dye, Marios Michaelides, and N. Alexander Christakis. 2014. "Co-laboratories of Democracy: Best Choices for Designing Sustainable Futures." In *Social Systems and Design T*, ed. by Kijima Kyoichi, Translatio, 00–99. Tokyo, Japan: Springer Japan KK.

Laouris, Yiannis, and Nikleia Eteokleous. 2005a. "Experiences from the Application of Knowledge Packets as Means for Educationally, Mentally, and Socially Balanced Instruction." *Recent Research Developments in Learning Technologies* 1: 485–489.

Laouris, Yiannis, and Nikleia Eteokleous. 2005b. "Successful Implementation of M-learning Depends on Well-defined Requirements." In *Proceedings IADIS International Conference Mobile Learning 2005*, Qawra, Malta, 103–110.

Laouris, Yiannis, and Nikleia Eteokleous. 2005c. "We Need an Educationally Relevant Definition of Mobile Learning." In *Proceedings of 4th World Conference on Mobile Learning, mLearn 2005, 25–28 October*, ed. by Herman Van Der Merwe, and Tom Brown, 1–13. Cape Town, South Africa: Cyprus Neuroscience & Technology Institute.

Laouris, Yiannis, Laouri Romina, and Aleco Christakis. 2008. "Communication Praxis for Ethical Accountability: The Ethics of the Tree of Action: Dialogue and Breaking Down the Wall in Cyprus." *Systems Research* 25: 331–348.

Laouris, Yiannis, Gayle Underwood, Romina Laouri, and Aleco Christakis. 2010. "Structured Dialogue Embedded Within Emerging Technologies." In *Emerging Technologies in Distance Education*, ed. by George Veletsianos, 153–173. Athabasca University Press.

Laouris, Yiannis. 1998. "Innovative Education for the New Millenium." In *A Leap into the New Millenium.' HILTON Nicosia, Organized by Max Nikias, Integrated Media Systems Center*, Los Angeles.

Lave, Jean. 1988. *Cognition in Practice: Mind, Mathematics and Culture in Everyday Life*. Cambridge: Cambridge University Press. DOI: 10.1017/CBO9780511609268

Liu, Chien-Jen, and Shu Ching Yang. 2012. "Applying the Practical Inquiry Model to Investigate the Quality of Students' Online Discourse in an Information Ethics Course Based on Bloom's Teaching Goal and Bird's 3C Model." *Computers & Education* 59 (2): 466–480. DOI: 10.1016/j.compedu.2012.01.018

Mitra, Sugata. 2013. "Sugata Mitra Shows How Kids Teach Themselves." *Ted.com*. http://www.ted.com/talks/sugata_mitra_shows_how_kids_teach_themselves.html. (last date of access August 2008).

Morrow, Lesly. 1989. *Literacy Development in the Early Years: Helping Children Read and Write*. Englewood Cliffs: Prentice Hall.

OECD. 2005a. *Organisation for Economic Co-operation and Development*. http://www.oecd.org/ (last date of access 5 September 2013).

OECD. 2005b. "The Definition and Selection of Key Competencies." *Oecd.org*. http://www.oecd.org/pisa/35070367.pdf. (last date of access 27 May 2005).

Ondrejka, Cory R. 2008. "Education Unleashed: Participatory Culture, Education, and Innovation in Second Life." Available at SSRN: In *The Ecology of Games: Connecting Youth, Games, and Learning*, ed. by Katie Salen, 229–251. MIT Press.

Papandreou, George. 2013. "Imagine a European Democracy Without Borders." *Ted.com*. http://www.ted.com/talks/george_papandreou_imagine_a_european_democracy_without_borders.html. (last date of access June 2013).

Pegg, Ann, Jeff Waldock, Sonia Hendy-Isaac, and Ruth Lawton. 2012. *Pedagogy For Employability*. York, UK: Higher Education Academy.

Petridou, Elia, Eleni Michail, Maria Georgiou, and Danae Psilla. 2012. *Reinventing Democracy in the Digital Era*. ed. by Yiannis Laouris, and Afonso Ferreira. Nicosia.

Polsani, Pithamber. 2003. "Use and Abuse of Reusable Learning Objects." *Journal of Digital Information* 3 (4).

Punch, Samantha. 2003. "Childhoods in the Majority World: Miniature Adults or Tribal Children?" *Sociology* 37 (2): 277–295. DOI: 10.1177/00380385030037002004

United Nations. 2000. "Millennium Development Goals." *Un.org*. http://www.un.org/millenniumgoals/. (last date of access 12 August 2013).

Vygotsky, Lev S. 1962. *Thought and Language (1934)*. Cambridge, Massachusets: MIT Press. DOI: 10.1037/11193-000

Vygotsky, Lev S. 1987. *The Collected Works of LS Vygotsky: Volume 1: Problems of General Psychology, Including the Volume Thinking and Speech*. New York, USA: Springer.

Wikipedia. 2013. "Socratic Circles." *Wikipedia.org*. http://en.wikipedia.org/wiki/Socratic_method#Socratic_Circles. (last date of access 13 September 2013).

Author's address

Yiannis Laouris MD, PhD (Neurophysiology), MS (systems Engineering)
Senior Scientist
Cyprus Neuroscience & Technology Institute
5 Promitheos, 1065 Lefkosia, CYPRUS
www.cnti.org.cy
www.FutureWorldsCenter.org
laouris@cnti.org.cy

Developing teachers' epistemic agency in a knowledge building community through cogenerative dialogues

Seng Chee Tan and Daryl Ku
National Institute of Education, Nanyang Technological University, Singapore

The aim of this study was to understand how cogenerative dialogues – reflective dialogues involving both teachers and students directing at improving the learning environment – might aid in the development of teachers' epistemic agency. To do so, we investigated how the epistemic agency of the teacher-participants in a postgraduate knowledge building course is manifested through cogenerative dialogues. We were able to identify two broad categories of actions related to epistemic agency: knowledge actions and community actions. In addition, we also uncovered one factor that could influence how their epistemic agency is manifested: their preoccupation with Knowledge Forum, an online forum tool used to support knowledge building.

1. Introduction

In this chapter, we describe a study aimed at understanding how the epistemic agency of teachers, as members of a knowledge building community, may be developed using cogenerative dialogue (Tobin 2006) as a strategy. Knowledge building refers to the continual production and improvement of ideas useful to a knowledge building community through the collaborative efforts of its members (Scardamalia and Bereiter 2006). Epistemic agency generally refers to one's ownership and capacity to engage in knowledge work. We view epistemic agency as an attribute of productive members in a knowledge building community, which is manifested in efforts that are collaborative, intentional, volitional and sustained, directed at advancing knowledge and characterized by progressive discourse involving reasoning and reflections. Cogenerative dialogues are dialogues focusing on collective reflection, involving both teachers and students but without the traditional classroom power differential, leading to action plans directed at improving the learning environment.

Our study was partly inspired by Scardamalia and Bereiter's (1999) call to transform schools into knowledge building institutions so as to prepare the next generation of workforce with the capacity to survive and operate in a knowledge-based economy. This call was later heeded by Tan (2010), who argued that to transform schools into knowledge building institutions, teachers have to be equipped with the skills and capacity for knowledge building. This is a challenging task as we currently lack the know-how to do so. The study in this chapter is thus an attempt to take up this challenge. We took a very specific approach by investigating how the epistemic agency of teachers may be developed. Our study was guided by the research question "How is epistemic agency manifested through cogenerative dialogues?" and was situated in the context of teachers as members of a knowledge building community. We chose to focus on cogenerative dialogues because we believe that the use of cogenerative dialogues may aid in the development of teachers' epistemic agency.

In the following sections, we will elaborate further on what knowledge building is to establish the theoretical premise of our study. After that, we will explain why we chose to approach the problem from an epistemic agency angle. As we specifically chose to use Tobin's (2006) cogenerative dialogue as a strategy to aid in the development of teachers' epistemic agency, we will also explain what cogenerative dialogue as a research method involves. Following that, we will describe our study method before presenting the findings from our research.

1.1 Knowledge building and its prerequisites

To prepare students for citizenship in a knowledge-based society, Scardamalia and Bereiter (1999) believe that we must first transform our schools into knowledge building institutions. In such institutions, students would be engaged in eliciting and improving ideas through collaborative and productive discourse. Such practices are not unlike that of the scientific community, which we considered a paragon of a knowledge building institution.

Members of a knowledge building community typically engage themselves in expressing and representing their ideas in a form that is accessible and manipulable by the members of their community. In knowledge building parlance, such representations are known as *epistemic artifacts* (Sterenly, 2004). They are important because it is only through such artifacts that the members of a community can share and subsequently develop their ideas. This notion can be traced to Popper's (1979) three world ontology: the first world is one that is physical, the second is one that is mental or psychological, and the third world is described as one that is an intersection of the first two worlds where mental objects are embodied or physically realized. Therefore, epistemic artifacts can also be thought of as reified ideas, or what Popper would refer to as World 3 objects.

As epistemic artifacts are essential to support knowledge building, Scardamalia and Bereiter (2006) proposed the process should be supported by technologies, and Knowledge Forum was developed for this purpose. Knowledge Forum is a computer-based tool specifically designed by Scardamalia and Bereiter to support knowledge building. It enables members of a knowledge building community to collaboratively engage in expressing, sharing and improving the community's epistemic artifacts.

The production and improvement of epistemic artifacts by students is a process many students are not familiar with, which requires intentional scaffolding effort by teachers. In order to transform schools into knowledge building institutions, Tan (2010) argued that we have to equip teachers with the skills and capacity for knowledge building. With the appropriate skills and capacity, teachers would be able to collaboratively improve ideas relating to the theories and practices of teaching and learning. Only then can they seek to positively influence the learning outcomes of their students in their new roles.

Currently, there is a lack of information about how a knowledge building culture can be engendered among teachers. Empirical research into the development of teachers' knowledge building capacity, for example, was observed to be lacking (Stahl 2004). To address this, Tan and his colleagues (Tan 2010; Chai and Tan 2009) specifically conducted a number of investigations with teachers as the focus. This involved having teachers examine cases relevant to knowledge building in the literature, work on authentic problems in schools, reflect on their practices, and participate in reciprocal teaching. Through the insights gained, Chai and Tan (2009) learned that there are two criteria that are essential for the development of teachers' knowledge building capacity. First, they must be provided with quality facilitation by an experienced instructor who has the capacity and experience with the knowledge building pedagogy. Second, such teachers must be provided with sufficient time to negotiate the theory-practice nexus of knowledge building. However, these conditions suggest a reliance on external agency (e.g., an experienced instructor). This means that the teachers who experience these learning activities may still not be a productive member of a knowledge building community. According to Bereiter (1994), there are three qualities that characterize a productive member of a knowledge building community: (1) committed to improve, (2) committed to strive towards common understanding rather than just mutual agreement, and (3) committed to expand the community's knowledge base. As such, a means to develop teachers' epistemic agency is by developing these qualities. This study builds on our previous efforts in developing teacher's capacity in knowledge building, in particular, developing the epistemic agency of teachers.

1.2 Epistemic agency

The pioneers of knowledge building, Marlene Scardamalia and Carl Bereiter, refer to epistemic agency as students' collective responsibilities towards the development of the community's knowledge artifacts and, self-directedness in setting and aligning learning goals with the community's knowledge advancement trajectory (Scardamalia 2002; Scardamalia and Bereiter 2010). According to Bereiter (2002) and Scardamalia (2002), epistemic agency is an important quality to possess for members of a knowledge building community because students with epistemic agency will deal "with problems of goals, motivation, evaluation, and long-range planning that are normally left to teachers or managers" (Scardamalia 2002, 79). Epistemic agency is also considered to be important in cognate fields such as learning as knowledge creation (Paavola and Hakkarainen 2005), which suggests it may have a vital role in the production of knowledge.

The multi-disciplinary treatise by Damşa, Kirschner, Andriessen, Erkens, and Sins (2010) on the theoretical concept of epistemic agency provides further insights into what epistemic agency entails. First, they reasoned that the term "epistemic" referred to "knowledge and what it means to know something" (149). As such, epistemic agency could generally be understood as referring to activities involving knowledge and knowing. They considered the meaning of "agency" from a philosophical perspective (Reed 2001; Schwartz and Okita 2004), a social-cognitive perspective (Bandura 2001), an activity theory perspective (Engeström 2008) and a sociological perspective (Emirbayer and Mische 1998), and concluded that epistemic agency is an expression of the "learner's intentional, goal-directed, and sustained involvement in knowledge-driven, object-oriented, collaborative activities" (149). Our understanding of epistemic agency is a synthesis of these ideas and Bereiter's (1994) notion of progressive discourse. We view epistemic agency as an attribute of productive members in a knowledge building community, which is manifested in efforts that are collaborative, intentional, volitional and sustained, directed at advancing knowledge and characterized by progressive discourse involving reasoning and reflections.

Damşa et al. (2010) held that there had been very little empirical research that focused on epistemic agency. As such, epistemic agency as a distinct concept is still not very well understood. As part of their plan to understand what characterizes shared epistemic agency, Damşa et al. (2010) investigated the actions of university students enrolled in an educational and instructional design course. In doing so, they were able to identify a list of actions that might indicate shared epistemic agency. The findings from their study suggest shared epistemic agency may be manifested as two broad categories of actions: epistemic and regulative. Epistemic actions are actions directly related to creating knowledge whereas regulative actions are actions that support the creation of knowledge. While our study did not focus on what Damşa et al. specifically referred to as "shared" epistemic agency, our analytical focus is similar in that we analyzed the actions of the participants as a class rather than as individuals. As such, Damşa et al.'s study was able to inform our study.

Knowledge building is not a new field of research. Nonetheless, despite the advancements that were made over the years, there remained little insights in the literature to inform how teachers' epistemic agency can be developed. The study we described in this chapter is thus an attempt to address this lack of understanding. At the same time, our study is also a very specific attempt to gain empirical insights into how Tobin's cogenerative dialogue can be used as a strategy to develop the epistemic agency of teachers situated in the context of a knowledge building community. It extends past research on epistemic agency beyond the context of professional work environment (Russell 2002) and group project work (Damşa et al. 2010). It also foregrounds the roles of discourse in developing teachers' epistemic agency.

1.3 Cogenerative dialogues

Cogenerative dialogues refer to "activities in which a small number of students and the coteachers review evidence from a recent class and 'cogenerate' collective resolutions regarding new rules for the class, changes in teacher and student roles, and responsibility for accomplishing changes" (Tobin 2006, 133). It is more than a group reflection in that there is intentional equalization of power between students and teachers, and a concrete focus on improving the learning environment through collaborative discourse. In a typical cogenerative dialogue session, researchers, teachers and students review video recordings of past lessons and discuss how the lessons could be improved subsequently. This method of improving students' learning and their learning environment through the use of discourse is coherent with the knowledge building principle of advancing shared knowledge through knowledge building discourse.

Studies involving cogenerative dialogues had yielded promising results. In the study conducted by LaVan and Beers (2005), they reported how the various stakeholders, students, teachers, co-teachers and researchers learned from one another through collaborative evaluation of lessons, identification of the tensions and contradictions in class, and suggestions involving the appropriate resolutions. The process provided the participants with valuable opportunities to learn from one another, resulting in symmetrical advancement in their personal understanding.

In our study, we used Tobin's cogenerative dialogue as a strategy to bring forth the latent epistemic agency of the teacher-participants. We believe that in doing so, it also engenders in the participants a propensity for efforts that are collaborative, intentional, volitional and sustained, directed at advancing knowledge and characterized by progressive discourse involving reasoning and reflections. Our study is also an attempt at extending the use of cogenerative dialogue to the development of epistemic agency, specifically in the context of teachers situated in a knowledge building community. This bridges two different fields of research, knowledge building and cogenerative dialogue. In doing so, we aimed to better understand how we can develop the knowledge building capacity of teachers.

2. Methods

2.1 Participants

The eighteen participants in our study were students enrolled in a knowledge building course offered as part of the Master of Education (Learning Sciences and Technologies) program at the National Institute of Education, Singapore. Knowledge building and the use of *Knowledge Forum*, a network-based online forum to support knowledge building, were not new to these participants. They were acquainted with the topic and the use of Knowledge Forum through a different course that they were previously enrolled in. In contrast, none of the participants was aware of what cogenerative dialogue is. This study was their first exposure to it.

As the participants were all students in the same Master program, they had similar academic experiences due to the courses they were required to enroll in. Another similarity among the participants was that they were all teachers by profession. But, in terms of knowledge building communities, the makeup of the participants' community was still considered a heterogeneous one. First, the participants' age range was diverse, ranging between twenty-five to fifty-two years old. Their years of teaching experiences were also diverse, ranging between two years to thirty-two years. They taught subjects such as mathematics, arts, chemistry, English, Chinese, and computing. In addition, while they were all teachers, only sixteen of them were teachers at K-12 schools. Two were lecturers at polytechnics.[1] The heterogeneity displayed here was considered ideal for a knowledge building community because idea improvement thrives on diversity and differences (Scardamalia 2002).

1. A polytechnic in Singapore is distinct from a university. It is a tertiary institution that mainly offers vocational study programs. These are typically full-time three-year programs leading to a diploma qualification. Unlike polytechnics in the UK or US, the highest qualification that can be awarded by a polytechnic is an advance diploma. However, advance diplomas are mainly awarded through select programs that are part-time only.

2.2 Context

The National Institute of Education (NIE) is the national teacher training institute in Singapore and is an autonomous institute of the Nanyang Technological University.

The postgraduate course the participants were enrolled in is named *Engaged Learning in Knowledge Building Communities*. This consisted of thirteen three-hour lessons that took place every week during the academic term. Lessons were conducted in a purpose-built computer laboratory with sufficient space for the participants to gather in a circular seating configuration during the cogenerative dialogue sessions.

2.3 Instructional approach

Lessons were conducted face to face, on campus in a computer laboratory designed to support more conducive learning. The instructor (the first author) had intentionally used knowledge building as the instructional method as this was in line with the aim of the course. This was also intended at providing the students with the opportunity to personally experience themselves as members of a knowledge building community.

The curriculum for the course was divided into three main phases. The first was the initiation phase. This spanned three lessons and was aimed at helping students form mental images of a knowledge building classroom. The second was the meaning making phase. This spanned six lessons and was aimed at providing students with the opportunities to make sense of the theories and the practical issues relating to knowledge building. The last phase was the consolidation phase. This made up the last four lessons of the course and was aimed at providing students with the opportunities to apply what they had learnt. Specifically, this involved students either designing a knowledge building curriculum or writing a position paper on topics relating to knowledge building communities.

The design of the course's curriculum was inspired by some of the knowledge building principles suggested by Scardamalia (2002). The principle "Real Ideas, Authentic Problems" suggests that students should work on authentic problems rather than contrived textbook problems. To enact this principle, students were required to study a case report as well as share their individual experiences implementing knowledge building as a teacher in their own classes. Another principle is "Constructive Use of Authoritative Sources of Knowledge". This was enacted by involving students in analyzing research papers concerning knowledge building communities to better appreciate the underlying theories and methodologies involved. "Community Knowledge, Collective Responsibilities" was another principle that inspired the design of the curriculum. With this principle, reciprocal teaching arrangements were made that involved students taking responsibility to lead part of the discussions in class. The students, in groups, chose the topics they were interested (e.g., technologies supporting knowledge building; theory of collaborative knowing). They were free to decide on the instructional strategy to help their peers understand the key ideas related to the topics. Most groups shared relevant journal papers with their peers, presented the key ideas and designed some questions to engage their peers in discussion.

As the class operated as a knowledge building community, there was a need to support the development of epistemic artifacts. This was supported by the use of Knowledge Forum, a computer-based tool resembling an online discussion forum. In Knowledge Forum, a series of discussions involving a specific topic are organized together and presented as a 'view', which could contain several 'threads' as in a typical online forum. See Figure 1 for an example.

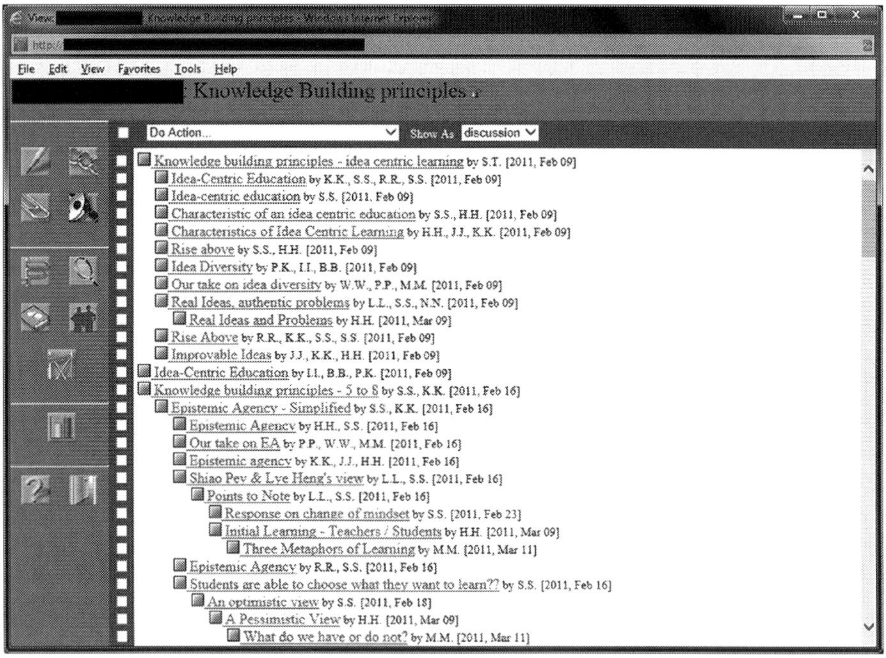

Figure 1. Screenshot of a 'view' taken from Knowledge Forum

As such, a view is also an organized presentation of epistemic artifacts concerning a specific topic. In Knowledge Forum, such artifacts are represented as 'notes', which are similar to 'posts' in a typical online forum. A note in Knowledge

Forum, however, can be invoked in one or more views while remaining unique. This means that if a note is amended, the amendment is reflected in all the views where the note is invoked. It is not simply different posts with the same content. See Figure 2 for an example of a note.

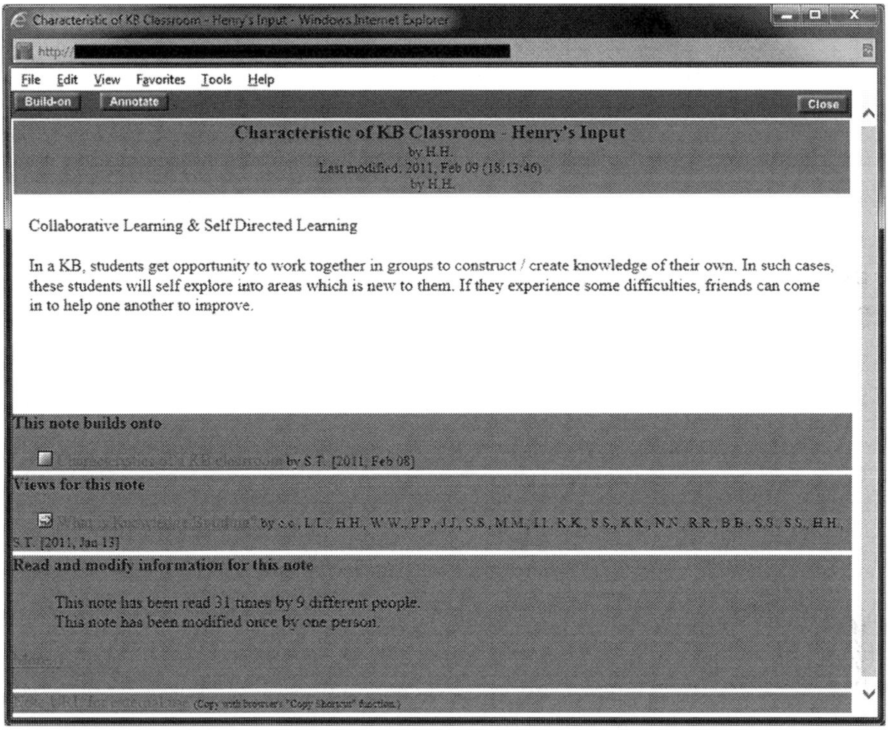

Figure 2. Screenshot of a 'note' taken from Knowledge Forum

A note can be created by any member of the community. However, only the member who created the note has ownership and write-access. One of the advantages of using Knowledge Forum to support knowledge building is that the flow and development of epistemic artifacts is made readily apparent through the sequential and hierarchical organizations of the notes in a view.

The activities associated with knowledge building using Knowledge Forum include members building on one another's notes, making references to notes, as well as annotating notes. Through such activities, the process of knowledge building for the community and individual members is made overt. Consequently, this provides an explicit trail of activities and interactions that may be investigated further.

Other than specifically supporting the development of epistemic artifacts, Knowledge Forum is also designed to support the scaffolding of thinking. This function can be accessed through the scaffold feature in Knowledge Forum and is also presented whenever a new note is being created. This scaffold takes the form of sentence starting phrases. A generic set of phrases are provided by default and can be customized according to needs. For example, to support better argumentation, the instructor might add customized phrases, such as "My claim is …," "My claim is supported by …," or "A counter argument is …." These scaffolds serve as cognitive cues to model thinking and promote more productive knowledge building discourse – as opposed to casual social conversations (Scardamalia and Bereiter 1993).

Knowledge Forum serves as an equitable platform that provides all students with the opportunity to voice their opinions. This changes the turn-taking structure typical in face to face settings and discourages the domination of discussions by individuals who are more vocal (Tan and Tan 2011).

2.4 Implementation of cogenerative dialogue

In our study, cogenerative dialogue was used as a means to facilitate dialogues involving knowledge building as well as dialogues involving the pedagogical implementation of knowledge building in class. Each cogenerative dialogue session commenced with the instructor asking questions such as "what went well in this class," "what did not go so well," and "what could be done to improve the next lesson."

Our specific implementation of cogenerative dialogue, however, had to be altered slightly to fit the needs and constraints of the study. First, the roles of researcher and teacher were fulfilled by the instructor instead of separate individuals. However, this did not diminish the value of cogenerative dialogue because the instructor was also an expert in knowledge building. As such, he possessed the necessary expertise to simultaneously facilitate and instruct students on issues relating to knowledge building. Second, instead of reviewing video recordings of previous lessons, the participants reviewed their immediate classroom experiences. This was made possible because the cogenerative dialogue sessions took place immediately after the class formally ended. The duration of each session ranges between nine to twenty minutes. Due to the limited duration in which the study could be carried out without severely inconveniencing the students, it was not possible to review past video recordings, as doing so would consume a lot of time. Furthermore, the three-hour lessons were scheduled in the evening. Therefore, it was already late into the night by the time the class had ended and the session began. Given these constraints, we had to adapt Tobin's cogenerative dialogue accordingly. While the participants did not benefit from the use of video recordings to support recollection and discourse, this was ameliorated by the temporal proximity of the cogenerative dialogue sessions to the lessons proper. As the participants' transition from the lesson to the cogenerative dialogue session was a seamless experience, it also helped maintain the context that was "still fresh" from the lesson. As such, our arrangements did not diverge from cogenerative dialogue as a research method.

2.5 Instructor's balancing act

One of the challenges faced by the instructor during the cogenerative dialogue sessions was learning how to balance facilitating with instructing. This concerns the idea of structure versus agency and is an important topic which had been addressed in several sociological theories (e.g., Giddens 1981). In using cogenerative dialogue as a strategy to develop the participants' epistemic agency, the instructor was effectively imposing a structure on the process. This structure was characterized by routine questions aimed at influencing the participants to evaluate their immediate classroom experiences and to take initiatives to improve their learning experiences in the subsequent lessons. As this structure was fundamentally concerned with directing the participants, and epistemic agency was construed as a learner's self-directedness in setting learning goals and aligning such goals to the needs of the community (Scardamalia 2002; Scardamalia and Bereiter 2010), using cogenerative dialogue to develop epistemic agency can, therefore, create tension in the process. As such, in imposing a structure, the instructor was consequentially limiting the expression and development of the participants' epistemic agency.

Giddens (1981), however, saw structure and agency as complementary rather than contradictory, arguing that structures are "both the medium and the outcome of the practices which constitutes social systems" (27). In other words, while social structures shape people's behaviors and practices, it is the people that enact such structures because it is their practices that constitute and reproduce such structures. As such, individuals can shape their social practices and in doing so, mediate the construction and reproduction of social structures (Giddens 1981). In this study, the participants, through their own agency, shaped the structure of their learning environment. This was achieved in a variety of ways, usually involving the participants proposing how subsequent lessons can be improved.

Another challenge that the instructor faced during the cogenerative dialogue sessions concerned balancing authority with empowerment. Rather than providing answers to all the questions raised by the students, the instructor would ask the students more questions to help them arrive at their own answers. This facilitation process was a precarious one requiring delicate balance. If the participants were provided with a roundabout instead of a direct response to their questions, they may not be satisfied with the response they were given. This may also have the consequence of inviting a negative emotional response from the participants. In addition, in providing a roundabout response, the instructor may inadvertently give participants the impression that he was being evasive because he was not knowledgeable enough. This possibility should not be underestimated because of the cultural context. In most Asian cultures, teachers are seen as the sole authoritative source of knowledge. Therefore, the notion of empowering participants as epistemic agents is antithetical since this challenges their perception of knowledge authority. In this study, the instructor tried to exercise rational authority (Driver et al. 2000) in the delivery of the lesson although it would be convenient to rely on tacit institutional power.

2.6 Data collection and analysis

The course consisted of thirteen weeks of lessons but cogenerative dialogue sessions were only conducted for the first nine lessons. Our analysis, however, was delimited to the first seven sessions because the structure of the sessions for the eighth and ninth lessons mainly involved the participants taking turns briefly sharing their learning reflections. We decided to exclude the data from these two sessions from our analysis because while the structure allowed the participants to review and share their learning reflections, it did not provide them with the opportunities to also cogenerate ideas to improve their learning environment. We were unable to let the participants do so because we needed every participant to review and share their individual learning reflections in the limited time we had to conduct the study.

Data was primarily collected using video cameras. Two video cameras were set up at opposite ends of the circular seating configuration and focused at the participants to record the discussions that took place. In total, more than one hundred minutes of video data were collected.

To facilitate analysis, we first transcribed the participants' dialogues. Following that, we used content analysis as a method to analyze the transcript for manifestations of epistemic agency. Our focus of analysis was the participants as a class. We did not discriminate epistemic agency between individuals. We (the two authors) analyzed the transcript using themes as our unit, where one theme refers to one identifiable idea (Aviv 2001, 59). In this case, an identifiable idea refers to a set of actions that are contiguous and directed at the same purpose. A theme may encompass one or more sentences spoken by one or more participants. The transition of the ideas underlying the participants' dialogues was generally clear-cut so we encountered no difficulties identifying the distinct ideas in the transcript. In addition, to achieve better validity and reliability, the literature on content analysis (De Wever et al. 2006; Rourke and Anderson 2004) was consulted beforehand.

We used Damşa et al.'s (2010) "Actions Indicating Shared Epistemic Agency" framework (175) as a starting basis for our analysis. This framework was constructed based on their treatment of the literature involving knowledge creation and agency, and then subsequently adjusted using empirical data collected from their study into shared epistemic agency and collaborative knowledge creation. Rather than analyzing the transcripts independently, our analysis process was an iterative, collaborative and reflexive one. The first author started with a draft framework and coding; the second author critiqued the framework and proposed a revised framework. The differences were discussed and a new framework was derived (See Table 1 for our final framework). The second author continued the re-coding with the new framework. All doubtful cases were discussed until consensual agreement was achieved between the two coders. The analysis concluded when we were satisfied that the refined framework, the data and our insights were coherent. This method relied on consensus of the coders (Bryman and Burgess 1994) to achieve dependability (Denzin and Lincoln 1994) of the coding rather than relying on the positivist criteria of reliability.

3. Findings and discussions

3.1 Manifestation of participants' epistemic agency through cogenerative dialogues

The outcome of our analysis was a refined framework representative of how the teacher-participants, as members of a knowledge building community, manifested their epistemic agency as a class. As cogenerative dialogues have specific intended actions – improving the students' learning and the learning environment – we labeled these as actions. Through our analysis, we were able to identify two broad categories of actions that we consider to be manifestations of their epistemic agency: knowledge actions and community actions. Refer to Table 1 for an outline of this framework.

Table 1. Framework of the manifestation of epistemic agency by teachers situated in a Knowledge Building community

Knowledge actions
1. Triggering Knowledge-related Dialogues a. Identifying Knowledge Gaps or Problems: To identify the knowledge gap or a problem, for the purpose of triggering further discussions. b. Highlighting Ideas for Discussion: To recount a specific idea that happened in class for further discussion. 2. Creating Shared Understanding a. Clarifying Understanding: To check the intended meaning of ideas; to clarify concepts or ideas for better understanding. b. Valuating Ideas: To appraise the value of ideas.
Community actions
1. Lesson Implementation: To evaluate how the lesson was pedagogically implemented and supported with tools and resources; and propose improvements. 2. Community Etiquette: To establish or practice conduct beneficial for the community such as laying out how members should function or summarily review such functions.

Knowledge actions are actions that are directly related to knowledge building. Community actions are meta-actions that are essential to support the process of knowledge building. We will elaborate what these two categories of actions involve in the next sections.

3.1.1 *Knowledge actions*

We identified two distinct categories of actions that are *directly* related to knowledge building for the teacher-participants. These two categories of actions involved the participants determining the nature of their community's epistemic artifacts as well as the creation and refinement of such artifacts.

The first category, *Triggering Knowledge-related Dialogues*, is associated with the participants determining the nature of their community's epistemic artifacts. This may be characterized by the actions *Identifying Knowledge Gaps or Problems* or *Highlighting Ideas for Discussion. Identifying Knowledge Gaps or Problems* involves the participants identifying knowledge gaps or problems in their knowledge base for the purpose of triggering further discussions. An example of this action can be illustrated through the following talk:

> You know what's the difference between the other module and this one? That one was continuous. This one we go back. You know, we may have the idea right now but when we go back we are swarmed with so many other things.

Highlighting Ideas for Discussion involves the participants recounting specific ideas that they had engaged with during the class for further discussion. This action is illustrated through the following talk:

> I think we see how the obstacle from the KB goes first. Because I think it's quite important that we understand what obstacles [are] out there. Otherwise, we can talk a lot, and sounds very good. But once like we go out, try to implement [in] reality, then we face obstacles, then how are we going to solve it? If not, it will forever is like that.

The second category, *Creating Shared Understanding*, is associated with the participants' creation and refinement of the epistemic artifacts of their community. Note that the participants did not use Knowledge Forum to create or refine notes during the cogenerative dialogue sessions. Our study did not require or allowed them to do so. Nonetheless, we consider that epistemic artifacts *were* created to the extent afforded by the cogenerative dialogues. This is because in expressing their ideas verbally, the participants were explicitly sharing their ideas with the engaged members of their community. Therefore, while such expressions were ephemeral and not as accessible as the notes produced using Knowledge Forum, they did serve as a knowledge building currency for the participants. In this case, the epistemic artifacts we refer to here were the ideas encapsulated in, and represented by, the participants' verbal utterances. These epistemic artifacts are consistent with Popper's notion of reified ideas as physical world objects (participants' utterances) intersecting with mental/psychological objects (participants' ideas). As such, epistemic artifacts *were* created and refined through the cogenerative dialogues. But, instead of being represented as notes using Knowledge Forum, they were represented as verbal utterances. The participants' creation and refinement of the epistemic artifacts of their community may be characterized by the actions *Clarifying Understanding* and *Valuating Ideas. Clarifying Understanding* involves the participants checking the intended meaning of ideas or clarifying an idea for a better understanding. The following talk concerns the participants having just studied cases of knowledge building in Hong Kong. A participant then attempted to clarify if there are cultural and contextual differences between Hong Kong and Singapore that would mediate their applications of the knowledge building principles:

> I mean like we want to actually like know how we, will it be applicable to like Singapore context. Because like if you look at Hong Kong context or whatsoever, it could be like slightly different, different culture and all that. So if we have a real life, happening right now, so I think it will be a better idea how we can better [unclear word] our own KB.

Valuating Ideas involves the participants appraising the value of their ideas. An example can be seen in the talk below:

> But even then the lesson idea today, when we talk about Henry's lesson right? We were saying what it was *not* rather than what it was. You understand what I mean? You understand what I mean? For example we were not saying that like this lesson … the key feature was idea diversity, for example. So we don't really know how it looks like for idea diversity. I mean in his case, when he presented, we were asking is this KB? And why it wasn't a KB. Rather than is this KB and what were the elements that's in. So I think there is a world of difference because I want to see how it is, or how we can make it real in the classroom.

Note that this is not the same as participants evaluating ideas in the "critique" sense. Instead, this had more to do with participants appraising the value of an idea. This action is contextually significant because the participants, being teachers, were predominantly concerned with the pragmatics rather than the academic of teaching theories and ideas. As such, they were more concerned with understanding how teaching theories and ideas add value to their teaching and how they can be effectively applied.

3.1.2 *Community actions*

Community actions are essential actions that support the knowledge building process of the community. If knowledge actions are actions that are directly associated with the development of epistemic artifacts, then community actions are meta-actions that support the development of epistemic artifacts. While we refer to them as supportive actions, we do consider them to be just as important as knowledge actions because such actions shaped the knowledge building dynamics of the participants' community.

The results of our analysis indicate two distinct categories of community actions. One is associated with the participants' evaluation and follow-up actions concerning the pedagogical implementation of knowledge building as an instructional method. The other is associated with the desired etiquette for the community.

The category, *Lesson Implementation*, is specifically concerned with participants' actions involving the evaluation of the instructor's pedagogical implementation of knowledge building and the measures to take for improvement. This includes how the instructor supported his instruction with tools and resources. The following talk illustrates a participant evaluating the instructor's use of Knowledge Forum to support knowledge building and his attempt to offer a solution:

> I think one of the, one of the things that we are using the Knowledge Forum right? I don't think it's really functioning as one. It's just more of your individual note, my individual note, but we haven't really gone in to use the other scaffolds to try

> to seek verification maybe, or to give our opinion about. So I don't think we have actually, although we have been exposed, we haven't really use it in that sense also, you see. So maybe we can explore that a little bit more.

This participant was not convinced Knowledge Forum was an appropriate tool to support knowledge building because he perceived the process of knowledge building as one of creating notes.

The category, *Community Etiquette*, is another category of meta-actions that is associated with the development of epistemic artifacts and is specifically concerned with establishing or practicing conduct beneficial to the community. This includes participants explicitly defining conducts that are expected and summarily reiterating such conducts. The cogenerative dialogues in the third session were particularly concerned with the use and value of Knowledge Forum and make for a case in point here. The following talk demonstrates one of the participant's agreement to make a contribution to the community through Knowledge Forum.

> Maybe give it one comment and … At least see maybe two views. Take a look of two people's, and then maybe give one comment at least, minimum.

Towards the end of the session, two participants voluntarily summarized the actions that the class had agreed upon. The aforementioned action was revisited in their dialogue:

> Participant 1: Try to make use of the Knowledge Forum.
> Participant 2: At least once.

The dialogues associated with the participants' community actions are strongly influenced by the structure of the cogenerative dialogue sessions (Tobin 2006). Their dialogues involving lesson implementation and community etiquette, for example, are logical responses to the standard cues used by the instructor to improve how the lessons were conducted. Even though they were not targeted at the conceptual understanding of knowledge building, they still reflected the productive agency of the participants (Schwartz and Okita 2004) who articulated concrete choice of actions, rules and structures to improve their learning process.

3.2 Relationship between knowledge building and the use of Knowledge Forum

We conducted additional analysis to further investigate if there was a relationship between the participants' understanding of knowledge building and their use of Knowledge Forum. This was motivated by the participants' apparent resistance towards the use of Knowledge Forum for supporting knowledge building as noted by the instructor personally; this resistance was also reflected in the transcript. One of the participants, for example, had questioned if Knowledge Forum was an appropriate tool for supporting knowledge building: "I don't think it's really functioning as one. It's just more of your individual note, my individual note [...]." We found this to be interesting since the participants had previous experiences using Knowledge Forum and yet had remained resistant towards its use. We had reasons then to believe that as the participants' understanding of knowledge building improve, so would their reception towards the use of Knowledge Forum. This led us to conduct an additional analysis into the dialogues that are specifically associated with knowledge building and Knowledge Forum.

The additional analysis we conducted was based on the themes in which we constructed our framework. To reiterate, a theme corresponds to a distinct idea in the participants' dialogues. We counted the number of themes associated with knowledge actions and the number of themes specifically associated with community actions related to Knowledge Forum. See Figure 3 for a visual presentation of the outcome from our analysis. The unshaded bars (*KB*) indicate the number of themes associated with knowledge actions. The shaded bars indicate the number of themes associated with community actions related to Knowledge Forum. There is a lighter shaded bar (*KF A*) and a darker shaded bar (*KF B*) because we were able to make further distinctions in the quality of the dialogues. The quality of KF A dialogues is mainly associated with technology perception and use, whereas the quality of KF B dialogues is mainly associated with the usability[2] of Knowledge Forum for knowledge building. The differences can be briefly explained with questions: "What can we do with Knowledge Forum?" (KF A) versus "What can Knowledge Forum do for us as productive and engaged members of this knowledge building community?" (KF B). Note that Figure 3 was not intended to be interpreted quantitatively. We intended for it to aid us in perceiving the relationship between knowledge building and the participants' reception towards Knowledge Forum.

Our analysis suggests the participants' knowledge actions generally increased over the weeks. Furthermore, this improvement was marked by a change in their disposition towards Knowledge Forum. In Figure 3, it can be seen that the number of KB themes were low in the first four sessions but increased more than double to five in the fifth and sixth sessions. This is interesting because at the same time, the

2. In ISO 9241-11 (1998), usability is defined as "the extent to which a product can be used by specified users to achieve specified goals with effectiveness, efficiency and satisfaction *in a specified context of use*" [italics ours]. In this case, the concern is with the value provided by Knowledge Forum, for the participants, in the context of knowledge building, for the purpose of creating and refining epistemic artefacts.

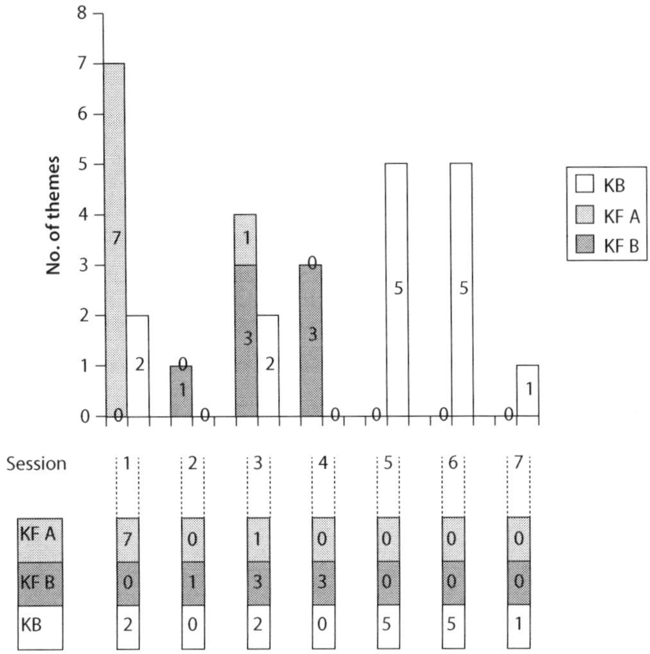

Figure 3. Number of 'knowledge' action themes and 'community' action themes related to Knowledge Forum in each session

number of KF themes were decreasing. But, not only were they decreasing, the initially high number of KF A themes were also transiting towards higher quality KF B themes. This shift is reflective of the participants' technological pedagogical knowledge (Mishra and Koehler 2006). We propose that the subsequent "absence" of KF themes may also be related to the participants' improvement in their understanding of knowledge building. This was an improvement characterized by a re-calibration of priorities resulting in their attention towards Knowledge Forum subsumed by their increasing focus on the more important aspects of knowledge building.

As highlighted earlier, we were able to observe a change in the quality of the dialogues associated with community actions related to Knowledge Forum. In our analysis, we found it useful to make a distinction and categorized these dialogues as higher quality dialogues (KF B) and lower quality dialogues (KF A). Lower quality dialogues are associated with technology perception and use. The thinking behind such dialogues can generally be thought of as "what can we do with Knowledge Forum?" and can be illustrated by the following exchange between a participant and the instructor:

Participant: I still find the knowledge forum a little, I mean it's like going through a labyrinth. I mean, honestly speaking, because I, because it's, it doesn't look, I mean from, I mean from this point of view, it doesn't look that savvy. I mean it's not intuitive, it's not intuitive. You have to go through cryptic, you know like some. And then you have to know through you must like wave through like jungles of mangrove or something.
Instructor: It's not user friendly.
Participant: Exactly.

Note how there was little attention towards knowledge building in the exchange. Instead, the focus was on how the participant personally felt about Knowledge Forum and its unsatisfactory design. Consequently, the participant was concerned with what he can do with Knowledge Forum given its lack of intuitiveness.

High quality dialogues are associated with the usability of Knowledge Forum for knowledge building. The thinking behind such dialogues can generally be thought of as "what can Knowledge Forum do for us as productive and engaged members of this knowledge building community?" The following talk is an example of such dialogues:

> I think the previous week I brought this up about we haven't actually used the Knowledge Forum per se. I think today's discussion went very well because a lot of questions were generated. But I feel that all those things that we asked were not captured, so if we were captured in the knowledge forum then I think it would have been something better. I think we had a lot of questions and there is a lot of discussions created but unfortunately it is all lost already unless we either remember it or for those who have taken notes will have [unclear phrase].

Unlike the previous exchange, the talk here reflects the participant's concern that the epistemic artifacts they had verbally created would be lost unless they were transcribed into notes using Knowledge Forum. The participant's concern clearly demonstrated the priorities he had accorded to knowledge building and Knowledge Forum, with the latter subsumed by his concern to preserve the epistemic artifacts that were verbally created through the cogenerative dialogues.

4. Conclusions

The aim of this study was to investigate how the epistemic agency of teachers situated in the context of a knowledge building community is manifested through the use of Tobin's (2006) cogenerative dialogue. Guiding the study was the research question: "How is epistemic agency manifested through cogenerative dialogue?"

We identified two broad categories of actions which we consider to be manifestations of the teacher-participants' epistemic agency. The first category of actions, knowledge actions, involves dialogues that are directly related to knowledge building. This includes dialogues to determine the nature of the community's epistemic artifacts as well as the creation and refinement of such artifacts. The characteristics of such dialogues are similar to Scardamalia's knowledge building principle "Knowledge Building Discourse" (81), which is aimed at improving shared ideas that are of interest to the community. The second category of actions, community actions, involves dialogues that are essential to support the knowledge building process of the community. This includes dialogues to evaluate the instructor's pedagogical implementation of knowledge building as well as the necessary follow-up actions, and dialogues to address the desired etiquette for the participants' community.

In addition to uncovering how the epistemic agency of the teacher-participants in this study was manifested through cogenerative dialogues, we also uncovered one other factor that could influence its manifestation, that is, the participants' preoccupation with Knowledge Forum as a tool to support knowledge building. In the initial cogenerative dialogue sessions, the participants were vacillating between the pursuit of technological knowledge and pedagogical knowledge. Initially, the participants were more interested in questioning the instructor's choice of Knowledge Forum as the course's official knowledge building tool, and expressing their interest in the use of alternative tools that they were more comfortable with. The participants' appreciation for the theory of knowledge building was a contrast in the later cogenerative dialogue sessions. Further analysis suggests there was an improvement in their understanding of knowledge building, which was marked by a simultaneous change in their disposition towards Knowledge Forum.

The findings in this study suggest cogenerative dialogue could aid in the development of the participants' epistemic agency. The dialogues explicitly engaged the participants in knowledge building discourse – reflect, listen, and talk about their understanding and the learning process – about their technological pedagogical knowledge. The study also illuminated the fluidity of epistemic agency, in that its manifestation is subject to the context of learning, the content of learning, and the structure of the learning environment.

Future studies could examine the manifestation of epistemic agency through various instructional activities (e.g., cogenerative dialogues versus reciprocal teaching), and interactions through different media (e.g., face-to-face versus online forum). In addition to the tension of structure-agency dialectics reported in this study, it would be valuable to investigate other tensions and contradictions that could have a bearing on how epistemic agency is manifested.

Acknowledgements

This study is funded by the National Institute of Education, Singapore, project RS 10/08 TSC. Appreciation goes to participants who provided feedback to the study in AERA 2012.

References

Aviv, Reuven. 2001. "Educational Performance of ALN via Content Analysis." *Journal of Asynchronous Learning Networks* 4 (2): 53–72.

Bandura, Albert. 2001. "Social Cognitive Theory: An Agenctic Perspective." *Annual Review of Psychology* 52:1–26. DOI: 10.1146/annurev.psych.52.1.1

Bereiter, Carl. 1994. "Implications of Postmodernism for Science, or, Science as a Progressive Discourse." *Educational Psychologist* 29 (1): 3–12. DOI: 10.1207/s15326985ep2901_1

Bereiter, Carl. 2002. "Subject Matter that Matters." In *Education and Mind in the Knowledge Age*, ed. by Alan Bryman and Bob Burgess, 275–313. Mahwah, NJ: Lawrence Erlbaum Associates, Inc.

Bryman, Alan and Bob Burgess. 1994. *Analyzing Qualitative Data*. London: Routledge. DOI: 10.4324/9780203413081

Chai, Ching Sing, and Seng Chee Tan. 2009. "Professional Development of Teachers for Computer-Supported Collaborative Learning: A Knowledge-Building Approach." *Teachers College Record* 111 (5): 1296–1327.

Damşa, Crina I., Paul A. Kirschner, Jerry E. B. Andriessen, Gijsbert Erkens, and Patrick H. M. Sins. 2010. "Shared Epistemic Agency: An Empirical Study of an Emergent Construct." *Journal of the Learning Sciences* 19 (2): 143–186. DOI: 10.1080/10508401003708381

De Wever, Bram, Tammy Schellens, Martin Valcke, and Hilde Van Keer. 2006. "Content Analysis Schemes to Analyze Transcripts of Online Asynchronous Discussion Groups: A Review." *Computers and Education* 46 (1): 6–28. DOI: 10.1016/j.compedu.2005.04.005

Denzin, Norman K., and Yvonna S. Lincoln. 1994. "Introduction: Entering the Field of Qualitative Research" In *Handbook of Qualitative Research*, ed. by N. K. Denzin, and Y. S. Lincoln, 1–18. London: Sage.

Driver, Rosalind, Paul Newton, and Jonathan Osborne. 2000. "Establishing the Norms of Scientific Argumentation in Classrooms." *Science Education* 84 (3): 287–312. DOI: 10.1002/(SICI)1098-237X(200005)84:3<287::AID-SCE1>3.0.CO;2-A

Emirbayer, Mustafa, and Ann Mische. 1998. "What is Agency?" *American Journal of Sociology* 103 (4): 962–1023. DOI: 10.1086/231294

Engeström, Yrjö. 2008. *From Teams to Knots: Activity-Theoretical Studies of Collaboration and Learning at Work*. New York: Cambridge University Press. DOI: 10.1017/CBO9780511619847

Giddens, Anthony. 1981. *A Contemporary Critique of Historical Materialism: Power, Property and the State*. vol. 1. London: Macmillan.

LaVan, Sarah-Kate and Jennifer Beers. 2005. "The Role of Cogenerative Dialogue in Learning to Teach and Transforming Learning Environments." In *Improving Urban Science Education: New Roles for Teachers, Students and Researchers*, ed. by Kenneth Tobin, Rowhea Elmesky, and Gale Seiler, 149–166. New York: Rowman & Littlefield.

Mishra, Punya, and Matthew J. Koehler. 2006. "Technological Pedagogical Content Knowledge: A New Framework for Teacher Knowledge." *Teachers College Record* 108 (6): 1017–1054. DOI: 10.1111/j.1467-9620.2006.00684.x

Paavola, Sami, and Kai Hakkarainen. 2005. "The Knowledge Creation Metaphor – An Emergent Epistemological Approach to Learning." *Science & Education* 14 (6): 535–557. DOI: 10.1007/s11191-004-5157-0

Popper, Karl. 1979. "Three Worlds." *Michigan Quarterly Review* 18 (1): 1–23.

Reed, Baron. 2001. "Epistemic Agency and the Intellectual Virtues." *Southern Journal of Philosophy* 39: 507–526. DOI: 10.1111/j.2041-6962.2001.tb01831.x

Rourke, Liam, and Terry Anderson. 2004. "Validity in Quantitative Content Analysis." *Educational Technology, Research & Development* 52 (1): 5–18.

Russell, Ann. 2002. "The Role of Epistemic Agency and Knowledge Building Discourse to Foster Interprofessional Practice in a Canadian Hospital." In *American Educational Research Association Annual Conference*, New Orleans.

Scardamalia, Marlene. 2002. "Collective Cognitive Responsibility for the Advancement of Knowledge." In *Liberal Education in a Knowledge Society*, ed. by Barry Smith, and Carl Bereiter, 67–98. Chicago: Open Court.

Scardamalia, Marlene, and Carl Bereiter. 1993. "Technologies for Knowledge Building Discourse." *Communications of the ACM* 36 (5): 37–41. DOI: 10.1145/155049.155056

Scardamalia, Marlene, and Carl Bereiter. 1999. "Schools as Knowledge Building Organizations." In *Today's Children, Tomorrow's Society: The Development Health and Wealth of Nations*, ed. by D. Keating, and C. Hertzman, 274–289. New York: Guilford.

Scardamalia, Marlene, and Carl Bereiter. 2006. "Knowledge Building: Theory, Pedagogy and Technology." In *The Cambridge Handbook of the Learning Sciences*, ed. by R. Keith Sawyer, 97–118. New York: Cambridge University Press.

Scardamalia, Marlene, and Carl Bereiter. 2010. "A Brief History of Knowledge Building." *Canadian Journal of Learning and Technology* 36 (1).

Schwartz, Daniel L., and Sandra Okita. 2004. "The Productive Agency in Learning by Teaching." http://aaalab.stanford.edu/papers/Productive_Agency_in_Learning_by_Teaching.pdf. (last date of access 19 Sept. 2013).

Sterenly, Kim. 2004. "Externalism, Epistemic Artefacts and the Extended Mind." In *The Externalist Challenge: New Studies on Cognition and Intentionality*, ed. by Richard Schantz, 239–254. Berlin, New York: de Gruyter.

Stahl, Gerry. 2004. "Building Collaborative Knowing: Elements of a Social Theory of CSCL." In *What We Know About CSCL: And Implementing It in Higher Education*, ed. by Jan-Willem Strijbos, Paul A. Kirschner, and Rob L. Martens, 53–86. Norwell, MA: Kluwer Academic Publishers. DOI: 10.1007/1-4020-7921-4_3

Tan, Aik-Ling, and Seng Chee Tan. 2011. "Conversation Analysis as a Tool to Understand Online Social Encounters." In *Handbook of Research on Methods and Techniques for Studying Virtual Communities: Paradigms and Phenomena*, ed. by Ben Kei Daniel, 248–266. Hershey, PA: IGI Global.

Tan, Seng Chee. 2010. "Developing 21st Century Teachers as a Knowledge Builder." *International Journal for the Scholarship of Teaching and Learning* 4 (2): 1–8.

Tobin, Kenneth. 2006. "Learning to Teach Through Coteaching and Cogenerative Dialogue." *Teaching Education* 17 (2): 133–142. DOI: 10.1080/10476210600680358

Authors' addresses

Seng Chee Tan
National Institute of Education
Nanyang Technological University
1 Nanyang Walk, Singapore 637616
sengchee.tan@nie.edu.sg

Daryl Ku
National Institute of Education
Nanyang Technological University
1 Nanyang Walk, Singapore 637616
daryl.ku@nie.edu.sg

PART III

Dialogic knowledge building

Potentials of dialogic technologies for knowledge building and negotiation

Mobile game-based learning in university education

Alexander Bartel, Paula Figas and Georg Hagel
Kempten University of Applied Sciences

Access to information and learning materials should be as independent and efficient as possible. Mobile Learning (m-learning) makes this happen as a consequence of the mobile diffusion. This new educational approach offers many chances to extend the possibilities of e-learning since learning is no longer dependent on a specific time of occurrence or a particular location. Besides an integrated pedagogical framework, the process of how sustainable knowledge can be transformed to students' minds seems to be the main challenge. To achieve this sustainability, gamification would be an appropriate method. Combining gamification-aspects and social interaction to increase the engagement of students, leads to an application for mobile devices. Its concept and the different scenarios of using the application in a university context will be presented in this contribution.

Introduction

While technology has become an omnipresent part of everyday life, its usage moves into the center of attention. This leads to unrecognized potential in the field of university education. Enforcing a higher level of engagement and a better learning experience amongst students enters into the limelight. As a result of the ongoing world-wide mobile diffusion during the last years, almost every student in industrialized countries owns a smartphone. According to a study of the University of New Hampshire, 70 percent of students use their smartphones more than three times during class periods (Alfano, Horowitch and Kitchen 2010). These findings cannot be considered as representative, but hint towards a common trend. Using this already familiar and available technology in the context of learning is, of course, a great opportunity to achieve a deeper involvement of the so-called digital natives. This assumption is supported by Kloos et al. (2012, 5) in their findings:

> Mobile devices really make a difference in education. Their possibilities allow defining new kinds of scenarios that improve motivation, increase retention, enhance creativity, facilitate more flexibility.

This paper consists of two parts: The first part provides an overview of the relevant terms and defines the basic aspect of learning games and mobile learning. It also points at pedagogical potentials and discusses further possible impacts on students. The second chapter will seek to clarify how learning games and mobile learning can be implemented in university contexts.

Learning games

The idea of learning by playing has fascinated scientists and teachers for many years. There are already numerous studies, didactic journals and pedagogical literature addressing the question whether it is possible to foster learning through games. But, there is still a large potential for controversy.

Definition of terms

The historian John Huizinga (1955) coined the term "*Homo Ludens*" – the playing man – and demonstrated that playing has many different faces and exists in almost every field of life. As Zimmermann (2010, 1) illustrates: "We play with toys. We play musical instruments and we play the radio. We can make a play on words, be playful during sex, or simply be in a playful state of mind". But, the terms "play" and "game" have different meanings: Huizinga (1955, 28) describes a play as a voluntary activity with "[…] its aim in itself and accompanied by a feeling of tension, joy, and the consciousness that it is 'different' from 'ordinary life'". Hence, play is not only a matter of what the actions are but also their performance (Wechselberger 2008, 3).

In contrast, a game can be defined as "[…] a system in which players engage in an artificial conflict, defined by rules, that results in a quantifiable outcome" (Salem and Zimmermann 2004, 80). This shows, that there are a number of differences between the terms: For instance, playing with a doll, only involves one person, while a game of chess needs at least two opponents (Wechselberger 2008, 4). Yet, a computer can serve as a party during play. So-called digital games can be played with electronic devices, like computers that set the rules of the game (Esposito 2005, 2). There are many different kinds of digital games: In action games, like in car races, the objective is to be the fastest. In contrast, puzzle games like "Tetris" focus on logical and conceptual challenges. In adventure games, like "Zork", the player has to perform tasks in dangerous environments. These are just a few examples of popular types of digital games.

The impulse to play does not have to come from the person itself. Since "[…] in play we feel most fully and intensely ancestral joys" (Hall 1904, 206), the Gamification approach integrates game elements in non-gaming situations to make them more enjoyable or to influence behavior. Therefore, games can also be used to transfer and consolidate knowledge in pedagogical practice. Murphy et al. (2011, 2) describe learning games simply as "[…] games that are used for non-entertainment purposes, specifically to teach material or reinforce learning". The idea of learning games, also called game-based-learning or education games, is not a new one. Due to the changed learning needs of the "Net Generation" (Whitton 2007, 1063), especially, digital learning games became the focus of closer attention. However, the discussions about games in pedagogical research are not comparable with those of the last few decades. The differences have become apparent in, for example, technical developments: New innovations enable complex 3D user interfaces or dynamic synchronous players' interaction. Also, the underlying philosophy is quite different and has shifted more and more from behaviorism (Jong et al. 2010, 2) to constructivism. In comparison to behaviorism, constructivist education assumes that students construct their own personal reality and that knowledge cannot be simply transferred from the teacher to the student. Hence, the constructivist approach enables students to construct their knowledge by themselves (Mottok et al. 2012).

According to Wechselberger (2008, 6), there are three main types of digital learning games: *Commercial off-the-shelf games* are developed by the games industry based on commercial interest with the intention to entertain. The pedagogical claim to learn something is not in the foreground. Nevertheless, games like "Civilization III" can give a better insight into old cultures and the historical contexts (Wechselberger 2008, 6). *Educational Games* have both an entertainment and didactic function. A well-known example is the game "Global Conflicts". In this game the player takes on the role of a journalist in crisis areas. He should report about the situation to both learn about journalistic work and the situation in crisis areas (Wechselberger 2008, 6). The third and most important kind of learning game, the so-called *Serious Game*, uses electronic devices for non-entertainment purposes. It clearly focuses on the transfer of knowledge and skill development (Tarja, Johannesson and Backlund 2007, 3).

Nevertheless, the obligatory use of learning games seems to run contrary to the basic idea of games. As shown before, a game is out of touch with reality, just serves an end in itself and has no consequences. In comparison, learning games focus on the transfer of knowledge. Sometimes even negative consequences like poor marks can follow if the aim of the learning game cannot be achieved. Therefore, one can reach the conclusion that an instrumentalization of play is inconsistent with its characteristics (Wechselberger 2009, 5). Considering this, it becomes clear that a learning game is something different from a "normal" game. It is played for another reason and is constructed differently. Still the question remains whether games can positively influence the learning success of students or not.

Possibilities and limits of learning games

In public debates computer games are in general controversial subjects. The main concern about using games in education lies mostly in the fact that it requires a lot of time, and that they may not be suitable for every learning content. Furthermore, some psychological approaches point out that not every student can learn through games, and that both children and adults can become addicted to computer games. But, whereas the opponents place computer games in context with aggressiveness, social isolation, addiction and violence (Fromme, Jörissen and Unger 2008, 1), the supporters see great opportunities in digital, game-based learning. Whitton (2007, 1063) even believes that they might have

> [...] the potential to transform the way in which students learn, and motivate and engage a new generation of learners in a way that traditional education does not.

From the pedagogical perspective, there are several aspects of educational games which must be considered. One aspect relates to the fun-factor of games in general: According to Zichermann and Cunningham (2011, 2) "everything has the potential to be fun". Many of the most popular games in the past include activities, which have no high "fun-factor" in the real world, like gardening (FarmVille), setting the table (Diner Dash), diapering babies or combing someone's hair (Sally's Salon). Those games are successful because of their design or their system of rewards (Zichermann and Cunningham 2011, 12). Scientists assume that this might even have an effect on learning content. With the help of games students are even motivated to learn material which is normally considered being tedious and difficult, like mythology or maths (Whitton 2007, 1064). Therefore, the vision of the teachers is that "[...] learning would happen almost without their realizing it, in pursuit of beating the game" (Prensky 2001, 12).

Beside the fun-factor there is the motivational aspect: Is it possible to motivate students with games? Many studies have shown that motivation could have a great impact on learning outcomes and that a lack of motivation negatively influences students' learning outcomes (Figas, Hagel and Bartel 2013, 1299ff.). Due to this, the idea becomes steadily more important that it may be "[...] possible to get learners of all ages totally involved in learning any subject matter" (Prensky 2001, 19). Naturally, this does not apply to all people in the same way. As the study of Whitton shows

> [...] it is clearly not the case that all individuals find computer games-based learning to be motivational, even in a key demographic of game players.
> (Whitton 2007, 1066)

Finally, the flow-experience has to be mentioned: Csikszentmihalyi (1990, 4) describes flow as "the state in which people are so involved in an activity that nothing else seems to matter". Therefore flow "[...] acts as a magnet for learning" (Csikszentmihalyi 1997, 33). Flow arises especially in digital games when they have been designed in such a way that distractions are minimized, challenges with player skill and time are balanced, the players receive feedback and clear tasks are given (Murphy et al. 2011, 6).

In summary, the usage of games in education is not appropriate for every learning context and might have some disadvantages, like the time aspect. However, games offer many possibilities to improve learning and teaching (Whitton and Moseley 2012, 197). The transfer of knowledge can be "[...] accompanied by an exciting adventure or amusing games function" (Meiers 2012, 7), competences like aiming, timing or strategy can be developed (Whitton 2007, 1063). This poses the question whether games can also be used in university education. Whitton gives a positive answer and argues that play is for both, adults and children. This becomes apparent when one looks at current learning games.

Examples

Games are already used as a didactic tool in an educational context. A survey in 2006 showed that both primary school teachers and secondary school teachers use games for teaching purposes (Sandford et al. 2006, 16ff.). Customized science games, commercial off-the-shelf historical games and, in general, games with multi-user environments are already used for school children (Whitton 2007, 1063). For example, in a game called "Math Blaster", students shoot at the right solution for a math problem. With every right solution, a balloon moves towards a needle. When the ball bursts, the student wins the game (Jong et al. 2010, 4).

In adult education learning games are being used in a range of different contexts for learning in almost any field of knowledge: For example, in healthcare they are used to improve physical fitness or to support patients with diabetics. Marines play games to prepare and train for operations, and in boot camp sailors of the US Navy train on the Damage Control Trainer (Murphy et al. 2011). Murphy et al. (2011, 33) summarize that "[l]earning games are all around us, being used in all sorts of innovative ways".

Mobile learning

As the previous chapter has shown, modern technology offers many possibilities to use games in education. Another modern, technology-based approach of learning is the so-called "mobile learning".

Definition of terms

Mobile learning, also known as m-learning, describes a form of education "[...] when the learner is not in a defined location [...]" (Meiers 2012, 2). Traditional education is frequently generalized in literature as face-to-face teaching in a classroom or a lecture hall. However, the idea of distance learning is not new. According to Winters (2006, 5), forms of distance education have existed for over 100 years.

Mobile learning is closely related to the term "e-learning" (electronic learning). Both terms describe forms of education using technology. In contrast to e-learning, m-learning mainly refers to mobile technology. According to Vosloo (2012, 10), it "[...] is education that involves the use of mobile devices to enable learning anytime and anywhere". Only a few years ago m-learning almost exclusively referred to laptops. Today it includes smartphones, tablet PCs or entertainment consoles. The goal behind this "[...] is learning what you want, where you want and when you want" (Meiers 2012, 2).

Possibilities and limits of mobile learning in education

In the last years, the number of students with mobile devices has increased continuously: Recent studies have shown that every third mobile phone today is a smartphone. In 2011 more than 10.1 million smartphones were sold in Germany. A similar development can be observed for tablets (Goertz 2012, 22f.). Thus, the use of mobile applications, and with it the interest of pedagogy and economy in these applications, continues to grow.

As illustrated in Figure 1, Google Scholar, as an example for a bibliographic database which is connected to WorldCat, shows the increasing popularity of the subject m-learning. The search query which was used to extract single values of that chart was: intitle: "mlearning" OR intitle: "mobile learning" OR intitle: "m-learning" OR intitle: "m(obile)-learning" (Google Inc. AG 2013).

But what are the advantages or disadvantages of m-learning? Does it make sense to integrate this new form of learning in education? Goertz (2012, 26) assumes that mobile devices will provide better access to study content because students can develop their skills almost anytime and anywhere and learn whenever

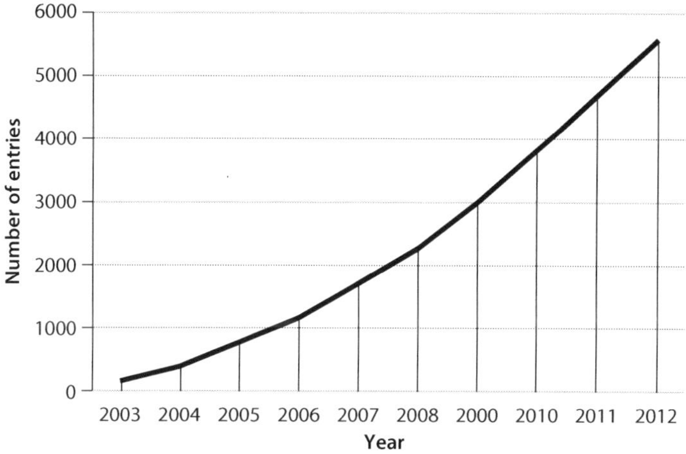

Figure 1. Development of search query hits for the term m-learning

and wherever they want: Learning does not have to take place in university courses, but it can also happen on a bus or subway, during waiting times or in bed before going to sleep.

Due to the fact that mobile learning can piece together individual information on different levels of complexity, one can focus more closely on each student's individual requirements. The whole learning process can be planned, designed and monitored in different ways (Schwertfeger 2012, 46f.).

A further aspect relates to the fact that through capacity of mobile phones knowledge content becomes easily available – only by touching the screen (Goertz 2012, 26). Therefore, it can be distributed more widely in less time, compared to other technology-supported learning arrangements. Communication media, like mobile phones, smartphones, tablet PCs or PDAs, are even used for supporting professional training as an additional channel to extend and deepen learning contents in existing blended-learning arrangements.

However, not every student owns such a device. In order to provide equal treatment to all students, a university has to establish the according technical environment. This results in high costs and administrative efforts. Furthermore, both students and lecturers might not be familiar with this new technology and its special characteristics and, therefore, probably refuse to work with it. Actually, aspects like these point out the limitations of m-learning arrangements.

In conclusion, it can be said that mobile learning does not replace existing learning concepts, but it extends didactical goals with modern technological possibilities. It offers opportunities and challenges for universities, their teachers and students (Cobcroft et al. 2006, 21) and may

> [...] support the social construction of knowledge amongst learners by enhancing their critical, creative, collaborative and communicative engagement within the sites of application of knowledge. (Cobcroft et al. 2006, 7)

Actually, several approaches are used in various contexts, as the following section shows.

Examples

Mobile Learning is used in industry as well as in educational contexts: The German Federal Ministry of Education and Research supports an application named "Flexicare 50+" which informs medical fieldworkers about new medical insights and procedures (Goertz 2012, 24). As an online collaboration, environment "Edmodo" has to be mentioned (Edmodo 2013). It connects lectures and students with each other and offers possibilities to measure the student's progress in learning. Furthermore, mobile learning is frequently used in driving schools to prepare students for the examination (Goertz 2012, 24).

Mobile game-based learning in the university context

Learning games and mobile learning have many advantages in education as summarized in Table 1. However, the two approaches have to be considered together: With the benefits of m-learning and the motivational aspects of learning games, education has the potential to improve teaching and study conditions. Learning can be more individual, pleasurable and more adapted to the technical development. According to Meiers (2012, 7) mobile devices "[...] are particularly suited for the use of learning games as they combine playful movements such as 'wiping', 'shaking' and 'zooming' with a discerning graphics design".

There are already a few research projects like the mobile-Game-Based-Learning project mGBL (2013) which have the aim to improve and change education through the development of innovative learning models. Prensky (2001, 5) also deals with the topic digital game-based learning and describes it as "[...] the coming together of serious learning and interactive entertainment into a newly emerging and highly exciting medium".

With mobile learning games, both generic and subject-related, competences can be developed. For instance, studies have focused on the link between creativity and learning games: The university of Northern Taiwan embedded a mind mapping strategy in several mobile devices for a university course and showed that mobile learning could significantly promote students' creativity (Hwang et

Table 1. Comparison between learning games and m-learning

	Characteristics	Pedagogical potentials
Learning games	Gaming-aspect Non-entertainment purpose	Fun-factor Motivation Flow-experience
M-learning	Learning anytime and anywhere Use of mobile devices	Mobility Availability of learning content Individuality

al. 2012, 242). However, some games are actually better suited to certain competences: To develop creativity for example, Prensky recommends puzzles and invention games. In contrast, to learn languages or to train communication role play games or reflex games might be useful (Prensky 2001, 1).

This can be seen by comparing several learning objectives: To measure, evaluate and develop competences, different levels of learning objectives need to be taken. One way to do this is by using a classification of educational goals like the competence-model of the German EVELIN-project (Abke et al. 2012).

Table 2. Taxonomy of the EVELIN-project

	Remember	Understand	Explain	Use	Apply	Develop
Content 1						
Content 2						
Content n						

It refers to well-known examples, like the taxonomy of Bloom (1956) or Anderson, Krathwohl and Bloom (2001) and has been specially developed for the teaching of Software Engineering, but can also be applied to other areas (Claren and Sedelmaier 2012, 647ff.). As shown in Table 2, the model subdivides different contents into several classes:

- Remember: At the first class of the taxonomy, the learner is able to remember information (Claren and Sedelmaier 2012, 648). To transfer the content of factual and theoretical knowledge several types of games like strategy games with multi-player interaction can be used.
- Understand: The second class is about understanding the meaning and sense of information for itself. It includes the ability to recognize connections and to see differences and similarities of information (Claren and Sedelmaier 2012, 648). This learning objective can be reached, for example, by using learning games with quiz content.

- Explain: Explaining describes the ability of students to provide own definitions about what they have learnt and to explain background-information and the context in their own words (Claren and Sedelmaier 2012, 648). Therefore, a learning game must contain communicative elements and stimulate students to state something in their own words.
- Use: To "use" something means to be able to carry out a certain practical activity either under instructions or according to a given pattern (Claren and Sedelmaier 2012, 649). Learning games can support this by taking up theoretical knowledge and giving tasks to work with in a simulated exercise, like it is the case in certain educational games.
- Apply: The class "apply" includes the ability to select and transform solution methods and to practically apply these to the study content (Claren and Sedelmaier 2012, 649). Hence, learning games should allow independent thinking and should offer a variety of individual solutions, as is the case in certain detective or strategy games.
- Develop: The last class consists of the ambitious learning objective to develop solutions independently (Claren and Sedelmaier 2012, 649). This aim can only be achieved if creativity and independence is permitted. Thus, well-designed games like puzzles and invention games can support the individual learning process.

This taxonomy can support the classification of learning contents for example in a mobile learning application.

Implementing mobile learning games in university education

As shown in the previous chapter, the use of m-learning as an innovative learning concept has high potential. Beside the pedagogical efforts, there is the technological view. In general, the special characteristics of mobile devices have to be considered. Limitations in media rendering and the user interface of such devices are caused by their concept and will continue to exist for the next years (Maske 2012, 138). In the past, mobile devices had less hardware power than a computer. This has changed in the last few years and is no longer a barrier.

Additionally, the complexity of developing a mobile application has decreased, so that mobile devices provide an appropriate development environment in information technology. In combination with modern programming languages, different disciplines can be connected to each other in one single application. This offers the opportunity to integrate up-to-date findings from disciplines like the didactic information technology faster than ever before. But still, an elaborated m-learning concept is needed. This section focuses first the thematic classification of such a concept in a technical way, giving an overview of the required, major steps to obtain the completed m-learning application. Furthermore, it depicts a mobile learning sample application, its potential scenarios of usage as well as the learning contents delivered by such an application. Finally, it clarifies the challenges that come along with using an m-learning application in a university context.

From vision to completion – An overview

First, there is the need for an initial concept. It should contain the vision, the aims which should be achieved by the application and, ideally, some first ideas what a future graphical user interface could look like. Based on this, it is recommended to develop the application using a top-down approach. This means that the initial concept has been improved and enhanced by a deeper view, mostly structured with time boxes, so-called iterations. Iterations are integrated in a development process, which is structured in phases. Those, however, have at least one activity and can be fulfilled with one or more iterations. Depending on the decision which process is used to develop the application, there is a definite input for each activity as well as a definite output. Starting with the initial concept as the first input for the first activity, it is necessary to set the frame of the application. The following main questions should be answered before continuing with any further steps:

- What is the scope of the application?
- Who are the stakeholders and how are they managed?
- What are the possible risks and what measures will be taken if they occur?
- Which activities are assigned to what phase in the developing process and what techniques are used to implement them?

Once answered, the questions above build the framework of the application in order to reach the next step: define the functionality of the application and how the underlying concept can be technically implemented. Functional requirements determine what the application will be able to perform and non-functional requirements define the characteristics and constraints (Rupp 2009, 32ff.; Robertson and Robertson 1999, 10ff.). For formulating both types of requirements literature recommends using several template structures as described in Rupp (2009, 161ff.) or Withall (2007, 51ff.).

In the context of mobile development, special attention should be given to the usability of the application. The look and feel, as one example aspect of the usability, plays an important role concerning the satisfaction of future users of the application. Due to this fact, it is necessary to actively integrate future users as early as possible in the development process. Their feedback to first drafts of graphical user interfaces, which are ideally designed together with them with techniques like storyboards, is valuable for the user-acceptance of the product. Another important factor could be the fast construction of a prototype with which they can test some interactions and get familiar with the handling of the application. Feedback also plays an important role, as it goes hand in hand with change requests for improving the present application.

The design part could also be divided into activities in which attempts are made to illustrate – often by using the Unified Modeling Language (UML) – the logical and physical dependencies and relations between functional units. Based on this, the application will be technically implemented and then tested until adequate code coverage and quality has been reached. Before it becomes available to the public, maintenance procedures (e.g. update distance, support) have to be finally developed.

M-learning application example

Having a theoretical view on the process of developing an application, this section shows what a concrete m-learning application concept could look like, followed by scenarios which seem practicable to integrate such an application in university education.

Students of several disciplines are sometimes confronted with topics which they are not interested in. This challenge is sometimes hard to handle for both, students and teachers. As shown before, having fun-experiences with learning subjects could be an appropriate solution to counteract this circumstance. But, this requires rethinking about existing learning arrangements. Prensky (2001, 4) even describes this overhaul as having a revolutionary character:

> The true 21st century learning revolution is that learning – training and schooling – is finally throwing off the shackles of pain and suffering which have accompanied it for so long.

Actually, m-learning-applications can vary in shape, form, content and background. There is no ultimate product strategy. The aim of developing such an application should rather meet students' needs as completely as possible, along with considering the pedagogical aims which should be achieved by it. Firstly, the aspects which are required for the success of the product have to be defined. Therefore, we present an m-learning concept with its main aspects as follows:

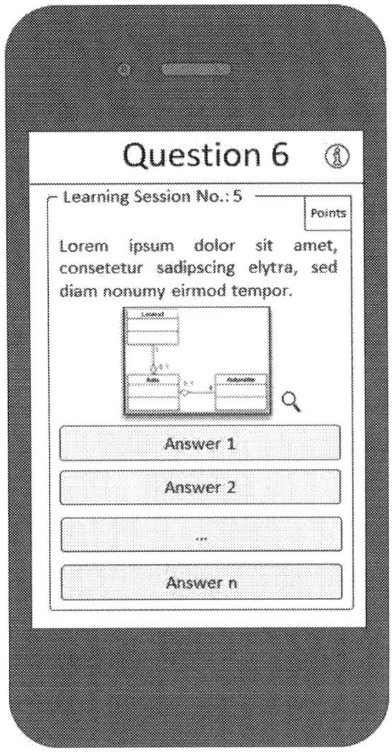

Figure 2. Example of a question

The context of the application and its focus should be defined and limited. As previously shown, a multitude of mobile learning games exists. However, there are a few types of games which provide additional benefit when using them in specific learning scenarios. One of them is the quiz game. In our context we define this type as a mobile application which can be played by at least two students simultaneously, each one of them on a mobile device. The participants have to answer questions with one or more possible answers.

Single choice and multiple choice answers are included and can be exchanged for every participant when answering (see Figure 2). Questions and related answers are consolidated into logical units, so-called learning session. Each session has at least one question connected to it. A learning session contains a special learning objective and the sequence of questions in a session follows a definite order. The lecturer specifies the order before the learning session is published to the students and rates a question according to its difficulty on a numeric scale. This can be used to generate statistics for each student. The individual scores of the students are compared on a leaderboard. At first glance, numeric values which are considered as experience points can be underestimated. However, according to Zichermann and Cunningham (2011, 39) they are very powerful because they "[...] never max out. A player continues to earn them as long as he or she plays the game." The results by using the global leaderboard to compare the competitors are a positive reputation. Students competing with each other could increase their engagement through social recognition (Zichermann and Cunningham 2011, 51). But still, this effect will only work if a player has some characteristics as Zichermann and Cunningham (2011, 51) describe: "For example, a player with a deep interest in leaderboard positioning is likely to be a more competitive player and can be guided accordingly". However, leaderboards can result in the opposite. Weaker students could lose interest when competitive participants extend their lead. For this reason the game mechanism should only be used if the lecturer is certain that it would be beneficial (evidence can be obtained by observing, surveying and sampling social interactions among students).

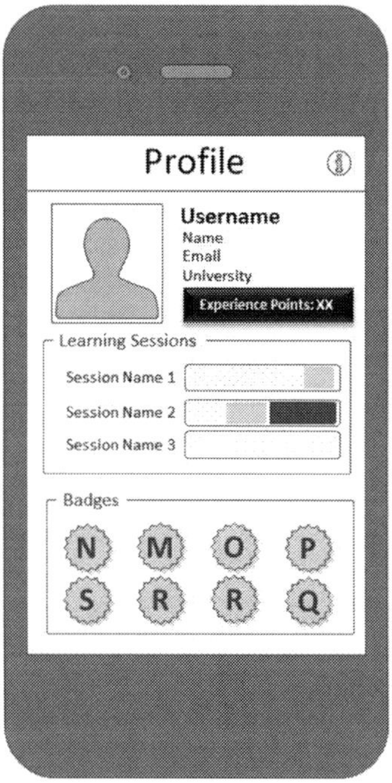

Figure 3. Profile of a user

All students have their own profiles (see Figure 3), consisting of a list of learning sessions he or she participated in, the related progress state of each session, the individual experience points earned by participating in learning sessions and an overview of gained badges. The progress state of each learning session is visualized by a progress bar. It shows the proportion between correct, wrong and unanswered questions in a learning session and provides visual feedback in colors according to the three states a question could have: correct (white), wrong (grey), not edited yet (black). Badges are another game mechanism to provide fun to "gamify" a quiz application. According to Kapp (2012, 33) "[...] it is fun to obtain a high score [...]" but "[...] it is just as fun to let others know you are the one who received the high score [...]". Badges will not only be awarded to students for reaching high scores because that would be overly success-oriented and the same difficulties could occur as in global leaderboards. Students should also be able to collect badges for tasks not directly linked to learning, like submitting assignments on time.

A previous study by Aljohani, Loke and Ng (2010) showed that a mobile quiz game has an additional benefit in learning and teaching when using it in a collaborative scenario. They state that the social-communicational aspect between students has a great influence on the understanding of a topic. Furthermore, this aspect should also be integrated in the application. Its integration seems to require more efforts than the game mechanics mentioned so far because the field of impact is being extended. As shown in this chapter, the game mechanisms and the quiz game itself as functional requirements are combined into an application. But, off-screen interaction, as a part of non-functional requirements which lead to a measurable outcome, is more difficult to implement. Therefore, another view of the entire application is necessary. It is a view which answers the questions how the application can be applied in a learning scenario and what pedagogical aims should be achieved?

Scenarios of usage

In fact, there are numerous ways to integrate mobile learning games into university courses. In our context there are two learning scenarios: the usage in class during lecture and outside university. Both can be regarded as a blended learning scenario: Blended learning is understood to mean a combination of face-to-face courses and electronic learning programs. A prerequisite for the use of the m-learning application during lecture is that every student has an own device. Otherwise it would not make sense because working together in groups with one device would adulterate the users' profile which is temporary in use. Learning sessions can be placed, for example, at the beginning of a lecture to repeat learning content taught before. They can also be used for deepen the understanding of abstract learning content during a lecture by illustrating it with media which can be part of questions. The advantages of this scenario are that the lecturer can receive instant feedback on the questions answered by them and, in addition, social-collaboration can be supported. If students are unsure about the answer to a question, they can discuss possible solutions with other students, in order to find the correct answer e.g. for exam preparation. In that way more than subject-related competences are promoted: implicitly generic competences like communication skills, problem-solving skills and conflict skills can be promoted, too. These assumptions are confirmed by the findings of Aljohani, Loke and Ng (2010). Additionally Prensky (2001, 5) pointed out that

> [p]erhaps the most important difference is that the 'stuff' to be learned – information, concepts, relationships, etc. – cannot be just 'told' to these people. It must be learned by them, through questions, discovery, construction, interaction, and, above all, fun.

This way of combining mobile technology in a playful or even competitive scenario with social-collaboration, leads to an innovative way of learning which can be differentiated in two phases. The first phase is the bilateral discussion of a topic in order to get to a collective understanding between the conversation partners (Scardamalia 2002, 67ff.). Sometimes the outcome of that conversation might differ from other conversation partners who discussed the same issue. At this point phase two comes in. It is about building a pool of collective understanding by getting it articulated by each group of conversation partners. These different understandings are discussed in public now, to extend the collective understanding from a small group to a public community-based understanding of the issue, ideally by resolving conflicting points of view (Scardamalia 2002, 67ff.). After these collaborative interactions with a learning issue, learners are able to create better solutions to a problem due to their deeper understanding about the subject (Mercer 2008, 90ff.).

The other scenario mentioned before is to integrate the usage of the application outside university. A typical use case would be to combine the lectures with follow-up test questions which shall be answered as an assignment (Meiers 2012, 6). In this scenario all the advantages of learning games and mobile devices can be combined. This scenario would extend the in-lecture-scenario by the independence of time and place. Learning sessions on a specific learning topic can be edited wherever and whenever students want to. Fischer and Smolnik (2012, 239) statement that "the traditional, lecturer-centric learning arrangement is often criticized for not including learners effectively as well as activating them". In these scenarios the learners are encouraged to participate actively, either by simply interacting with the mobile device or discussing possible solutions. Nevertheless, both scenarios should be used to achieve a pedagogical aim by using the advantages this learning arrangement has to offer. Therefore, the content in form of questions plays an important part.

Content for learning objectives

Referring to the taxonomy which has been introduced before, learning objectives are taught with learning content (Claren and Sedelmaier 2012, 647ff.). As shown in Table 3, the students simply answer questions by remembering factual and theoretical knowledge.

Table 3. Mobile game-based-learning in the taxonomy of the EVELIN-project

	Remember	Understand	Explain	Use	Apply	Develop
Content	X	X	X			

Their success can be measured by comparing their experience points for the learning sessions they participated in. Furthermore, the second class of taxonomy (understanding) can be reached for a learning objective. When answering a multiple choice question, students have to know the difference between quite similar answers in order to answer the question correctly.

Thus, they need to understand the learning content previously taught. Even the next class of the taxonomy can be achieved. Students explaining correlations between learning topics when answering a multiple choice question have to know how to explain the matter and which direction of discussion is useful for answering the question correctly. With all of these learning classes the issue still remains that every class is connected to the learning content. To explicitly address a class, the questions have to be asked by using a special formulation.

Challenges

Actually there are some structural challenges in m-learning arrangements. Lectures as well as teachers have increased efforts to maintain such products. In addition, learning units have to be created by responsible instructors of a course. Organizational tasks may occur, such as managing the rental of mobile devices in case an institution can provide each student the opportunity to use an m-learning application. Problems like that can be reduced by creating an application which is not bound to one single platform or operating system. Additionally, the effort for creating a learning unit is supposed to decrease with the growing amount of learners participating in a course. Although these problems currently exist, they are supposed to vanish over time and once m-learning plays a more important role in university education.

Summary and outlook

Technology supported learning arrangements have already been in the focus of learning institutions and economy for a long time. Still research in this field has not reached an end yet. We support the thesis of Pivec and Dziabenko (2004, 1) that "[…] novel approach in the area of universities and lifelong learning, gaming is becoming a new form of interactive content, worthy of exploration". As we have shown, the shift from e-learning to m-learning has just started and will probably last for the next few years. M-learning as a 21th century learning approach combined with game elements and used in a collaborative way offers great potential. It can engage students and can support the creation of sustainable knowledge. Especially learning games being "[…] part of children's growing up and formal education […]" (Pivec and Dziabenko 2004, 1) have proven their value in pedagogical practice.

However, m-learning with mobile devices also causes some problems. Existing e-learning content cannot be just transferred to m-learning scenarios. It has to be adapted to the restrictions mobile devices have. Formalizing this transfer in a defined process could be a research field which also has relevance to this work. The technical implementation and the method of promoting it in a student environment present further fields of interest. The promotion can be compared to a marketing concept when introducing a new technology in a company. A concept of that type is considered as a critical step in order to gain the curiosity of future users. Furthermore it can be essential to reach their satisfaction with the application. We conclude that m-learning has to be regarded as a serious way of technology supported learning with high potential, even though it has not yet arrived at every institution of education.

Acknowledgment

This work is supported by the Federal Ministry of Education and Research, project number 0PL12022C.

References

Abke, Jörg, Philipp Brune, Wolfram Haupt, Dieter Landes, Volkhard Pfeiffer, Yvonne Sedelmaier, Georg Hagel, Jürgen Mottok, Michael Niemetz, Irmgard Schroll-Decker, and Reimer Studt. 2012. "EVELIN. Ein Forschungsprojekt Zur Systematischen Verbesserung Des Lernens Von Software Engineering" In *Embedded Software Engineering Kongress*, Sindelfingen, 653–658.

Alfano, Lauren, Megan Horowitch, and Natalie Kitchen. 2010. *Cell Phone Use and Concentration During Class.* Whittemore School of Business and Economics. University of New Hampshire. http://www.unh.edu/news/docs/2010CellphoneUsageStudy.pdf. visited on 25-03-2013.

Aljohani, Naif, Seng Loke, and Wan Ng. 2010. "A Mobile-Based Group Quiz System to Promote Collaborative Learning and Facilitate Instant Feedback". In *9th International Conference on Mobile Learning*, Valletta, 1–5. http://eprints.soton.ac.uk/272088/1/Naif_F_-Short_Paper_F.pdf. visited on 11.12.2013.

Anderson, Lorin W., David R. Krathwohl, and Benjamin S. Bloom. 2001. *A Taxonomy for Learning, Teaching and Assessing: A Revision of Bloom's Taxonomy of Educational Objectives.* New York: Longman.

Bloom, Benjamin. 1956. *Taxonomy of Educational Objectives Book 1: Cognitive Domain.* New York: Longman.

Claren, Sascha, and Yvonne Sedelmaier. 2012. "Ein Kompetenzrahmenmodell für Software Engineering". In *Embedded Software Engineering Kongress*, Sindelfingen, 647–652.

Cobcroft, Rachel S., Stephen J. Towers, Judith E. Smith, and Axel Bruns. 2006. "Mobile Learning in Review: Opportunities and Challenges for Learners, Teachers, and Institutions". *Proceedings Online Learning and Teaching Conference (OLT)*, Queensland University of Technology, Brisbane.

Csikszentmihalyi, Mihaly. 1990. *Flow: The Psychology of Optimal Experience.* New York: Harper & Row.

Csikszentmihalyi, Mihaly. 1997. *Finding Flow: The Psychology of Engagement with Everyday Life.* New York: Basic Books.

Edmodo. 2013. *Edmodo. Where Learning Happens.* http://www.edmodo.com/. Visited on 03.04.2013.

Esposito, Nicolas. 2005. "A Short and Simple Definition of What a Videogame Is: Printversion". In *Changing Views – Worlds in Play*, ed. by Digital Games Research Association, 1–6. http://www.utc.fr/~nesposit/publications/esposito2005definition.pdf. Visited on 09.02.2013.

Figas, Paula, Georg Hagel, and Alexander Bartel. 2013. "The Furtherance of Motivation in the Context of Teaching Software Engineering". In *Proceedings Global Engineering Education Conference. Institute of Electrical and Electronics Engineers*, IEEE, Berlin, 1299–1304.

Fischer, Nikolaus, and Stefan Smolnik. 2012. "Das Potential Von Tablets in Der Universitären Lehre". In *Proceedings e-Learning Fachtagung Informatik Der Gesellschaft Für Informatik e.V (DeLFI)*, vol. 207, ed. by Jörg Desel, Jörg M. Haake, and Christian Spannagel, 237–242. Bonn: Gesellschaft für Informatik.

Fromme, Johannes, Benjamin Jörissen, and Alexander Unger. 2008. "Bildungspotenziale Digitaler Spiele Und Spielkulturen: Printversion". *Zeitschrift Für Theorie Und Praxis Der Medienbildung* 15 (16): 1–23.

Goertz, Lutz. 2012. "Lern-Apps Für Tablet-Computer Und Smartphones: Möglichkeiten Und Grenzen Für Die Digitale Weiterbildung im Unternehmen". *Personalführung* 4: 18–24.

Google Inc. AG. 2013. *Google Scholar Database.* http://scholar.google.de/. Visited on 22.03.2013.

Hall, G. Stanley. 1904. *Psychology of Adolesence.* New York: Appleton.

Huizinga, Johan. 1955. *Homo Ludens: A Study of the Play Element in Culture.* Boston: Beacon Press.

Hwang, Gwo-Jen, Chih-Hsiang Wu, Iwen Huang, and Fan-Ray Kuo. 2012. "A Mind Map-Oriented Mobile Learning Approach to Promoting Creative Thinking Ability of Students in a Business Course". In *Proceedings Seventh International Conference on Wireless, Mobile and Ubiquitous Technologies in Education (WMUTE)*, IEEE, Takamatsu, 242–248.

Jong, Morris, Junjie Shang, Fong-Lok Lee, and Jimmy Lee. 2010. *Learning through Computer Gaming*. http://www.cse.cuhk.edu.hk/~jlee/publ/10/constructivistIGI10.pdf. Visited on 22.03.2013.

Kapp, Karl M. 2012. *The Gamification of Learning and Instruction: Game-based Methods and Strategies for Training and Education*. San Francisco: John Wiley & Sons.

Kloos, Carlos D., Carmen Fernández-Panadero, Mª B. Ibáñez, Mario Muñoz, and Abelardo Pardo. 2012. "M-learning will Disrupt Educational Practices". In *Proceedings Global Engineering Education Conference (EDUCON)*. IEEE, Marrakesh, 1–6.

Maske, Philipp. 2012. *Mobile Applikationen 2: Interdisziplinäre Entwicklung Am Beispiel Des Mobile Learning*. Hannover: Gabler.

Meiers, Christina. 2012. "From E-learning to M-learning". *eLearning Papers* 32: 1–10. http://elearningeuropa.info/sites/default/files/asset/From-field_32_3.pdf. Visited on 22.03.2013.

Mercer, Neil. 2008. "Talk and the Development of Reasoning and Understanding". *Human Development* 51 (1): 90–100. DOI: 10.1159/000113158

mGBL. 2013. *Project Description mGBL – Mobile Game-Based Learning*. http://www.mg-bl.com/index.php?id=57\&no_cache=1. Visited on 05.04.2013.

Mottok, Juergen, Irmgard Schroll-Decker, Michael Niemetz, Georg Scharfenberg, and Georg Hagel. 2012. "Internal Conferences as a Constructivism Based Learning Arrangement for Research Master Students in Software Engineering". In *Proceedings International Conference on Frontiers in Education: Computer Science and Computer Engineering (FECS)*, Las Vegas.

Murphy, Curtiss, Dustin Chertoff, Michael Guerrero, and Kerry Moffitt. 2011. *Creating Flow, Motivation and Fun in Learning Games*. http://www.goodgamesbydesign.com/Files/CreatingFlowMotivationFun_MurphyEtAl_2011.pdf. Visited on 02.04.2013.

Pivec, Maja, and Olga Dziabenko. 2004. "Game-Based Learning Framework for Collaborative Learning and Student E-Teamwork". *E-Mentor* 2. http://www.e-mentor.edu.pl/_xml/wydania/4/42.pdf. Visited on 10.02.2013.

Prensky, Marc. 2001. *Types of Learning*. http://www.marcprensky.com/writing/Prensky%20-%20Types%20of%20Learning%20and%20Possible%20Game%20Styles.pdf. Visited on 21.01.2013.

Robertson, Suzanne, and James Robertson. 1999. *Mastering the Requirements Process*. New York: ACM Press.

Rupp, Chris. 2009. *Requirements-Engineering und -Management*. München: Hanser.

Salem, Katie, and Eric Zimmermann. 2004. *Rules of Play: Game Design Fundamentals*. Cambridge: MIT Press.

Sandford, Richard, Mary Ulicsak, Keri Facer, and Tim Rudd. 2006. *Teaching with Games. Using Commercial Off-The-Shelf Computer Games in Formal Education*. Bristol: Futurelab.

Scardamalia, Marlene. 2002. "Collective Cognitive Responsibility for the Advancement of Knowledge". *Liberal Education in a Knowledge Society* 67–98.

Schwertfeger, Bärbel. 2012. "Mobile Learning: Wie Sinnvoll Sind Lern-Snacks? Ashridge-Studie." *Wirtschaft + Weiterbildung* 6: 46–48.

Tarja, Susi, Mikael Johannesson, and Per Backlund. 2007. *Serious Games: An Overview*. Skövde.

Vosloo, Steven. 2012. *Mobile Learning and Policies. Key Issues to Consider*. Paris: UNESCO.

Wechselberger, Ulrich. 2008. "Einige Theoretische Überlegungen Über Das Pädagogische Potential Digitaler Lernspiele: Autorenversion". In *Wie Wir Spielen, Was Wir Werden*, ed. by Tobias Bevc, and Holger Zapf, 1–24. Konstanz: UVK.

Wechselberger, Ulrich. 2009. "Lernspiele Aus Pädagogischer Sicht". In *Geteilter Bildschirm – Getrennte Welten? Konzepte Für Pädagogik Und Bildung*, ed. by Berward Hofmann, and Hans-Joachim Ulbrich, 145–152. München: Kopaed.

Whitton, Nicola. 2007. "Motivation and Computer Game Based Learning". In *Providing Choices for Learners and Learning*, 1063–1067. ICT.

Whitton, Nicola, and Alex Moseley. 2012. *Using Games to Enhance Learning and Teaching: A Beginner's Guide*. New York: Routledge.

Winters, Niall. 2006. "What is Mobile Learning?" In *Big Issues in Mobile Learning*, ed. by Mike Sharples, 5–9. University of Nottingham.

Withall, Steven. 2007. *Software Requirement Patterns*. Washington: Microsoft Press.

Zichermann, Gabe, and Christopher Cunningham. 2011. *Gamification by Design: Implementing Game Mechanics in Web and Mobile Apps*. Sebastopol: O'Reilly Media.

Zimmermann, Eric. 2010. *Narrative, Interactivity, Play, and Games: Four Naughty Concepts in Need of Discipline*. http://www.ericzimmerman.com/texts/Four_Concepts.html. Visited on 01.05.2013.

Authors' addresses

Alexander Bartel, B.Sc. M.Eng.
Research Fellow, PhD Candidate
Project EVELIN
Kempten University of Applied Sciences, Germany
Bahnhofstraße 61, D-87435 Kempten
Phone: +49 (0)831 2523-236
alexander.bartel@fh-kempten.de

Paula Figas, B.A.
Research Fellow, PhD Candidate
Project EVELIN
Kempten University of Applied Sciences, Germany
Bahnhofstraße 61, D-87435 Kempten
Phone: +49 (0)831 2523-9251
paula.figas@fh-kempten.de

Prof. Dr. Georg Hagel
Software Architecture, Design Patterns and Requirements Engineering
Project EVELIN
Kempten University of Applied Sciences, Germany
Bahnhofstraße 61, D-87435 Kempten
Phone: +49 (0) 831 2523-471
georg.hagel@fh-kempten.de

Dialogic knowledge building

The making of a narrative inquiry teacher education discourse community

Darlene Ciuffetelli Parker and Debbie Pushor
Brock University / University of Saskatchewan

In this chapter we examine conceptually how we have formed an online narrative inquiry teacher education discourse community over the last year and a half with emphasis on: (1) the beginning process of developing and inviting an online community; (2) the trials and tribulations of building an online community, and; (3) the dialogue process and the obstacles of dialogic interaction online. We focus our attention on building a safe community and use Schwier's (2002) framework and elements of community building for online collaboration and dialogue. In doing so, we draw on our methodological work in narrative inquiry as well as other scholars' work in creating communities (Campbell, Schwier, & Kenny 2005; Connelly 2011; Craig 2011). We further use the 'combined communal interplay' of dialogue (Weigand 2010), and how to begin such a process online, to define the process, dilemmas, and complexities that we work through and conceptualize in this chapter.

1. Introduction

In this chapter we examine conceptually how we have formed an online narrative inquiry teacher education discourse community over the last year and a half with emphasis on: (1) the beginning process of developing and inviting an online community; (2) the trials and tribulations of building an online community, and; (3) the dialogue process and the obstacles of dialogic interaction online. We focus our attention on building a safe community and use Schwier's (2002) framework and elements of community building for online collaboration and dialogue. In doing so, we draw on our methodological work in narrative inquiry as well as other scholars' work in creating communities (Campbell, Schwier, and Kenny 2005; Connelly

2011; Craig 2011). Further, we are cognizant of Edda Weigand's (2008, 2010) scholarship on dialogue and action and, in the Italian phrase *un giocco misto*, the art of dialogue that builds community from what Weigand describes as a mixed game. In this chapter, we interpret *un giocco misto* (Weigand 2010, xii) to mean (and we use and interpret this term too from Ciuffetelli Parker's own Italian heritage/roots) the interplay (giocco/game) of dialogue as misto (combined, tossed, gathered together). In this manner, we use the 'combined communal interplay' of dialogue, and how to begin such a process online, to define the process, dilemmas, and complexities that we work through and conceptualize in this chapter.

In 2011, we published an edited book about teacher education and narrative inquiry with colleagues entitled, Narrative inquiries into curriculum making in teacher education (Kitchen, Ciuffetelli Parker and Pushor). In the foreword, Michael Connelly wrote, "This book could be a start for making a narrative inquiry teacher education discourse community" (p. xiii). The significance of this chapter is to illustrate the step by step process, led by two authors of the book, of forming an online discourse community in order to build dialogic knowledge in the area of narrative inquiry as it is applied to teacher education. The online community to build international dialogic knowledge is significant because: (a) teacher education and teacher education programs globally are facing curriculum and programmatic dilemmas of the 21st century (Ben-Peretz, 2009; Cochran-Smith and Lytle 2009; Cochran-Smith and Zeichner 2005; Grimmett and Chinnery 2009), (b) quantitative, directly evidential investigations, stripped of teacher experience, are taking front and center stage in the field of education and; (c) narrative inquiry, with its excavation of teacher knowledge, is uniquely positioned to address the pressing challenges in teacher education (Craig 2011). As teacher educators cope in an increasingly complex world, in a rapidly shifting diverse society, in an information age of new pressures, and in a climate of accountability, an international narrative inquiry teacher education discourse community facilitated by an online site will help them "attend to this complexity by grounding [their] teacher education practices in experience" (Ciuffetelli Parker, Pushor, and Kitchen 2011, 5). Connelly (2011) writes,

> Living and reliving are altogether unlike telling and retelling, the latter two of which might be thought of as the theoretical, textual, side to a narrative journey. ...[R]eliving comes down to teaching against the narrative grain embedded in ... educational narratives. (p. xi)

It is the living and reliving of our stories of teaching against the narrative grain that have brought us together in a narrative inquiry teacher education discourse community, an educative place to pursue questions and dilemmas which arise in the living and reliving of our practices. How can we do teacher education better? How can narrative theory and practice inform our work?

In the education field, we believe we need now more than ever to attend to how educators are equipped, or not, with strategies that enable knowledge building and reciprocal critical thinking as curriculum makers. How is knowledge building supported in a discourse community that values dialogue? Making an international narrative inquiry teacher education discourse community is our response to concerns not only regarding the state of teaching and teacher education but how we engage relationally with others through discourse. The dialogic nature and collaborative inquiry of participants are critical to this response.

2. Theoretical insights

Three vitally interconnected concepts underpin the methodology of the making of our online discourse community: narrative inquiry, curriculum making, and teacher education.

Clandinin and Connelly (1996, 2000) and Connelly and Clandinin (1988, 2006) foregrounded the importance of experience in education (Dewey 1938) as a means through which teachers develop personal, practical knowledge of children, teaching and learning. Narrative inquiry, as a research methodology for understanding experience as lived and as expressed through stories, is therefore an essential way to inquire into questions of teacher knowledge, as Craig (2011, 22) asserts,

> The prevalent, politically charged conception of knowledge for teaching is that of a codified script detailing what teachers must know and do. In that technical rationalist view, knowledge is a possession dictated, controlled, and tested by others. In stark contrast to this publically understood view stands[...] a narrative understanding of teacher knowledge based on meaning constructed over time.

In this same technical rationalist view, curriculum is often understood and taken up as a mandated course of study to be taught and learned. In contrast, we take up Connelly and Clandinin's (1988) notion of curriculum as "one's life course of action" (1). Believing that curriculum is made alongside students, curriculum, in this perspective, is made through the intertwining of the teacher educator's life course of action with their teacher candidates' life courses of action. Teacher education curriculum can thus be understood as a *curriculum of lives*, curriculum that is centered in the experiences of several individuals living in relation (Huber and Clandinin 2005; Downey and Clandinin 2010) who are affirming, co-constructing and expanding their teacher knowledge through carefully planned and scaffolded experiences.

Darling Hammond (2006) suggests that powerful teacher education programs are those that help teacher candidates confront deeply seated beliefs about the world in order to learn about the experiences of different people in our diverse 21st century world. The teacher education methods suggested to address these critical components are methods of self reflection, autobiographical writing, and writing that interrogates the personal, practical, and professional experiences of teacher candidates. Such methods "invite curriculum making that arises out of the lives of our teacher candidates as they intertwine with our lives as teacher educators" (Ciuffetelli Parker, Pushor, and Kitchen 2011, 13). A narrative approach to teacher education is consistent with goal-oriented practices in teacher education (Darling-Hammond and Bransford 2005; Darling-Hammond 2006) that adapts the personal practical of life and storied experience (i.e. a narrative approach) where a focus on *adaptive expertise* is not merely imparted but is lived out alongside teacher candidates and nurtured by teacher educators. We are strongly committed to discussions of the improvement of teacher education internationally via narrative inquiry. Dialogue is critically important to this community. Dialogue, as Bohm, Factor, and Garrett (1991) suggest, is an opportunity for a group of people to participate in process and listening must become a key factor in the process of dialogue. Dialogue, in its true form, allows for thought, reflection, deeper meaning and communication, where there is no hierarchy at play, and no place for control of a particular right solution. We believe and take into account that, "the underlying success [is] that the dialogue of all members of the group [is] respected (Ciuffetelli Parker 2008, IEJLL.mht). In this sense, we desire to build an authentic knowledge community that is a "safe storytelling place where educators narrate the rawness of their experiences, negotiate meaning, and authorize their own and others' interpretations of situations" (Craig and Olson 2002, 116). We follow in Olson's (1995) notion of narrative authority, that through such narration, negotiation, and authorizing "made manifest in relationships with others,…[narrative] authority [arises] from experiences … as each person shapes his or her own knowledge and is shaped by the knowledge of others" (Olson and Craig 2001, 670). In this manner, we wish to establish an authentic dialogic knowledge community.

The following section details the beginning phase of establishing our online narrative inquiry teacher education discourse community and how we were mentored by leading theorists in the field of narrative inquiry as it related to our desire to create a dialogic knowledge community. We want to illustrate our *giocco misto* in action, our 'combined communal interplay' of dialogue online between Debbie and Darlene, and with Cheryl Craig and Michael Connelly as leading scholars, responding to our inquiries in how to develop the online community. We take forward into the next section of the chapter Weigand's (2010) explanation of dialogic action from the Mixed Game (i.e. *giocco misto*). She puts forward a notion of dialogic action that constitutes three types of action: dialogic action (which discusses plans, purposes of an idea, in this case our development of the online discourse community; practical action (which has a concrete purpose, in this case the 'how to' of beginning an online discourse community and inviting members' participation), and; mental action (which is based on Debbie's and Darlene's cognitive actions to decide how to proceed with the online discourse community). Weigand (2010) asserts that, "[p]ractical, mental and dialogic actions are mutually connected" (52). As we narrate the development of our online narrative inquiry teacher education discourse community, we make visible the dialogic, practical, and mental actions that were embedded in our dialogue.

3. The beginning phase

3.1 The origins of the discourse community

In a teacher education symposium at the American Education Research Association (AERA) conference in New Orleans in 2011, arising out of our edited volume *Narrative Inquiries into Curriculum Making in Teacher Education*, we took up a notion proposed by Michael Connelly, by saying:

Darlene: Michael Connelly, in the foreword of our book, suggests that "this book could be a start for making a narrative inquiry education discourse community" and further suggests the entire book as "a centrepiece for a discourse community" (Connelly 2011, xiii). With this in mind, we would like to enact with everyone present today a discourse community where we invite you into our conversation. As we [the book's editors] have been engaged in a narrative inquiry teacher education discourse community throughout the last year and a half with our authors, we have at times lived against the grain to understand fully the storied experiences amongst us all, the landscape from where we came, the stories we live by, our respective identities. We also echoed one another's experiences along the way. We interacted with one another and instead of attempting to answer the 'what to do next' question, we all became a knowledge community (Craig 1995) for discussion, for one another and with our authors. Through this shared experience we came to better understand the context we live, the reverberations of our narratives, the call of our stories, and the many options to explore in curriculum making of teacher education.

Debbie: From [our authors' chapters] we see that curriculum is provisional (Grumet 2009). Our lived experiences, contextualized by relationships with peoples, things, and events and situated in place, shape our

> narrative authority – in Olson's (1995) words, what we know, how we know, how we come to know, why we choose to know in particular ways. [Our writing contributions] call us to attend to what knowledge – and whose knowledge – counts, and why, as we make a curriculum of lives in teacher education. We can rethink curriculum reform in a new way: as curriculum re-formed, curriculum always in the process of being formed and reformed as it is made and remade by particular people in particular relationships and places at particular points of time, an act to "revolutionize their practices" (Connelly and Clandinin 1988, xv) in the context of the particular.

The conversation which ensued was one of excitement amongst our audience members, a call to action from the results of our book launch, the symposium, and the audience participation. One member suggested that we form our discourse community in order to continue with a next phase of our work, a second volume of the book for example. Another audience member proposed notions of an organically made community in which the members, who often feel isolated in their academic institutions as lone narrative inquirers, would have like-minded colleagues with whom to discuss how narrative inquiry is used within teacher education programs. In this manner, ideas were generated and considered. With our simulation of a dialogic knowledge community, and as well the immediate invitation of members to join in, the idea of an online discourse community was born.

3.2 Mentors guiding our development of the discourse community

Following AERA, we met to discuss and consolidate the purposes of the narrative inquiry teacher education discourse community. As we desired mentorship on our beginning steps, we reached out to scholars Michael Connelly and Cheryl Craig, whose seminal works in narrative inquiry have informed our work in the field of teacher education. This intellectual genealogy was important to our work as was the work of theorists (whom we call Master Teachers) such as Schwab, Dewey, McKeon, Plato, Aristotle, and Crites who we also considered critical to the dialogue piece we imagined online. We sought Connelly's and Craig's ideas about how to bring together teacher educator narrative inquirers who puzzle about how to do teacher education better, how discussion about Master Teachers from the genealogy line could add intellectual perspective to the community, and how using exemplars and published writings/prototypes could help inform the discourse online to form a dialogic knowledge community. Michael Connelly had some suggestions as he responded to our ideas:

> I think if you are to capture the attention of a group beyond our authors you may want to have a single why with some emotive punch[…]. One way to think about this is to put yourself in the shoes of someone who is being invited to join a discourse community and then think back to some of your lonely fearful moments as you set out on the teaching journey and imagine what you might find attractive. Your first bullet ['how do we make teacher education better'] might be all your need here to get things started. (Email Correspondence, June 15, 2011)

Michael suggested that perhaps the members, rather than us, begin asking the what, why, and how of a discourse community in order to gain commitment. By "not over thinking it to begin with," Michael suggested that this would make room for all members of the community to have a voice in shaping the community" (Michael Connelly, Email Correspondence June 15, 2011).

Cheryl's suggestions were also rich and wise:

> I do think an effort to create a discourse community would be time well spent. The idea reminds me of my own work (Craig 1995) and the idea that these knowledge communities can be both found and made. To my way of thinking, you would, on the surface, be making a community, but I suspect there are many unacknowledged communities beneath the surface to be found[…] For me, discourse or knowledge communities bridge personal and professional knowledge for individuals as well as work as avenues of knowledge exchange among teachers/teacher educators. I would be inclined to start quite small but provide opportunities for your initial participants to bring others in their realm of interactions on board. I think it would be enormously interesting to follow how the spread of community as well as knowledge and practices within it happen.
> (Email Correspondence, Cheryl Craig, July 22, 2011)

But Cheryl cautioned us too:

> My final comment would be a caution. It has to do with the seductive idea of professional learning communities that presently has a great deal of currency, particularly in the US. Lastly, I have been writing about how such unblemished theoretical ideas about community have become tainted as they have become realized in practice[…] Others have taken the organic ways that teachers and teacher educators interact and have replicated them through administrative and consultative imperative. So, there is a delicate line you will be walking.
> (Email Correspondence, Cheryl Craig, July 22, 2011)

In line with Cheryl's thinking, we very much intended our narrative inquiry teacher education discourse community to be a knowledge community in the sense that aligns with her organic conceptualization rather than a professional learning community directed by imperatives we imposed on the community. It was important to us to stay true and genuine to a safe community of trust and care. To this end, we take note of Weigand's (2008, 17) explanation of the Mixed Game theory:

> What becomes evident is the fact that human beings only in part interact rationally and reasonably; occasionally they are massively influenced by the turmoil of emotions that can even gain the upper hand.

We acknowledged, just as Cheryl noted, that individuals will bring their personal and practical knowledge to our discussions; they also will bring their passions, emotions, and their hopes and dreams for themselves as teacher educators and for teacher education more broadly. We affirmed that it is such a discourse community that we desire, one in which members will tell their stories, their stories of success and of vulnerability, and they will feel comfortable to be their authentic selves in this dialogic space.

Encouraged by Michael and Cheryl's support and guidance, we moved forward in our conceptualization of an online discourse community that would be inquiry-based (Craig 2009). We invited ten members[1] to take part in our narrative inquiry teacher education discourse community. We invited these particular teacher educators because they are individuals with whom we have personal and professional relationships and we wanted to begin from a place of some familiarity and trust. We also invited these individuals because they work narratively and in relationship with teacher candidates and colleagues, they inquire narratively into their own practice as teacher educators, and they are teaching against the narrative grain, working to incite an intellectual transformation. In inviting these ten colleagues to join us in the discourse community, we held close Michael Connelly's (2011) words written in the foreword of our book:

> It often comes down to teaching against the narrative grain embedded in student teachers' educational narratives, and it often comes down to going against the narrative grain of one's university landscape of teacher education. (p. xii)

As we envisioned establishing a community of scholars in which we could engage in difficult and complex dialogue, such as would be necessary to take up Connelly's call, we felt it would be important to complement our online dialogue with face to face meetings in real time when opportunities prevailed. We imagined that the impact of our work within the discourse community could result in developments such as but not limited to: the creation of teacher education courses; invitations to be visiting scholars within each other's organizations; new

1. Invited members of the discourse community remain anonymous for the purposes of this chapter manuscript and as per ethical review processes during the timeline of the written manuscript.

research ideas in narrative inquiry; and the shaping of sections for a new book. So, with the invitations extended, and with a sense of purpose combined with a desire to have the community shaped by those individuals who decided to join, we proceeded into an action phase.

4. The action phase

4.1 Developing the site

With Darlene as the principal investigator for the project, we sought financial and technical support through her university to establish a website for our online discourse community. Despite the research assistance that we secured, an extensive amount of time passed in the process of the development, design, and creation of the website. In the interim, we wrote to our members who had responded to our invitation with excitement and agreement to be a part of the online discourse community:

> We have had phenomenal response from everyone regarding the development of an online narrative inquiry teacher education discourse community. Virtually everyone [all ten] responded with excitement and energetic interest to be a part of this narrative community. We would like to begin a simple, user-friendly discourse online very soon, and then develop our community as we go along with interested new members, ideas, insights, and knowledge sharing for our work as teacher educators and narrative inquirers. We are exploring various forms of easy online sites in order to better organize our response trails and conversations that are composed online. We envision a conversation that flows easily, that may be generated in small groups, creating narrative threads that pertain to members' interests in their narrative work alongside students[...] As we shape our narrative discourse from conversation online, we also envision an opportune time and space that we can gather physically together[...] Our discourse question remains the same and we would like to begin our community discussion by asking everyone: how can we make teacher education better?
>
> (Email to Members, January 30, 2012)

Our website was designed with links/taglines that speak to our intention for dialogue: *Home, Community of Scholars, Topic of Conversation, Read This, Sharing our Photos, and Sharing our Videos*. There are visuals/photographs that feature prominently on all pages that reflect conferences the invited scholars have been to together, featured articles by members, or videos of presentations by members. Once the site was completed, we wrote another email to our members entitled, First Topic of Conversation:

> We are so very excited to finally report that our online narrative inquiry discourse community site is ready to launch! Here are a few easy steps [for online access]: (a) navigate each link to become familiar with the site. It should take no longer than five minutes; (b) please provide your response to the topic discussion question in this link, *Topic of Conversation*. We desire a short response by all members. Deb and Darlene will assimilate the information as we move forward for future work together and as our online community broadens; (c) please write a bio of yourself and any other pertinent information in the *Community Scholars* link; (d) please post any photos in the *Sharing our Photos* link[…]; (e) please post any videos that you think would pertain to your work in the *Sharing our Videos* link. This link will become more active we imagine as there arises person to person meeting places of our teacher education work, via conferences, special meetings, or retreat forums we plan in the future; (f) please post any links or references to publications that you have written or from others that you think are valuable to this site in the *Read This* link. (Email to Members, February 15, 2013)

With the site finally launched, and our instructions to members communicated, we were excited to engage meaningfully in dialogic knowledge building. But then came silence.

4.2 Silence: Response was minimal

Although we had immediate interest and acceptance by all ten members to join in our online site, there was a lack of response by members to post comments or responses on our over-arching theme/topic of conversation – the very reason the site was established in the first place. Members indeed had taken the opportunity to log on and register on the new private site, almost all posting photos and short biographies. Most members, however, did not respond to the dialogue thread/topic we titled, "How do we make teacher education better?"

Together we puzzled over what was happening and why. Had we been negligent to attend to members' narrative authority (Olson 1995)? Did we listen carefully enough to Connelly's suggestion to have our members, rather than us, ask the questions first (about the discourse community) in order to gain commitment? As a result of this puzzling, we turned to literature on dialogue, and specifically on online dialogue learning communities. We were awakened to a number of complexities in relation to the establishment of an online discourse and what must precede the opportunity to engage in deep discourse, or any discourse for that matter. We were drawn in particular to Schwier's (2002) work on shaping community in online learning environments. Schwier reasoned that, by intentionally creating a community, there is possibility for richer and deeper dialogue than would occur in other formal settings, such as conferences. Important to the development of successful communities, he described the formative stage of development of online communities as malleable, with participants likely hesitant at first to join in with other community members. His finding was, indeed, indicative of the silence we experienced in the early stage of formation of our own online discourse community. Schwier suggested that time is needed to build community in order for members to feel comfortable with the purpose of the online community: "A mature stage of life in the virtual community is ultimately achieved once the purpose, shape, and operation of the community are settled" (2002, 5).

We were reminded of Michael Connelly's advice to us above, to have our own members puzzle themselves, alongside us, about the purpose of the community,

> One way to think about this is to put yourself in the shoes of someone who is being invited to join a discourse community and then think back to some of your lonely fearful moments [...] and imagine what you might find attractive.

Michael's advice was wise indeed, and perhaps we were not as attuned to how to build community through the communicative partnership of all members, as we had originally thought. As Schwier reasoned, "Communication is the brick and mortar of virtual communities, and communities only exist as long as communication is available to participants" (Schwier 2002, 3). We realized we had to slow down and build a sense of community among the members of our online community before we could begin to engage in deep discourse about teacher education. We also reminded ourselves, as Michael suggested earlier, that even before the rich dialogic knowledge building, our members needed the opportunity to ask the what, why and how questions too.

5. The deliberation phase: Getting the ball rolling again

In order to make sense of this dilemma of silence, we turned to what we knew best: narrative inquiry and its premise of relational knowing. What we had lost in the interim of the year gone by while we designed the site was the original continuity of the group.

Taking advantage of the AERA annual meeting that was forthcoming in San Francisco, USA, in May 2013, and at which many of our members were presenting papers, we decided to invite an in person meeting of our discourse community. We made plans to review our intentions face to face, have a conversation with the discourse community members in which we could respond relationally to their questions (i.e., the what, whys, and hows) and, most important, begin to develop the trust needed amongst members to move forward asynchronously as the online forum developed.

What we discovered when we met was that members of our discourse community were not as attuned to the purposes of the discourse community as we thought. Our conversation with members at AERA caused us to go back to our initial purposes and ask the question, "Now what?" Together, as a wider community, we agreed that the purpose of the online community was three-fold: to build community; to advance narrative inquiry in the field of teacher education, and; to advance scholarship in the group. We needed to juxtapose this newer vision with the original inception – to have a safe place for novice and veteran teacher educators to come together to dialogue about tensions in teacher education in a narratively-oriented manner. We needed to create a sense of the "tangible and intangible assets that [may be] accrued" (Schwier 2002, 5), the social capital, for each member individually and for our community collectively through our engagement in the narrative inquiry teacher education discourse community. Like Schwier said, we "need trust to invest or receive social capital" (2002, 5). Trust is vital, and we knew we needed to build trust within our membership in order to move to a place of dialogue, to a place where members could invest social capital in this undertaking and receive social capital in return from their engagement.

To re-vitalize the group and to contribute to building relationships between and among our online community members, Debbie suggested that we both post our narrative beginnings on our site, and invite others to do the same. Knowing one another's scholarship, we realized, does not equate necessarily to knowing one another. We felt a need to share the personal as well as the professional (see Appendix A for Debbie's and Darlene's postings).

After we posted the entries on our online discourse community site, we then emailed our members this message to make visible our intentionality in regard to the online community and to invite their engagement, reading in part:

> There's a list of things/happenings we want to share. While at AERA, we (Deb and Darlene) met with discourse community members who were in San Francisco for the conference. Here is a summary of some important items we discussed:
>
> - We reviewed the purpose of our community and we discussed three areas: to begin creating (small scale first) an international narrative inquiry online community; to advance our scholarship as a community; to nurture narrative inquiry in the field of teacher education.
> - We discussed our community as being a safe place for narrative inquirers (beginning educators as well as veteran educators).
> - Ethical issues were brought up (i.e. how much do we share, how can it be trusted, who's it for[…]) and this discussion led to the larger umbrella ethical issues of narrative inquiry research in general[…] a good topic we think to take up online itself.

> - Deb and Darlene wanted to emphasize that at this beginning stage it is very important to create a safe space to interact both in person and online[…] The purpose for meeting in person would be to extend online interaction and the three pillars of: scholarship; advancing NI in the field; creating community (online and in person).
> - To begin creating the safe space, Darlene and Deb suggested that they would post online a short professional/personal narrative beginnings. These could be shared as an invitation for everyone to post their own and a way to feel safe doing so.
> - It was suggested that directions for how to post items (including regular posts, pictures, articles, a video, etc.) would help all community members. Darlene is on that task [with our research assistant].
> - It was also suggested that if everyone has pictures (i.e. from a conference or other photos in general, i.e. we took a few in our meeting, they turned out great and will be posted soon!) they could also be posted as well as one of your favourite pieces of writing that you have authored/co-authored that speaks to your NI scholarship at this time/interests.
>
> We wish to remind everyone why we're doing what we're doing in forming this online community. Deb and Darlene are reminded of Mick's and Cheryl's original reflections on what the discourse community can provide: (1) a way for easing as well as unravelling the tensions that first time as well as veteran teacher educators feel in the academy with the NI work they do with their students and that many of us as narrative inquirers are alone in our academic spaces and need to face these kinds of issues alongside other narrative inquirers in a safe community place. The discourse community would be immensely valuable to first timers and old pros alike, in order to discuss problems, solutions, etc, (2) for the special quality of narrative inquiry oriented teacher education. (3) The notion of the narrative inquiry online discourse community being an innovative pedagogy approach that is inquiry-based. (May 13, 2013)

In inviting all of our members to share their narrative beginnings, we were working to enhance the sociability aspect of our online community. Sociability, according to Daniel, Schwier, and Ross, "nurtures the learning environment in important ways" (2007, 472). Not only is it associated with common hospitality, it is an essential element of community (2007, 472). In Pushor's and Ruitenberg's (2005) research on parent engagement, two key strands that arose as critical to creating a strong and reciprocal connection between parents and educators were "invitation and hospitality" (35) and "trust and relationship" (45). We came to see how significant it was for us to understand our work within our virtual online community in the same way in which we understand our work within the actual face to face communities in which we are members.

While we attempted to begin our online discourse by moving directly to posting and inviting response to our overarching question, "How do we do teacher education better," we learned that our first and most critical work in building the online community needed to be extending repeated invitations to our members, in multiple ways, to encourage their active and collaborative engagement with us (Pushor and Ruitenberg 2005, 38). It is through generating collaborative engagement that we will ultimately create a feeling of trust and relationship within our community. We are just now in this process.

We have invited engagement through our online communications and again in conversation with those who were present in our face to face meeting at AERA. By posting our narrative beginnings on our website and by asking others to do the same, we are extending yet another invitation which we hope will contribute to creating a social environment conducive to dialogue. By consciously working to develop this aspect of sociability among our online community, we hope to "encourage members of the [discourse] community to relate to each other informally, and develop strong social networking, which is an essential ingredient of community sustainability" (Daniel, Schwier, and Ross 2007, 472). First we have to know and trust one another, we realized, before dialogue and the creation of dialogic knowledge will ensue. This effort entails an enactment of moral agency in an online community.

6. Moral agency in our online community

The work we intend to take up in our narrative inquiry teacher education discourse community, responding to the question, "How do we do teacher education better?" is a question laden with intentions and values. Just as Campbell, Schwier, and Kenny noted in speaking of instructional designers, "[T]he [teacher educator] is an agent of social change at the personal, relational, and institutional levels. …[Teacher educators]…act in purposeful, value based ways with ethical knowledge, in social relationships and contexts that have *consequences in and for action*" (2005, 243). We acknowledge that these consequences affect the dialogic, practical, and mental (Weigand 2010) well being of all members and that this is directly tied to teaching, learning, and teacher education. The establishment of our discourse community is purposeful in that we intend for it to lead to action that will influence, shift, or change teacher education as it is currently being lived.

As we push against the narrative grain, we push against dominant discourses in which, as we cited earlier, "the prevalent, politically charged conception of knowledge for teaching is that of a codified script detailing what teachers must know and do" (Craig 2011, 22). Thus, we use narrative inquiry as our methodology for understanding experience as lived and as expressed through stories, and as an essential way to build dialogic knowledge. In our work within our online narrative inquiry teacher education discourse community, then, we are

> acting from ethical knowledge – with moral agency – [drawing on] reflexive knowledge of self in action, an understanding of 'one's biography, present circumstances, deep commitments, affective investments, social context and conflicting discourses. (Britzman 1991, p. 8)' (Campbell, Schwier, and Kenny 2005, 244)

We are taking a moral stance; we are exerting our moral agency.

7. Narrative inquiry and dialogic knowledge building: A pedagogical inquiry approach

We believe our online teacher education discourse community is vitally important to the future of teacher education, internationally. Cheryl Craig has referred to our beginning work of this project as an innovative pedagogical approach that is inquiry based. We hold true to this notion, even in our dialogic knowledge community's infancy stages. The inquiry notion of our community can be likened to Olson's (1995) term narrative authority, where each member's contribution is indeed relational and based on experience. We also are reminded of other narrative inquiry theorists before us who have written about the process of knowledge building based on relationship, such as Conle's (1996) work on narrative resonance. Narrative resonance, much like the interplay of communication, takes into account "dynamic, complex, [and] metaphorical relations" (Conle 1996, 313). The echoing of one person's dialogic rhythm brings forth ideas, insights and knowledge construction which intersect with another member's dialogic rhythm, and so it goes. We hope to discover such resonances as our discourse community continues and as it builds upon each and every member's contribution. In this fashion, and for the purpose of asking the bigger question of "How can we make teacher education better?" we believe that, indeed, our online discourse community is an innovative pedagogical inquiry based approach.

Akin to Conle's term narrative resonance, Weigand (2010) takes up the definition of the dialogic principle based on reciprocal action:

> Dialogue involves taking a position, and needs a reaction by the interlocutor, either carried out in the mind or explicitly expressed. This is precisely what human beings normally do...They inevitably reflect upon and take a position regarding what has been said. Dialogue is therefore constituted by the interactive purpose of *coming to an understanding* which is based on the sequence of action and reaction. (2010, 80)

What we have gained from the insights of both Conle's and Weigrand's work that, although we are still in the process of knowledge building within our new online discourse community, is the importance of staying awake to what it means, how it feels, how it ought not to be, and so on, when there is only a one-sided conversation. We, in the midst of organizing, modeling for our members, inviting conversation online, etc., have understood firsthand what it means to be in a dialogic relationship while building and planning an authentic knowledge community that has the potential to be both found and made, as Craig advised us in our consultation processes. This process, within the process of building, is in itself a pedagogical inquiry piece in our work that we wish to continue to track.

8. Looking to the future

Although it has been two years that we have been envisioning and working to enact an online narrative inquiry teacher education discourse community, in many ways we are still in the early stages of this undertaking. As with any new endeavor, our learning has been significant, arising from our lived experiences, from our mentoring by esteemed narrative inquiry colleagues, and by turning to a body of literature on online learning environments that, until now, was not the literature we drew upon in underpinning our research inquiries. As we move forward as a community (given the busy-ness of our academic lives, and the reality that for most members of our online community this is just one strand in our programs of research), working to maintain continuity of our communication in order to get to a place of deep dialogue will be a critical point of attention for us. There are two approaches to communication that we intend to put in place to establish and preserve a sense of continuity in our dialogue.

The first approach we are establishing is the use of both asynchronous and synchronous forms of communication. Given the limited postings we have to date on our website, in response to our question about how to make teacher education better, postings that have been invited as asynchronous forms of communication, we feel that scheduling regular synchronous conversations may be a valuable means to jumpstart the dialogue. As Schwier and Balbar noted, synchronous communication enhances the sense of community as it enables connections, develops or strengthens relationships, creates energy, and invites the opportunity for passionate expression and interchange (2002, np). When we are members of grant or research teams who connect in actual time, we attend meetings at set times. Perhaps key to the continuity of our communications as an online discourse community is to schedule such regular synchronous engagements for ourselves, using technology such as scheduled videoconferences, teleconferences, Skype conversations, or Collaborate forums as a means of connecting us with one another and capturing our conversation as research text. Early in our planning, Michael Connelly suggested an online conference with a theme:

> It occurs to me that you might try to host something like a three hour conference on a specific teaching theme emerging from the book. The conference might have as its title theme: The Makings of a Narrative Discourse Community, or some such. That way you would be focusing directly on a topic of reasonably wide interest and piggybacking the idea of the formation of the community on the theme. The online conference might have two hours devoted to the theme and an hour in which participants evaluate the conference and discuss future possible ways of community addressing such issues, which you will call a discourse community[…] The reason I think you need a theme or themes to revolve discussion is that the idea of a discourse community might be too abstract for some.
>
> (Email Correspondence, June 15, 2011)

Michael's comments provide one concrete example of what a synchronous interchange may look like. His proposal makes it possible to see how such communication could be a "forum for professional discussion and enriched learning" (Schwier and Balbar2002, np) and how it may invite the exploration of ideas that a member may hesitate to commit to paper in an asynchronous entry. Importantly, such a synchronous exchange has the potential to contribute to the vitality of the community (Schwier and Balbar 2002, np) and to the commitment and connection members feel to one another and to the community.

At the same time, the opportunities to post asynchronously continue to be important. Again, given the busy-ness of everyone's lives, there is a convenience to being able to post at a time that is relevant and personally-determined by the community member. In being provided this time, "participants [are able] to develop coherent, well thought-out arguments, [enabling] more substantive discussion to emerge" (Schwier and Balbar 2002, np) within the community. Members are able to write when they are in the midst of troubling an idea or experience, when they are celebrating a recent happening in their teaching, when they are working with a new conceptualization, as examples. Asynchronous communication leads to the deep discourse and dialogic knowledge we are hoping to promote and to capture in our discourse community.

The second approach we want to establish, through the attainment of research funding, is the opportunity for face to face interchanges in real time to complement the work we are doing virtually in our online discourse community. As researchers situated in teacher education and using narrative inquiry methodology, many of us frequently attend similar research conferences. With funding to support travel, we would have the opportunity to attach a day or two to the conference and to have the personal, professional exchange that some of us recently experienced at AERA in San Francisco. In person, we advance our trust and relationships as well as deepen our dialogue about teacher education.

What we are learning as we move forward with the enactment of our online discourse community is that "it is necessary for [us] to take advantage of, and in some cases invent, a process for engaging ideas, negotiating meaning and learning collectively" (Schwier 2002, 1). What at first we thought was straightforward has turned out to be complex. To address the complexity and to attend to the specificity of our community, and the particularities of the individual members within it, we may need to find or invent our own processes for moving to the place of deep dialogue. Thinking about the kind of honest and vulnerable conversations we hope to have, but also holding close the desire for a community which is formed on trusting and ethical relationships, we move forward, intent on engaging with ideas ruthlessly but engaging with each other gently (Schwier and Balbar 2002, np).

We have learned a bit about the giocco misto, the Mixed Game. While indeed it can be said that the Mixed Game is an art of persuasion, a back and forth dialogue based on action and reaction, we are also attuned to the Italian translation of giocco misto. We have played to the game of persuasion, perhaps, showing our members how we want to begin a sequence of 'action and reaction' in dialogue. We will see where this leads us as we continue with such a process. We found we had to pause and puzzle over the silence from our members, a lull in dialogue as it were. We learned, in that process, how important it is that the back and forth within the dialogue reflects the narrative authority of our members, and that we know one another off line, as well as online in our discourse community. We understand experientially now that it is narrative resonance that will continue the flow of new insights, ideas, and the rhythms of dialogic knowledge. The interplay of conversation – a reflection of ideas combined, tossed out for consideration, or gathered together with coherence and authority – is the hope for our combined communal dialogue. We continue this work with the intention of engaging with and better understanding the processes, dilemmas, and complexities which are all a part of building and sustaining our dialogic knowledge community. We believe that by constructing meaning and building knowledge through an online discourse community we will generate rich contributions to the vital conversation about how we can make teacher education better.

References

Ben-Peretz, Miriam. 2009. *Policy Making in Education: A Holistic Approach Responding to Global Changes*. Lanham, MD: Rowan & Littlefield.

Bohm, David, Donald Factor, and Peter Garrett. 1991. "Dialogue – A Proposal." http://www.davidbohm.net/dialogue/dialogue_proposal.html. (last date of access 28 August 2007).

Britzman, Deborah P. (1991). *Practice Makes Practice: A Critical Study of Learning to Teach*. Albany, NY: SUNY press.

Campbell, Katy, Richard A. Schwier, and Richard Kenny. 2005. "Agency of the Instructional Designer: Moralcoherence and Transformative Social Practice." *Australasian Journal of Educational Technology* 21 (2): 242–262.

Ciuffetelli Parker, Darlene. 2008. "Literacy Leadership and the Administrator: Relationship as Moral Agency from within." *The International Electronic Journal for Leadership and Learning* 12 (9).

Ciuffetelli Parker, Darlene, Julian Kitchen, and Debbie Pushor. 2011. "Narrative Inquiry, Curriculum Making, and Teacher Education." In *Narrative Inquiries into Curriculum Making in Teacher Education*, ed. by Julian Kitchen, Darlene Ciuffetelli Parker, and Debbie Pushor, 3–18. Bingley, UK: Emerald Publishing. DOI: 10.1108/S1479-3687(2011)00000130004

Clandinin, Jean D., and Michael F. Connelly. 1996. "'Teachers' Professional Knowledge Landscapes. Teacher Stories – Stories of Teachers – School Stories – Stories of Schools." *Educational Researcher* 25 (3): 24–30.

Clandinin, Jean D., and Micheal F. Connelly. 2000. *Narrative inquiry: Experience and Story in Qualitative Research*. San Francisco, CA: Jossey-Bass.

Conle, Carole. 1996. "Resonance in Pre-service Teacher Inquiry." *American Educational Research Association Journal* 33 (2): 297–325. DOI: 10.3102/00028312033002297

Connelly, Michael F., and Jean D. Clandinin. 1988. *Teachers as Curriculum Planners: Narratives of Experience*. New York, NY: Teachers College Press.

Connelly, Michael, F., and Jean D. Clandinin. 2006."*Narrative Inquiry.*" *Handbook of Complementary Methods in Educational Research*, ed. by J. Green, G. Camilli, and P. Elmore, 477–489. Washington, DC: American Educational Research Association.

Connelly, F. Michael. 2011. "Foreword." In *Narrative Inquiries into Curriculum Making in Teacher Education*. ed. by Julian Kitchen, Darlene Ciuffetelli Parker, and Debbie Pushor, xi–xvi. Bingley, UK: Emerald Publishing, UK. DOI: 10.1108/S1479-3687(2011)00000130003

Craig, Cheryl. 1995. "Knowledge Communities: A Way of Making Sense of How Beginning Teachers Come to Know." *Curriculum Inquiry* 25 (2): 151–175. DOI: 10.2307/1180185

Craig, Cheryl. 2009. "Research in the Midst of Organized School Reform: Versions of Teacher Communities in Tension." *American Educational Research Journal* 46 (2): 598–619. DOI: 10.3102/0002831208330213

Craig, Cheryl. 2011. "Narrative Inquiry in Teaching and Teacher Education." In *Narrative Inquiries into Curriculum Making in Teacher Education*, ed. by Julian Kitchen, Darlene Ciuffetelli Parker, and Debbie Pushor, 19–42. Bingley, UK: Emerald Publishing. DOI: 10.1108/S1479-3687(2011)00000130005

Craig, Cheryl, and Margaret Olson. 2002. "The Development of Teachers' Narrative Authority in Knowledge Communities: A Narrative Approach to Teacher Learning." In *Narrative Inquiry in Practice: Advancing the Knowledge of Teaching*, ed. by Nona Lyons, and Vicky LaBoskey, 115–129. New York, NY: Teachers College Press.

Cochran-Smith, Marilyn, and Susan L. Lytle. 2009. *Inquiry as Stance. Practitioner Research in the New Era*. New York, NY: Teachers College Press.

Cochran-Smith, Marilyn, and Kenneth Zeichner (eds). 2005. *Studying Teacher Education: The Report of the AERA Panel on Research and Teacher Education*. Upper Saddle River, Mahwah NJ: Lawrence Erlbaum Associates.

Daniel, Ben K., Richard A. Schwier, and Heather M. Ross. 2007. "Synthesis of the Process of Learning through Discourse in a Formal Virtual Learning Community." *Journal of Interactive Learning Research* 18 (4): 61–477.

Darling-Hammond, Linda, and John Bransford (eds). 2005. *Preparing Teachers for a Changing World: What Teachers Should Learn and Be Able to Do*. San Francisco, CA: Jossey Bass.

Darling-Hammond, Linda. 2006. *Powerful Teacher Education: Lessons from Exemplary Programs*. San Francisco, CA: Jossey-Bass.

Dewey, John. (1938). *Experience and Education*. New York, NY: Macmillan Co.

Downey, Charles A., and D. Jean Clandinin. 2010. "Narrative Inquiry as Reflective Practice: Tensions and Possibilities." In *Handbook of Reflection and Reflective Practice: Mapping a Way of Knowing for Professional Reflective Inquiry*, ed. by Nona Lyons, 383–397. XXVII (Chapter 19). New York, NY: Springer. DOI: 10.1007/978-0-387-85744-2_19

Grimmett, Peter, and Ann Chinnery. 2009. "Bridging Policy and Professional Pedagogy in Teaching and Teacher Education: Buffering Learning by Educating Teachers as Curriculum Makers: A Review." *Curriculum Inquiry* 39 (1): 125–143. DOI: 10.1111/j.1467-873X.2008.01441.x

Grumet, Madeleine. 2009. "Commentary: The Politics of Curriculum Creativity." *LEARNing Landscapes* 2 (2): 25–30.

Huber, Janice, and D. Jean Clandinin. 2005. "Living in Tension. Negotiating a Curriculum of Lives on the Professional Knowledge Landscape." In *Learning from Research on Teaching: Perspective, Methodology and Representation*, ed. by J. Brophy, and S. Pinnegar, 313–336. Bingley, UK: Emerald.

Kitchen, Julian, Darlene Ciuffetelli Parker, and Debbie Pushor (eds). 2011. *Narrative Inquiries into Curriculum Making in Teacher Education*. Bingley, UK: Emerald Publishing.

Olson, Margaret. 1995. "Conceptualizing Narrative Authority: Implications for Teacher Education." *Teaching and Teacher Education* 11 (2): 119–135. DOI: 10.1016/0742-051X(94)00022-X

Olson, Margaret, and Cheryl Craig. 2001. "Opportunities and Challenges in the Development of Teachers' Knowledge: The Development of Narrative Authority through Knowledge Communities." *Teaching and Teacher Education* 17 (7): 667–684.
DOI: 10.1016/S0742-051X(01)00023-3

Pushor, Debbie, and Claudia Ruitenberg, with co-researchers from Princess Alexandra Community School. 2005. November. *Parent Engagement and Leadership*. Research report, project #134, Dr. Stirling McDowell Foundation for Research into Teaching, Saskatoon, SK, 79. http://www.mcdowellfoundation.ca/main_mcdowell/projects/research_rep/134_parent_engagement.pdf. (last date of access 18 Sept. 2013).

Schwier, Richard A. 2002. "Shaping the Metaphor of Community in Online Learning Environments." Paper presented to the *International Symposium on Educational Conferencing*. The Banff Centre, Banff: Alberta.

Schwier, Richard A., and Shelly Balbar. 2002. "The Interplay of Content and Community in Synchronous and Asynchronous Communication: Virtual Communication in a Graduate Seminar." *Canadian Journal of Learning and Technology* 28 (2): 21–30.

Weigand, Edda. 2008. *Dialogue and Rhetoric*. Amsterdam: John Benjamins Publishing.
DOI: 10.1075/ds.2

Weigand, Edda. 2010. *Dialogue: The Mixed Game*. Amsterdam: John Benjamins Publishing.
DOI: 10.1075/ds.10

Authors' addresses

Dr. Darlene Ciuffetelli Parker, PhD
Associate Professor
Brock University, Faculty of Education
1842 King St. East, Hamilton, Ontario, Canada L8K 1V7
905 547-3555 3605
darlene.ciuffetelli-parker@brocku.ca

Debbie Pushor, PhD
Curriculum Studies
College of Education, University of Saskatchewan,
28 Campus Dr., Saskatoon, SK. S7N 0X1
(306) 966-7573
Debbie.pushor@usask.ca

Appendix A

Debbie posted:

Hi everyone!

I began my doctoral work at the University of Alberta with Jean Clandinin while I was on a parenting leave from my work as an educator with Edmonton Public Schools. At the time my son Cohen was just beginning his formal schooling and my twin sons, Teague and Quinn, were about two years old. It was my experience of taking Cohen to school, and for the first time experiencing what it felt like to be a parent on a school landscape, that caused me to pursue doctoral research on parent engagement. Although I had worked as a teacher, consultant, principal, and a central services supervisor; and although I had taught in Canada and overseas, I found myself in a position of not knowing school any longer when I entered the school as a parent. This began a very rich research journey for me, which is still underway!

My partner, Laurie, is a senior advisor with our provincial government and spends much of his week traveling between our home in Saskatoon and our province's capital city of Regina, 250 km from Saskatoon. My oldest son Cohen is 22, turning 23 in September, and is an avid cyclist. He hopes to set off on a big bike trip this fall Quinn, one of my 19 year olds, plans to leave midsummer for a trip to the Yukon., He is looking forward to canoeing, hiking, and exploring the beautiful North. Teague, my other 19 year old, just completed his first year of university in an Arts program, taking history, English, Native Studies, and political studies courses. My personal and professional life and passions have been very much intertwined throughout my academic career. Being a mother informs my work and my thinking about teacher education every day. Thank you for being a part of this rich community! I am very much looking forward to getting to know each of you more deeply, both personally and professionally. I know how thoughtfully each one of you engages with your teacher education work and I am excited about all I will learn with you and from you!

Darlene posted:

I began my Master of Education work at the Ontario Institute for Studies in Education / University of Toronto (OISE) under Michael Connelly's supervision while at the same time beginning a career in teaching, and giving birth to my beautiful daughter Maddie. While Maddie grew up, and with my career as an elementary school teacher, literacy consultant, and vice principal, I completed my PhD. All this last bit happened amidst a new marriage and a new baby, Max. Maddie and Max have both seen their share of OISE, tagging alongside me to my meetings with Michael, or during Works in Progress community sharing sessions[...] and I saw so many doctoral students doing the same as me. We wonder how we did it all[...] while we were doing it all!

Maddie is now 18 years old. Max is 11. My husband Craig, a businessman working in the city, appreciates the discipline of scholarship – and happy perhaps that he isn't in it himself! Ha! I guess what's important is that my love for narrative inquiry plays out in my personal as well as professional life. My family sees the value of my work topics of poverty, literacy, and education and the value of storied experience in this world. We 'talk' in stories[...] I'm sure this is not uncommon for many narrative inquiry 'families'!

My parents' humble beginning as immigrants to Canada keeps me grounded, I think, when I'm finding or fading or familiarizing myself with tensions, new thoughts, ideas about my research, my life with family and friends, my world. It's all a process. That's where I'm at now in my work. I'm trying to dig through the origins of historical context of places/milieus of climate, culture in the topics of poverty, literacy, teaching, learning, and schooling. At least for now.

Knowledge negotiation using technology

Potentials of technology and the knowledge negotiation model

Ilker Yengin
A*STAR – Institute of High Performance Computing, Singapore

In everyday social interactions, we negotiate knowledge in order to minimize knowledge differentials between us and other people. Although this takes place in everyday life, it is not widely studied and there are few supporting technologies.

This paper analyzes the process of knowledge negotiation and the current state of supporting technologies. It aims to provide a knowledge negotiation model (K-NeMo) that elucidates the essentials of the process. It also provides practical ideas for possible applications of 21st century technologies for the implementation of K-NeMo.

This paper will be of utility especially to teachers, technology developers, and researchers seeking a model for the essentials of knowledge negotiations.

Introduction

Knowledge exists both 'out there' and in our minds. Is our existing knowledge on a particular thing exactly same as the knowledge of others with regard to the same thing? Why is there a difference or similarity? If we do not think similarly about the same thing, how do we operate with regard to that thing together?

We need to communicate with others in order to tell them how we think about that same thing and, inversely, need to learn how they think about it also. We need to converse with others in order to express our point of view and learn about theirs. Also, we need to find a way to agree upon a common ground by decreasing the difference between different points of view, if there is any. This is why we must communicate in order to negotiate. If these points of view serve knowledge building, then the process of negotiation is actually a process of knowledge negotiation. Knowledge negotiation processes are constantly going on around us in our everyday social environment, e.g., we may need to negotiate regarding our ideas in order to build the knowledge required for a decision. Consider the situation of you and taxi driver communicating in order to decide upon the best route for reaching a destination. The knowledge of the best route was not there initially because the taxi driver did not know your destination until you reveal it. After disclosing the destination, you and the taxi driver should come to be in agreement on what parameters are to be taken into consideration while deciding the best route. Thus, it is required to build knowledge about which parameters affect the best route. If the route is new knowledge for the taxi driver, he may not know the pertinent parameters for the given destination. Then, the taxi driver and yourself need to communicate in order to build that new knowledge by considering how the variables time, distance, traffic, etc. affect the given route. Deciding upon the parameters is a process of negotiation, e.g., you may not know the traffic conditions, but the taxi driver might, and could, thus, propose taking heavy traffic conditions into consideration because it is currently rush hour in the city. Moreover, you might suggest using toll roads since you know that you are willing to pay the extra fees to use them. After deciding what constitutes the best route, the taxi driver may suggest a route that is the best taking the knowledge of the pertinent parameters into consideration, however, his knowledge of the best route may not be same as yours. You may know an alternative way that is better. Subsequently, there follows another process of negotiation regarding the knowledge of the best route until you and the taxi driver come to an agreement. Once an agreement has been reached on the proposed knowledge chunks related to the parameters, the negotiation process ends. During this process of negotiation, however, you and the taxi driver have built knowledge together.

Is there any technology to support this kind of everyday social process of negotiation? The purpose of this chapter is to find some answers to that question. This chapter investigates technologies supporting knowledge negotiation, analyzing the process of knowledge negotiation in order to provide a model for future reference, and ultimately providing a perspective for viewing knowledge negotiation henceforth.

First, this chapter shortly discusses what knowledge negotiation is, the aims of the knowledge negotiation process, and how to teach knowledge negotiation processes. Subsequently, some of the very few currently available technologies designed specifically for knowledge negotiation are introduced.

After putting forward a perspective on knowledge negotiation, this chapter provides a new knowledge negotiation model that describes the essentials of knowledge negotiations. Then, it discusses implementations of 21st century technologies as the possible applications of the knowledge negotiation model put forward here.

This chapter will be of utility especially to teachers who like to teach knowledge negotiations using technology, technology developers, and researchers seeking a model for the essentials of knowledge negotiations.

Knowledge negotiation

In everyday social environments we communicate with each other and build knowledge together. Building knowledge is a social process enabling us to operate together. We need to know and understand our own thought processes and gain insight into other people's ideas in order to be successful in everyday social life.

If we comprehend why other people's and our thought processes veer in a certain direction, we can communicate more easily and resolve differences of points of view more efficiently. Moreover, we can begin negotiating our ideas in a manner so that we can establish probable points of equilibrium in social occasions in which mutual cooperation is required.

Knowing and understanding others and ourselves requires us to know the meaning and reasoning behind the concepts we attempt to communicate to each other. Such an understanding, gives us the flexibility of differentiating between the concepts of others that are the same or different from ours, helping us to extrapolate different points of view.

In the knowledge of these points of view, we can work with and around them allowing common ground to be found, especially in negotiations. If common ground has not yet be found, there should be a way to get there. Knowledge of diverse points of view enables us to determine where we are in relation to one another and where we need to go in order to reach consensus.

Stahl (2006) argues that "collaborative knowledge building, itself, can be viewed as fundamentally a knowledge negotiation process".

Discussing ideas is the first step to initiate knowledge negotiation processes in a group. In group discussions, we usually put forward our personalized knowledge in order to illustrate our perspective. All the personalized and perspective based knowledge that is offered up should be conjoined in order to be processed into a blend of completely new knowledge. This new created knowledge serve as a group's knowledge artifact. The knowledge artifact of the group is created due to a shared process in which the personalized and perspective-based knowledge of each participant is processed several interactions with activities such as critiquing, brainstorming, discussions, and meetings. The group's knowledge artifact is a new and unique piece of knowledge because it is created using the knowledge pieces of all the group members. It comes about due to the collaborative effort of the group and, thus, belongs to it.

During the creation of the group knowledge artifact, the participants are not just exchanging their personal knowledge and/or talking about their perspectives. They also combine and transform these perspectives. In fact, the act of creating the group knowledge artifact requires participants to perform many high-level cognitive activities in order to integrate each group member's ideas into a single representation, thus, carrying shared meaning of the group.

The production of shared meaning in a group knowledge artifact also involves the act of negotiation. Negotiation is a process that enables the activities of combining and transforming the ideas of each group member. The negotiation process is necessary because participants need to reach an understanding and resolve different viewpoints in order to reach a common ground upon which the creation of the group knowledge artifact can take place as a combination of the personalized knowledge put forward.

Moreover, the final form of the group knowledge artifact should satisfy all parties involved in the negotiation process in order to avoid conflicts (Bingham, Nabatchi and O'Leary 2005). Thus, the negotiation process is critical to the success of combining and transforming personalized knowledge into a group knowledge artifact.

Negotiation is more than a joint decision and a dialog process. It includes the process of understanding ourselves and our knowledge about the world, communicating it to others and understanding them and their knowledge. It also includes reaching a compromise.

Understanding ourselves is a self-reflexive process requiring meta-cognitive language in a monologue. In contrast, expressing ourselves to others and negotiating our ideas requires the active participation of others in order to transform the process into a dialog. If we understand why other people's and our own thinking follows a certain path we can communicate more easily about ideas and resolve knowledge differences by engaging in negotiation processes.

Teaching knowledge negotiations

Communicating ideas and discussing them to reach an agreement in order to collaboratively build knowledge is the knowledge negotiation process. The knowledge negotiation process is a very important part of our lives. It helps us discover the meaning inherent to others and ourselves. As an important life skill, knowledge negotiation should be passed on to our students. However, what should we teach in order to enable learners to engage in knowledge negotiations? Although there are many possible answers here, let us consider the fundamental skills required for successful knowledge negotiation. The process requires students to be active participants in the knowledge negotiation activity in order to carry the dialog for negotiations actively. Thus, firstly, we should teach students that the aim of dialog for knowledge negotiation is to create awareness for all participants. In knowledge negotiation dialogs in which the objective is to create awareness, the ultimate aim of the dialog participants should be to understand the general point of view of the others on the concepts that are present in a given situation. It should be made clear to dialog partners that the ultimate aim here is not to prove and/or disprove the ideas of others.

Second, we should teach the learners how to conduct the dialog in order to resolve differences of point of view. After understanding each other's ideas and the respective points of view, participants should be able to proceed with the dialog and discuss outcomes in order to come to an agreement. As mentioned before, the aim is not to prove and/or disprove the respective ideas, but rather finding common ground that the participants can agree upon.

Knowledge negotiation technologies

There are many systems developed to support negotiation (Pommeranz, Wiggers, Brinkman and Jonker 2012) such as Negosist (Schoop, Jertila and List 2003), Negotiation Support Systems – NSS (Sungsoon, Boltom, Rothrock and Brosig 2010), and Family Winner (Belluci and Zeleznikow 2005) etc., but there are few systems developed to support the knowledge negotiation process itself.

We should keep in mind that negotiation support systems are different from knowledge negotiation systems. Knowledge negotiation systems deal with the process of negotiation and creation of knowledge artifacts. Negotiation systems basically deal with supporting decision-making processes during negotiations, but not the creation of new knowledge or negotiation of the knowledge artifact of a given group.

Knowledge negotiation is one of the core components of collaborative knowledge building, but is rarely supported in online systems (Stahl 2006). There are a few examples of knowledge negotiation technologies. One is provided Stahl's (2003) paper, which illustrates the design and development of a knowledge negotiation tool in asynchronous learning networks. The tool is a new software system for K-12 classroom support named Basic Support for Collaborative Learning (BSCL). BSCL is designed for shared knowledge building in small groups. Using BSCL, group members interact with each other to create knowledge that is negotiated by the group. Knowledge proposals are collated in the form of a folder in which documents containing the personalized knowledge proposals function as knowledge artifacts. Further group knowledge artifacts supporting the negotiation process are multi-user discussion threads and portfolios. Using the discussion threads, group members negotiate the ideas and the modifications of the group knowledge artifact, the discussion threads being tools for a participant to indicate his/her reasoning and reactions to group knowledge artifact's current state.

Another example of relevant software is "Reality Check" which is purported to be software that supports knowledge negotiations (Petraglia and Glass 1999). "Reality Check" is developed to provide a platform for the teacher and students to participate in the process of knowledge negotiation. It supports the exchange of stamens and clarifications of positions to provide better understanding. Unlike BSCL, "Reality Check" does not provide a mechanism to create a shared knowledge artifact. Rather, it provides a mechanism to compare the participants' perceptions and ideas to create a platform to recognize the knowledge gaps and to negotiate them.

Furthermore, Herrera and Fuller (2005) describe a prototype tool designed for knowledge negotiations. Using this prototype tool, users in work groups may be engaged in different group projects in which there is nevertheless a need for the negotiation of knowledge. Users can propose their ideas using an interface providing shared and group workspaces. Using the group space, users' ideas are submitted for discussion and revision in a proposal format. These proposals are designed in a private workspace. An interactive map illustrates the relationships of proposed concepts and all proposals can evolve during the negotiation process. This prototype tool provides support for discussion of each group member's ideas and proposes a mechanism for group consensus. However, it is not clearly indicated how the prototype tool supports the development of an ultimate knowledge artifact of the group.

The problem of negotiation

When there is a traditional practice of negotiation, this entails each party taking a position and arguing in its defence. This kind of negotiation requires each party to avoid making concessions as much as possible, pushing the other party to make them give up some of their initial interests in order to reach to a compromise. This kind of traditional practice of negotiation successively puts forward and discards positions, producing inefficient results and endangering ongoing relationships (Fisher and Ury 2011). Obviously, producing inefficient results and damaging relationships between parties is a problem in the negotiation process. The same problem may occur during knowledge negotiation in a social and collaborative learning setting (Stahl, Koschmann and Suthers 2006; Stahl and Herrmann 1999).

Any proposed activity for knowledge negation should provide mechanisms to address this issue. These mechanisms should change the parties' attitudes towards the negotiation process and their thinking towards the aim of finding a common ground. This will support students to accrue prudent and efficient knowledge negotiation skills. Gaining prudent and efficient knowledge negotiation skills will help them to have awareness during knowledge negotiation discussions. It will also help students to easily communicate ideas and resolve knowledge differentials.

We need to understand how knowledge negotiation works in order to design technology to enable students to develop prudent and efficient knowledge negotiation skills. Currently, there is no fundamental guideline or model describing the principles of knowledge negotiation. A model may describe the ideal roles and interactions processes of participants during knowledge negotiation. Using such a model would be of utility in understanding the negotiation process and could guide research on knowledge negotiation.

A few technologies do support knowledge negotiation processes and yet none of them are designed on the basis of a fundamental model. Software systems based on such a model should be designed according to the requirements of the negotiation process and the participators' needs/roles therein.

Knowledge negotiation model (K-NeMo)

Fisher and Ury (2011), the authors of the book "Getting to YES", discuss the process of negotiation defining successful negotiation as an activity in which the goal is having a prudent outcome reached in an efficient and friendly manner. They also describe the role of negotiators. According to their description, negotiators:

1. are problem solvers;
2. separate the people from the problem;
3. are soft on the people, hard on the problem;
4. proceed independent of trust;
5. focus on interests, not positions;
6. explore interests;
7. avoid having a bottom line;
8. invent options for mutual gain;
9. develop multiple options to choose from; decide later;
10. insist on using objective criteria.

Fisher and Ury propose a method for successful negotiation processes. Although it is designed for the negotiation of interests, it also has utility in comprehending how negotiation in general can be optimized. Their method focuses on the central issue that "basic interests, mutually satisfying options and fair standards typically results in a *wise* agreement". Their method stipulates four directives for the process of negotiation:

1. Separate the people from the problem.
2. Focus on interests, not positions.
3. Invent options for mutual gain.
4. Insist on using objective criteria.

Using this method as a starting point, it is possible to design a new method for the knowledge negotiation process. There are some basic differences and similarities between negotiation per se and knowledge negotiation processes. Before designing a new method on the basis of an extant one, these differences and similarities should be clarified.

The differences are:

1. participators in knowledge negotiation are idea generators;
2. the knowledge negotiation process is much more related to utilizing negotiation dialog in order to create new knowledge and generate ideas rather than discussing defending existing ideas;
3. knowledge negotiation deals with understanding negotiators' points of view by exploring their reasoning and the meaning behind their ideas proposed during the negotiation process. They do not negotiate with regard to interests or positions;
4. rather than focusing on problem solving, knowledge negotiation functions by discovering new knowledge and ideas. In fact, the selfsame discovery process can be found in activities of discovering new problems (Dunbar 1997);
5. knowledge negotiation participators invent options to combine, associate and connect their ideas. The process and outcomes are all shared by the participants;
6. knowledge negotiation does not need to avoid bottom lines because there is no negotiation on interests at all.

Similarities are:

1. the goal is to have an outcome which is wise, efficient and, amicable for all participants;
2. both processes do not support ad hominem attacks. They promote being soft on people and separating people from the problem or the ideas/knowledge proposed;
3. both processes proceed independent of trust;
4. both process supports developing multiple options. Also, they promote delaying the decision phase until all the possible options have been taken into consideration;
5. both processes advise using objective criteria if necessary.

After defining differences and similarities, we can discuss the design of the new knowledge negotiation method. The new proposed knowledge negotiation method is called "Knowledge Negotiation Model (K-NeMo)". K-NeMo visualized in the Figure 1.

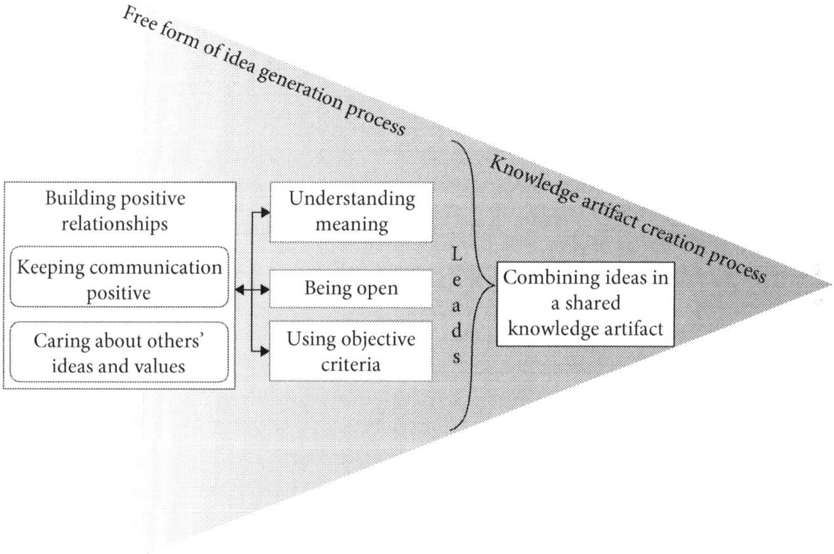

Figure 1. Knowledge Negotiation Model (K-NeMo)

K-NeMo explained

K-NeMo consists of two main parts which are the 'free form of idea generation process' and the "knowledge artifact creation process". "Free form of idea generation process" has four subcategories that are "Building Positive Relationships", "Understanding Meaning", "Being Open", and "Using Objective Criteria". "Knowledge artifact creation process" has one subcategory "Combining ideas in a shared knowledge artifact". These categories are not representative of the steps of knowledge negotiation, rather they represent its constitution. The categories are mutually interconnected. For example, being open to others' ideas is helpful for building a positive relationship because it is needed for showing care with regard to others' ideas and values. On the other hand, in order to demonstrate being open, it is necessary to keep communication positive.

In order to put these categories into practice, there are certain activities and roles in which the participants of the knowledge negotiation process should partake. These acts and roles are listed in Figure 2 and explained in detail in the following.

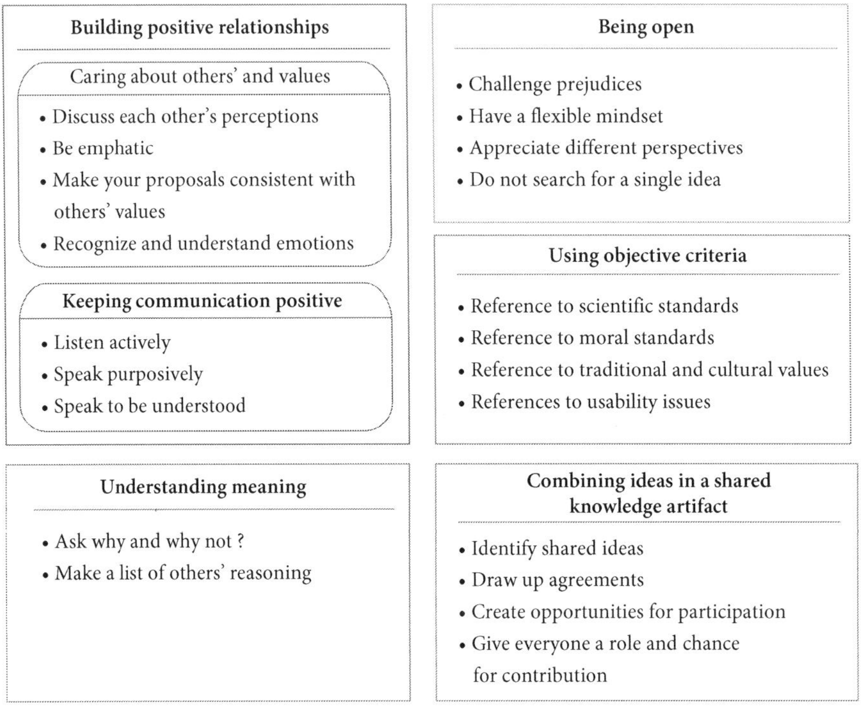

Figure 2. Acts and roles to facilitate the categories of K-NeMo

Processes of knowledge negotiation

The "free form of idea generation process" deals with the most important part of the negotiation activities. Within this process, participants' main objective is to generate ideas while maintaining positive relationships. They discuss each other's ideas in order to grasp the meaning behind them in an open and objective environment. There is no well-defined set of steps or procedures for the discussions. Dialogs may continue until participants feel they have found some common ground.

After participants decide to terminate the "free form of idea generation process", they can proceed to the "knowledge artifact creation process" in which the objective of participants is to combine ideas to create a knowledge artifact. The "free form of idea generation process" leads into the "knowledge artifact creation process". The knowledge artifacts of the latter process cannot be created without the ideas discovered and agreed upon in the former process.

Steps and sequences

The participants of knowledge negotiation should communicate with each other in order to generate ideas with the aim of creating a shared knowledge artifact as a first step. After the knowledge artifact is created, the negotiation process sequence may come to an end.

Building Positive Relationships: Knowledge negations should build positive relationships. It is not an activity like a debate where participants need to prove or disprove ideas. Knowledge negotiation is a collaborative activity in which it is absolutely necessary to be polite. Thus, participants should insist on positive relationships. Building positive relationships is interconnected with other subcategories of the idea generation process since it is also one of the main objectives of the overall negotiation process.

Caring about others' ideas/values and keeping communication positive are essential to helping participants build positive relationships in the knowledge negotiation process. Relationships are susceptible to being damaged when this is not the case. Participants should discuss each other's perceptions to be able to show they are caring and invested in others' ideas and values. Knowing other people's perceptions will help to determine individual differences and motivations providing powerful assets to determine other points of view within the negotiation process. In most cases, we realize that different thinking is down to individual differences that create the gaps between our points of view and theirs. If we determine the viewpoints we can work on them and try to negotiate in order to reduce the gaps. More importantly, people perceive that we care about their ideas and they will be willing to work with us towards the knowledge negotiation process (Wentzel 1997).

Moreover, understanding perception of others will help to form an approximate safe zone where certain themes can and cannot be discussed, e.g., there may be some sensitive themes (e.g., religion, race, cultural values, etc.) that participants should be very careful around while voicing criticism. Discussing different perceptions will assist in investigating how other people react to such taboo or difficult topics.

If we are aware of the perception of other people and safe-risky topical zones, it becomes easier to form ideas and proposals consistent with others' values and ideas in these zones. This will also help to demonstrate that we care about others and to maintain the discussion without unnecessary conflicts that may be damaging to relationships.

The majority of our ideas are connected to emotions. We are somewhat open to being hurt when our ideas are challenged and criticized in a negative and destructive way. Recipients of destructive criticism may feel anger and tension causing them to not collaborate or compromise (Baron 1988). There are many emotions involved in social interactions (Ekman 1999), and, thus, the process of negotiation may also be affected by our emotional reactions. For example, some ideas may induce sadness in others for some reason unbeknownst to us. If we wish to maintain our positive relationships in order to sustain knowledge negotiation through the participation of others we need to recognize and understand their emotional reactions.

Understanding others' emotions may help us to form an emphatic perception of them. It also aids the perception of differences. Being emphatic enables us to experience similar thinking processes in others aiding the maintenance of mutual positive relationships.

Keeping communication positive: Communication is an essential skill as the motor of dialog. Listening with the aim of understanding and speaking to be understood are two fundamental parts of positive communication. Dialog participants speaking without understanding are aimless and wasting time and energy. Positive communication requires us to listen actively because it helps us to confirm what we heard and reaffirm our understanding of the other parties. An active listener gives feedback to the speaker by using methods such as paraphrasing or restating (Rogers and Farson 1979). As long as communication at hand is a mutual interaction process, we also need to ensure whether others understand our ideas. Feedback is useful for confirming mutual understanding in order to avoid building dialogs on misleading and/or misunderstood premises about ideas in each other's heads. Misunderstandings may cause conflicts in the proceeding phases of dialog leading to negative communication overall in the knowledge negotiation process.

Positive communication requires participants to distinguish which points are specifically related to the main objective of the discussions, that being the generation of ideas. Having a main objective provides a method of keeping participants 'on track'. Otherwise, dialogs may stray away from the main aim of ongoing knowledge negotiation. Once the dialog has strayed, there is the additional problem of expending extra effort and time to get back on track. Spending too much time on unnecessary points decreases the allocated time for other important activities in the knowledge negotiation process. Speaking within the framework of a main objective may solve such problems. Participants should structure their thinking and monitor the path of their points of view in the unfolding dialog in order to constantly evaluate their current purpose for speaking. Structuring thinking before responding includes the process of clearly understanding the idea to be responded to. It also includes understanding our own reasoning of why we need to respond to that certain idea. While evaluating our purpose, we should not forget our roles and our objectives in the knowledge negotiation process, and also not lose sight of the current theme of the ongoing discussion. If the current theme is not directly related to the overall objectives of knowledge negotiation, we may not want to spend too much time on it.

Understanding meaning: The negotiation process is sustained until common ground in the form of the knowledge artifact is reached that is created as a result of the process. The knowledge artifact is created by combining the ideas of the participants of the negotiation. Understanding the ideas of the participants and the meaning behind them requires us to cycle through a number of questions–answers loops. "Why" and "Why not" types of questions are the best fit in order to investigate meaning within these loops. Once we discover what others mean, we may gain a common ground to critically think about it. Without digesting the meaning behind the ideas, it requires a great and wasteful amount of 'blind effort' to work around others' not fully understood ideas.

Knowledge negotiation sessions may include many participants. Making a list of all the ideas put forward and the reasoning behind them will help to grasp the overall picture. Lists will also be useful for keeping track of discussion flow as well as understanding overall connections between all the ideas presented at a particular time. Ideas that are common, different, or extreme outliers can be discovered by examining the list. This kind of a list may also be reused when the collaborative knowledge artifact needs to be created.

Being open: Knowledge negotiation should take place in an environment open to the discussion of any kind of ideas as long as they are pertinent and not in conflict with the values of others. An open environment is essential because it gives everyone a chance to reveal a variety of ideas and reasonings. Without an open environment, participants may feel distress when uttering their ideas in anticipation of social judgments within the group.

Open environments cannot exist by themselves, the participants must make them happen. Participants of knowledge negotiation should be aware of their roles and responsibilities to create an open environment. To do this, it is important for participants to challenge prejudices. Prejudices lock the mind into a fixed point blocking the possibility of taking the point of view of others and their proposed ideas.

Many of us bring our prejudices to knowledge negotiation. It is difficult to avoid, because we already have many ideas and attitudes toward the world. This difficulty notwithstanding, we should attempt to challenge prejudices.

Having a flexible mindset will also help. A flexible mindset frees us from a limited way of viewing complexities in the world. However, a flexible mindset does not mean that we should change our ideas, but that we should work with them in a flexible manner in order to make them work in changing situations. In the knowledge negotiation process, we need to work together with many different people which increases the complexity. A flexible mindset will make working with different people more easy.

Working with different people is a great opportunity for the creation of knowledge since a variety of people is also a valuable resource of diverse knowledge, with each person bringing a different perspective to the table. Different perspectives increase the chance of creating an entirely unique knowledge artifact. Thus, it is a creative approach that is required in order to appreciate the different perspectives and, since different perspectives contribute different ideas, it is not a prudent approach that searches for one single idea.

Using objective criteria: For the knowledge negotiation process, it is suggested building positive relationships and investing effort into understanding the meaning behind the ideas put forward in an open environment. However, times of conflicts are likely at which participants find it difficult to find common ground and/or clear disagreement on some ideas. Moreover, there may be many different ideas related to the same topic due to different perspectives. For example, there might be a conflict when deciding the definition of an object's color as blue or purple. Some participants may perceive it as being bluer than purple or vice versa. In such situations, there should be some points of reference, that can be used during the decision process of selecting ideas that are to be kept or discarded. These points of reference cannot be selected alongside the ideas generated by the participants, or even the ideas of any moderator (such as a teacher, forum manager, etc.). Rather, they need to be sufficiently objective and have enough authority in order to satisfy all of the participants with regard to the final decision. Scientific judgments and standards, moral standards, and traditional – cultural values fit this description to some degree. Another point of reference for decision-making could be the usability of generated ideas. In some cases, ideas simply may not be usable as a part of the shared knowledge artifact. In those cases, they may need to be discarded or postponed for future applications, for which these ideas may be a better fit. The ideas are usable, if they are practically applicable to real life practices and/or applicable to the current situation (note that not all the ideas are necessary for the application to real life); if they are effective enough for achieving their purpose (e.g., proposing an idea that does not match what it is really meant for); if they are efficient enough so that they do not require too much effort for their implementation in real life and/or current conditions, and if they are satisfactory in the view of all the participants.

Combining ideas in a shared knowledge artifact: Knowledge negations have an ultimate goal, which is to reach a final agreement. After discussing the ideas, it is necessary to decide which of them are going to be represented in a knowledge artifact. There may be several discussed ideas and for some it may not be possible to represent them independently from each other. Ideas should reflect the common ground found by the participants, forged together in a combinatory process whose outcome is the shared knowledge artifact. The combinatory process starts by identifying shared ideas. In knowledge negotiation sessions, there will have been times at which participants would have already presented similar ideas. These shared ideas should be categorized under a single item and collated in a list. Furthermore, this list can also include ideas that participants come to agree upon.

If there are no agreed or shared ideas, then the negotiation process should continue to put forward possible agreement options. This requires creating opportunities for participation and giving everyone a role and chance to contribute. When all the participants have no or little chance to contribute to the process, there is much less chance to reach an agreement. Moreover, participants who play a role in the process will also feel a sense of ownership motivating them to come up with more ideas and persevere with the knowledge negotiation process.

21st century technologies for knowledge negotiation

K-NeMo is not a model for technology development. Rather, it is a model for describing the roles and interactions processes of participants during the knowledge negotiation process. K-NeMo may be helpful for understanding negotiation processes in general in order to guide the design of technologies for knowledge negation process in particular. In addition, K-NeMo may be helpful for identifying the technological tools necessary for carrying out knowledge negotiation successfully.

Figure 2 describes acts and roles to enable the categories of K-NeMo. Acts and roles may help to inform our decisions while selecting technological support for knowledge negotiation. Using K-NeMo as a reference, it is possible to select 21st century technologies that are viable for promoting the essentials of the knowledge negotiation process.

Web 2.0 tools are ideal technologies for the knowledge negotiation process because they provide a way to work online collaboratively and to integrate different services. Integration is very important because different parts of K-NeMo require different kinds of solutions to work together at the same time. Web 2.0 services are usually simple enough to be used by end-users utilizing the "mash-up" method, which combines different services in one place. Mostly focusing on Web 2.0 technologies, the following paragraphs will describe some services that are viable as utilities for promoting essential phases of knowledge negotiations as described in K-NeMo.

Knowledge negotiation requires having mechanisms to help participants build positive relationships. Caring about others' ideas/values and keeping communication positive are essential, whereas maintaining positive relationships is much more related to our attitudes when we communicate with each other. However, technological tools can only create a platform for carrying communication and provide some guidelines (e.g., templates and forms to format our thought processes), and cannot fully direct our attitudes during the communication process. Rather than seeking a magic solution, we must view technologies as assistive tools in knowledge negotiation.

Technological solutions and services for communication should be positioned in an open environment in order to give everyone a chance to reveal all sorts of ideas and reasoning during the knowledge negotiation process. These solutions and services should provide a mechanism for questioning ideas and reasoning, as well as a mechanism for responding to these questions.

Personalized live discussion forums may match these requirements. Discussion forums may assist users to sustain communication (usually as threads) but be able to question each others' reasoning by replying to messages posted that have been posted. Moreover, some forums provide a system for user roles that could be helpful in knowledge discussion sessions. Some users play the role of forum moderator who can monitor the message traffic and the forum to ensure that relationships remain positive and the forum is free from negative patterns of communications (e.g., using bad language).

Another tool to discuss ideas would be brainstorming tools. Unlike dialog forums, brainstorming tools do not enable the questioning of ideas. However, they are especially ideal for creating an open environment. Web 2.0 tools are also available for brainstorming purposes.

Because not all the ideas are easy to describe just using text formats, some diagrams and visual illustrations may be used as a supplementary communication method. There are many Web 2.0 services allowing sharing and the discussion of knowledge in different representation formats (e.g., graphs, charts, diagrams, presentations, etc.).

The knowledge negotiation process also makes it necessary to look to objective criteria when looking for points of reference. Although technology itself cannot be a reference point, only the message or the knowledge it carries can be. Objective points of reference may be web resources that are publically accepted as authoritative and an objective source of knowledge. Some public and socially created web resources such as Wikipedia may be a source for points of reference if they are accepted as authoritative and objective by the group members of the knowledge negotiation discussion. Government websites and databases are other possible resources.

The usability of the generated ideas is another point to be considered, albeit not always easy to do. For some ideas, it is not possible to evaluate their usability before they have been implemented. In such situations, a voting technique may be useful in which participants vote on the usability of the ideas according to their perceptions. A Web 2.0 polling service may be embedded into the forum to allow participants to vote on the threads.

The idea generation and discussion process leads into knowledge artifact creation. The knowledge artifact may be represented in many formats such as a webpage, presentation, video, animation, 3D model, audio, etc. The format depends on the group's needs. The most important factors in creating the knowledge artifact are that it is shared and modifiable by all group members. Web 2.0 technologies allow both sharing and modification in collaborative ways, enabling students to create knowledge collaboratively in the form of wikis, blogs, world quests, stories, videos, audios, animations, virtual worlds, 3D objects, presentations, office documents, games, illustrations, graphs, etc. The shared knowledge artifact of the group may take on one or many of these formats as long as group members collaboratively create and share it according to their agreements drawn up in their negotiation of knowledge dialogs.

All the technologies suggested here are easy to find with a simple web search. These technologies may be used as a single service or combined to create an integrated webpage. However, there is currently no technology providing all the discussed solutions as a single service, although, in the future, there may be software or web services that might combine them. In addition, these services do not cover all the necessities of K-NeMo. For example, there is no software service that helps students sustain their communication while remaining empathic to others or no software is designed to support checking our own understanding of others' ideas. However, in the future, this may change with the development of new services and technologies.

Conclusion

We communicate with others in order to find a way to reach a common ground, we communicate to negotiate knowledge in our everyday social environment. In this chapter, the few technologies supporting this everyday social process have been discussed and a perspective on knowledge negotiation and teaching knowledge negotiation has been provided, a new knowledge negotiation model (K-NeMo) introduced and explained.

K-NeMo may be a model for future reference describing the roles and interaction processes of participants during the knowledge negotiation process. Here, it has been considered and explained the two main parts of K-NeMo and their respective categories.

In the final section of this paper, 21st century technologies were considered as possible applications of K-NeMo. Web 2.0 technologies were found to be suitable for the knowledge negotiation process because of their affinity for providing an open and shared platform for building knowledge artifacts in a collaborative manner.

References

Baron, Robert A. 1988. "Negative Effects of Destructive Criticism: Impact on Conflict, Self-Efficacy, and Task Performance." *Journal of Applied Psychology* 73 (2): 199. DOI: 10.1037/0021-9010.73.2.199

Bellucci, Emilia, and John Zeleznikow. 2005. "Developing Negotiation Decision Support Systems that Support Mediators: a Case Study of the Family_Winner system." *Artificial Intelligence and Law* 13 (2): 233–271. DOI: 10.1007/s10506-006-9013-1

Bingham, Lisa Blomgren, Tina Nabatchi, and Rosemary O'Leary. 2005. "The New Governance: Practices and Processes for Stakeholder and Citizen Participation in the Work of Government." *Public Administration Review* 65 (5): 547–558. DOI: 10.1111/j.1540-6210.2005.00482.x

Dunbar, Kevin. 1997. "How Scientists Think: On-line Creativity and Conceptual Change in Science." *Creative Thought: An Investigation of Conceptual Structures and Processes* 461–493. DOI: 10.1037/10227-017

Ekman, Paul. 1999. "Basic Emotions." In *Handbook of Cognition and Emotion 4*, ed. by Tim Dagleish, and Mick Power, 5–60. New York, et al.: Wiley.

Fisher, Roger, and William L. Ury. 2011. *Getting to Yes: Negotiating Agreement without Giving in*. Penguin.

Herrera, Oriel, and David A. Fuller. 2005. "Shared Knowledge: The Result of Negotiation in Non-Hierarchical Environments." In *Groupware: Design, Implementation, and Use*, ed. by Hugo Fuchs, Stephan Lukosch, and Ana C. Salgado, 255–262. Berlin Heidelberg: Springer. DOI: 10.1007/11560296_20

Park, Sungsoon, Gary E. Bolton, Ling Rothrock, and Jeannette Brosig. 2010. "Towards an Interdisciplinary Perspective of Training Intervention for Negotiations: Developing Strategic Negotiation Support Contents." *Decision Support Systems* 49 (2): 213–221. DOI: 10.1016/j.dss.2010.02.007

Petraglia, Joseph, and Bryce Glass. 1999. "Technological Support for Knowledge Negotiation." In *HICSS-32. Proceedings of the 32nd Annual Hawaii International Conference on System Sciences*, IEEE, 1999. http://citeseerx.ist.psu.edu/viewdoc/download?doi=10.1.1.129.2613&rep=rep1&type=pdf. (last date of access 19 Sept. 2013).

Pommeranz, Alina, Pascal Wiggers, Willem-Paul Brinkman, and Catholijn M. Jonker. 2012. "Social Acceptance of Negotiation Support Systems: Scenario-based Exploration with Focus Groups and Online Survey." *Cognition, Technology & Work* 14 (4): 299–317. DOI: 10.1007/s10111-011-0181-8

Rogers, Carl, and Richard E. Farson. 1979. "Active Listening." In *Organizational Psychology*, ed. by David Kolb, Irwin Rubin, and James MacIntyre, 108–116. New Jersey: Prentice Hall.

Schoop, Mareike, Aida Jertila, and Thomas List. 2003. "Negoisst: A Negotiation Support System for Electronic Business-to-Business Negotiations in e-Commerce." *Data and Knowledge Engineering* 47 (3): 371–401. DOI: 10.1016/S0169-023X(03)00065-X

Stahl, Gerry. 2003. "Knowledge Negotiation in Asynchronous Learning Networks." In *Proceedings of the 36th Annual Hawaii International Conference on System Sciences*, IEEE, 2003. http://www.hicss.hawaii.edu/HICSS36/HICSSpapers/CLALN02.pdf). (last date of access 19 September 2013).

Stahl, Gerry. 2006. *Group cognition: Computer support for building collaborative knowledge*. Cambridge, MA: MIT Press.

Stahl, Gerry, and Thomas Herrmann. 1999. "Intertwining perspectives and negotiation." In *Proceedings of the international ACM SIGGROUP conference on Supporting group work*, 316–325, ACM.
Stahl, Gerry, T. Koschmann, and D. Suthers. 2006. *Computer-supported collaborative learning: An historical perspective*. Cambridge handbook of the learning sciences, 2006.
Wentzel, Kathryn R. 1997. "Student Motivation in Middle School: The Role of Perceived Pedagogical Caring." *Journal of Educational Psychology* 89 (3): 411–419. DOI: 10.1037/0022-0663.89.3.411

Author's address

Ilker Yengin, PhD
Research Scientist
A*STAR – Institute of High Performance Computing
Computational Social Cognition
1 Fusionopolis Way, #16-16 Connexis, Singapore 138632
yengini@ihpc.a-star.edu.sg

Teaching and learning as explorative action games

Guidelines for the design of dialogic educational technology

Sebastian Feller
Institute of High Perfomance Computing, Singapore

In this chapter, I develop a view of teaching and learning as explorative action games (TaLEAG). The concept of the action game is borrowed from Weigand's (2010) Theory of Dialogic Action Games or Mixed Game Model (MGM). The MGM rests on two basic assumptions: communication is dialogic and language is action. These two assumptions are adapted to teaching and learning in general and to what I call explorative action games in particular. The ensuing discussion revolves around the question of how educational technology should be designed in order to facilitate learning in the context of explorative action games.

The chapter is structured as follows: Following the introduction, I will outline a theory of teaching and learning that is derived from the main assumptions of the MGM. The focus here is on the dyad of action and reaction in TaLEAG. I will describe the main features of the initial speech act in the game, which I call the explorative speech act, as well as of the discover speech act being the reaction to the explorative. In the second step, TaLEAG is connected to a view of learning as conceptual change learning (CCL). In the final step, this will lead us to a set of preliminary guidelines for the design of educational technology. The chapter concludes with an outlook on research and development in the area of dialogic educational technology.

1. Introduction

Die Bildungskatastrophe (The education catastrophe) – this is the title of a chapter in Richard David Precht's (2013) latest book *Anna, die Schule und der liebe Gott* (Anna, school, and the Dear Lord). Precht's book is a wake-up call: the German education system is outdated. Radical change is needed if we want our children to be prepared for the requirements of modern everyday life. Education should be about actual questions, real problems, and the attempt to tackle these with creative and innovative solutions. The *status quo* of the German education system lies on the opposite end of the spectrum: rote learning and what might be called *pseudo*-learning are at the top of the education agenda. Students are confronted with Ohm's law, the ablative in Latin, and infinitesimal calculus. In fact, the word "confronted" very much hits the nail on the head. As Precht describes it from his own classroom visits, the teacher presents the curriculum in isolated islands, without any clear connection between the topics of a single school subject, let alone across different school subjects. Furthermore, students usually have difficulties applying what they learn at school to their everyday lives.

Precht tackles this disheartening situation in multiple ways. For example, he suggests that students should learn in project-based learning groups. These groups should tackle topics such as the greenhouse effect or genetically modified food from an interdisciplinary standpoint, combining the curriculum and methodology of different school subjects right from the start.

Another idea is the so-called "flipped classroom", also known as "flip teaching". In a flip teaching context, the student initially learns a new topic through video lectures at home. Subsequently, in the classroom, she applies her new knowledge to specific problems. The teacher has a passive role here, providing only guidance if the student gets stuck. It is the student who is in the active role, finding solutions to a problem through higher-level thinking. Here, it is not sufficient to learn off by heart and regurgitate knowledge, rather students are required to transfer what they learn in the video lessons to new problems and new situations.

Of course, this kind of rethinking is not restricted to the German context. There are many countries that feel the need for revising their existing education systems. Singapore is a good example. One of the central themes for policy makers in Singapore like the National Institute of Education (2009) are so-called "21st century skills". These skills include, among others, critical thinking, collaborative problem solving, creative and innovative thinking, and information and communication skills. When tackling a specific problem, students should exchange their different viewpoints, question information that is presented to them by other parties, go off the beaten track and think out of the box.

In sum, this view of teaching and learning promoted by Precht and Singapore, to name but a few of its proponents, could be paraphrased as exploration. Students should explore a topic with the aim of making new discoveries for themselves. That said, the question arises of how this new concept can be implemented in the classroom of the 21st century. In search of an answer, I will firstly outline a basic model of teaching and learning in terms of what I call explorative action games.

2. Teaching and learning as explorative action games (TaLEAG)

One of the central key concepts behind teaching and learning as exploration is dialog. Teaching and learning should be dialogic in the sense that teacher and learner, just like learner and peers, should communicate about a topic (Alexander 2006; Arnett 1998; Wegerif 2010). All dialog partners are thereby equal. As a consequence, the traditional master-novice relationship gives way to a more egalitarian guide-explorer relationship.

This dialogic conception is based on Weigand's (e.g., 2000, 2010) Theory of Dialogic Action Games or Mixed Game Model (MGM). The following section gives a brief overview of Weigand's basic assumptions.

2.1 The basic assumptions of the Mixed Game Model (MGM)

The MGM rests on three basic principles: (i) the action principle, (ii) the dialogic principle, and (iii) the coherence principle. In short, (i) holds that speakers carry out mutually related actions when they use language in communication. (ii) means that there are always one or more speakers that react to an initial communicative act. In addition, (iii) captures the fact that the speakers construct meaning on the basis of words-in-use, i.e. words as they occur in natural language use, namely in the co-text of other words and the context of a particular communicative situation.

From this theoretical framework of the MGM I derive a model of communicative interaction for teaching and learning as exploration. I term this model teaching and learning as explorative action games (TaLEAG). In the sections that follow, I will outline the overall make-up of the model.

2.2 The explorative action game: Acts of exploring

Following the MGM's basic assumptions, I hold that teacher-learner interactions are based on (i) communicative actions that are part of what I call the explorative action game. I will describe the types of communicative actions of the explorative action game in this and the following section. In accordance with (ii) I hold that the minimal unit of the explorative action game is dialogic:

Explorative speech act ⟷ Discover speech act

Figure 1. The minimal explorative action game

This minimal communicative unit consists of the mutual dyad of two speech acts: (a) the explorative speech act and (b) the discover speech act. By "mutual" I mean that each speech act is fully definable only in relation to the correlating speech act. This means that in order to arrive at a proper understanding of (a), one must take (b) into account, and vice versa.

In this section I will take a closer look at (a), (b) will be dealt with in the next section. In order to arrive at a clear understanding of (a), we need to answer the following two questions:

1. What is (a) used for, i.e., what is its communicative function?
2. What is (a) about, i.e., what propositional content does it feature?

In general terms, the answer to (1) is that we use (a) for what I call acts of exploring. My definition of exploring goes hand in hand with the idea behind 21st century skills (cf., e.g., Trilling and Fadel 2009). To give an example, let us take a look at critical thinking. We explore the world through critical thinking. This happens when we question conceptualizations and theories that we encounter in our conversations with others. Exploring means here not to take things at face value, but to look behind the scenes and find out how things seem from different perspectives.

Creative thinking is another act of exploration. Leaving beaten tracks and being creative in this sense means to explore new ways of thinking or of doing something. For example, the other day I observed how my two-year old son would convert a small child's soccer goal into a rocking boat. By doing so, he explored the object, testing out different, i.e., unconventional functions of the object (see also Hargreaves 2012, for a more detailed account on creativity). An explorative speech act mediates and initiates such acts of exploration in communication.

2.3 What acts of exploring are about: Epistemological foundation

Question (2) regarding the propositional content of the explorative speech act points us towards the world and the objects therein. Surely "the world" as an object of investigation is a bit too broad to get a grip on, however, there is no reason to despair as help is on the way. Epistemology being the science of knowledge supplies us with a more orderly view of things. As I have argued (Feller 2013), it is especially Aristotle's epistemology that provides a working epistemic framework in the context of TaLEAG. Aristotle's (1992) epistemology is based on *aitiae* of which he differentiates four types:

a. constitutive: relating to objects and its parts
   (1) A car has four wheels.

b. formal: defining what distinguishes an object within a larger domain
   (2) This elephant is grey just like any other elephant but it has exceptionally large ears.
c. telic: referring to an object's purpose or function, i.e., what it is used for
   (3) A car is for driving.
d. efficient: indicating forces outside of an object, causing change or movement or bringing it into existence
   (4) A car is assembled in a car factory.

According to Aristotle, these four *aitiae* or, causes, lie at the heart of our understanding of things in the world. They give an answer to the question *Why?* and are thus the basic building blocks of our understanding or definition of things. Thus the four *aitiae* provide a plausible categorization for the answer to question (2) mentioned above. As the basic building blocks of explanation, they are the road signs on the cognitive "paths" we traverse when we explore things. By "path" I mean epistemic strategies that help us process and structure the world.

In the next section, we will look into how these cognitive paths are constructed in more detail. I will derive different kinds of cognitive paths, which I call enablers, from the above-mentioned *aitiae*.

2.4 Cognitive paths of teaching and learning: Enablers

Based on the above-described *aitiae*, we can now derive a number of correlating enablers. See Table 1 for a list of candidates. This list is not exhaustive, but suffices as a preliminary starting point.

Table 1. Deriving enablers from *aitiae*. "x" indicates that enabler and *aition* correlate with each other

enabler/*aitiae*	a. constitutive	b. formal	c. telic	d. efficient
A. part-of	x			
B. has-a	x			
C. general-specific		x		
D. specific-general			x	
E. similar-different		x		
F. is-for			x	
G. cause-effect				x
H. effect-cause				x
I. antecedent-consequent				x
J. is-at				x

In the following, I will briefly discuss each enabler separately beginning with (a) constitutive. (a) is about the parts or components of an object. Conceptualizations run here along the following lines, amongst others:

A. part-of relation: this relation defines an object as being part of a larger object. Consider the following example:

   (5) The wheel is part of the car.

B. has-a relation: compared to (A), this relation starts off from the opposite end. It is now the larger object, which is at the center of the conceptualization. Remember the example from before:

   (1) A car has four wheels.

We continue with enablers under (b) formal. Here I distinguish between the following relations:

C. general-specific relation: this is the relation between an umbrella concept, the so-called hyperonym, and its subordinate, the so-called hyponym. The relation between hyperonym and hyponym is defined by conceptual inheritance: the hyponym inherits all the features from the hyperonym. In addition, it possesses further features that are only presupposed as potentials in the hyperonym but not *per se* part of it. The following example with "car" being the hyponym and "vehicle" being the hyperonym illustrates this:

   (6) A car is a vehicle with four wheels.

D. similar-different relation: this relation is similar to (C). It is based on an intersecting set of features of two or more objects contrasted against a subset of object-specific features. As opposed to (C), where the intersecting set of features is derived from the hyperonym, here the intersecting set is derived from a concept on the same conceptual level as the base concept. Here an example:

   (7) A Porsche is like a Ferrari made in Germany.

Let us move on to (c) telic.

We can construct the relation in (6) in the opposite direction, resulting in the new relation (E) specific-general.

   (8) A car is a vehicle.

In contrast to (6), in (8) the hyponym is defined in terms of the more abstract hyperonym. Specific features are not mentioned. Here it is rather the basic functions common to all vehicles such as the transportation function that are entailed by this conceptualization.

F. is-for relation: this relation refers explicitly to the purpose or function of an object. To give an example, consider (3) discussed earlier:

(3) A car is for driving.

Finally, we can take a look at (d) efficient. These are the correlating relations:

G. cause-effect relation: this relation points to a force outside the object, i.e., the cause, which brings about something, namely the effect. The following sentence illustrates this relation:

(9) The street is wet because it was raining.

This relation can be turned around, resulting in (H) effect-cause:

(10) It was raining, so the street is wet.

In a wider sense, we can also derive temporal relations from (d). For example, (I) antecedent-consequent relation:

(11) First I went to the bank, then I visited Laurie.

The event structure is, similar to the causal structure in (9) and (10), an external "force". I hold the same for location or what I call (J) is-at relation:

(12) The car is parked on the other side of the building.

Correlating time and location with this and not another *aition* or even a completely new epistemic category is a heuristic decision. I do not claim that any of the above-mentioned correlations reflect cognition as it really is. Rather, the proposed structure is a working hypothesis for coming to grips with the cognitive processes in learning from a theoretical point of view.

3. Connecting epistemology and language

3.1 The structure of the explorative speech act

Having defined the communicative function and propositional content of the (a) explorative speech act, we arrive at the following representation:

EXPLORATIVE(enabler)

Figure 2. The explorative speech act

This structure is based on Searle's (1969, 33) formula F(p), where F stands for the communicative function (i.e., in our case exploring a topic) and p for the propositional act (i.e., the content of the explorative speech act, which I have structured along the distinct enablers introduced earlier). In Figure 2, EXPLORATIVE is equal to F and enabler is the propositional act p.

However, the structure is not yet complete. In addition to the structure so far, every teacher-learner interaction is also about a particular topic. In other words, the act of exploring by using a specific cognitive path (enabler) is directed towards a particular something, which is the topic of the explorative action game. To give an example, the speakers might explore the function of electrons in a physics class, the role of photosynthesis for the ecosystem in a biology class, or the effect of higher income taxation on the domestic buying power in an economics class. A directed explorative action game is made up by directed speech acts including a directed explorative speech act of the following form:

TOPIC[EXPLORATIVE(enabler)]

Figure 3. The directed explorative speech act

But this is still only half of the story. In order to arrive at the full picture, we need to take into account the dialogic nature of the action game. The directed explorative speech act is only the initial communicative action. In the following section I will, therefore, take a closer look at the reactive speech act of the action game: the discover speech act.

3.2 The discover speech act

The (b) discover speech act is the counterpart of the (a) explorative speech act. While (a) is about initiating the finding out of things, (b) is about the very act of finding something out. In other words, it is the act of discovering something that we are dealing with here. As the object of discovery lies within the domain of the act of exploration, TOPIC of DISCOVER should be similar to TOPIC of EXPLORATIVE. In addition, both speech acts share the same enabler.

TOPIC[EXPLORATIVE(enabler)] ⟷ TOPIC[DISCOVER(enabler)]

Figure 4. The directed explorative action game

There is a major difference, however: the discover speech act aims at learning. This raises the question of what "learning" actually means in this context. In the following section I will give an overview.

3.3 Conceptual change learning (CCL)

Taking what has been said so far seriously, especially my strong emphasis on learner-centeredness and 21st century skills, we are in the need of a view of learning that matches this kind of teaching and learning philosophy. Conceptual change learning is a good candidate for the following reasons: conceptual change learning is based on Conceptual Change Theory (Thagard 1992) (CCT), which revolves around the individual learner and her existing knowledge state. The basic assumption is that we are not blank slates (Pinker 2002). Rather, we always possess some sort of idea or theory about something. These theories and ideas manifest themselves as concepts in our knowledge base. What we do when we learn something is that we change our existing concepts. Conceptual change comes in three different variants (cf., e.g., Hewson 1992, 3f.):

1. An existing concept is extended.
2. An existing concept is truncated.
3. An existing concept is partially revised, i.e., parts of it are replaced with new parts.

Let me give a short example of each variant.

1. The learner knows that honeybees produce honey. In her biology class, the teacher explains that honeybees also produce propolis, i.e., bee glue, which they use to repair cracks in the hive. This new information is added to the original concept in the learner's knowledge base.
2. The learner believes that male bees have a sting. In her biology class, the teacher explains that in contrast to female bees, male bees do not have a sting. She thus truncates her original concept of a male bee.
3. We imagine the learner thinks that the honeybee has eight legs. In her biology book, she discovers the illustration of a honeybee showing only six legs. The learner hence revises this part of her existing concept.

3.4 Thinking patterns: Correlating enablers with conceptual change

Having derived the enablers (A) to (J) from the *aitiae*, we can now tackle the question of how enablers are connected to conceptual change. The basic assumption is that we can use specific enablers in communication to potentially trigger particular types of conceptual change. Here the word 'potentially' is of utmost importance. If enablers do in fact trigger conceptual change is contingent on factors that lie beyond the scope of the *aitiae* and enablers. Another decisive factor here is the learner's existing knowledge. An enabler will not result in conceptual change, if the learner already possesses the knowledge entailed by the enabler. Thus, a precondition of conceptual change is that the learner has an actual need to change her existing knowledge. Depending on the exact type of conceptual change, this need differs in nature: In the case of (1) concept extension, the need comes in the form of a knowledge gap; in the case of (2) concept truncation, the learner must be aware that an existing concept in her knowledge base contains superfluous information that should be deleted; additionally (3) concept revision presumes that the learner is aware that parts of an existing concept are inaccurate and should be replaced with new information.

Table 2 gives an overview of the specific correlations between enablers and conceptual change:

Table 2. The relation between enablers and specific types of conceptual change. "x" indicates that the enabler directly triggers the corresponding type of conceptual change. "(x)" indicates that the enabler must be specified further in order to trigger the corresponding type of conceptual change

enabler/conceptual change type	extension	truncation	revision
part-of	x	(x)	(x)
has-a	x	(x)	(x)
general-specific	x	(x)	(x)
specific-general	x	(x)	(x)
similar-different	x	(x)	(x)
is-for	x	(x)	(x)
cause-effect	x	(x)	(x)
effect-cause	x	(x)	(x)
antecedent-consequent	x	(x)	(x)
is-at	x	(x)	(x)

3.4.1 *Concept extension*

Let us begin with (A), the part-of relation. Returning to (5) *The wheel is part of the car.*, we can split up the complex proposition expressed in (5) into smaller parts: first, the base concept "the wheel" and, second, "the car", which extends the base concept. Here "the wheel" is put into its broader "ecological" context. This enabler thus correlates with (i) conceptual extension.

(B) has-a relation functions similarly. Compared to (A), base concept and extension are switched: in the corresponding example, (1), it is “a car” that is now the base concept and “four wheels” extending this concept.

(C) general-specific also adds information to the base concept. As illustrated in (6), new information is added in terms of the hyperonym “vehicle” and the specific feature “four wheels” of the hyponym. (E) specific-general works along similar lines, except that specific features are not provided but information in the form of the set of general features inherited from the hyperonym.

(D) similar-different differs only slightly from (C). While in (C) information is added by the hyperonym, in (D) two or more objects of the same hierarchical level are compared with each other. Idiosyncratic features that distinguish the base concept in the contrast relation are added to the base concept. We can see in (7) how the base concept “Porsche” is specified by the intersecting set of features it shares with “Ferrari” and the additional distinct feature “made in Germany”.

Moving on to (F) is-for relation, the base concept is extended by the object’s specific function, see (3) earlier.

As for (G) cause-effect, the base concept, i.e., the effect, is specified by the cause and vice versa for (H) effect-cause.

The temporal order expressed in (11) by (I) antecedent-consequent relation specifies the events expressed in the proposition. The events are presented in a sequence that is not inherent to the single events *per se*. The chronological order can be changed without causing any sort of contradiction, for example, *First I visited Laurie, then I went to the bank* works just as well.

Location is another case of concept extension. As illustrated in (12), the base concept “the car” is extended through (J) be-at relation by the locative information “on the other side of the building”.

3.4.2 *Concept truncation*

Concept truncation occurs when the propositional content of enablers is fully or partially negated. As an example, let us take a look at our earlier case under (E) specific-general and contrast it with a slightly extended version:

(6) a. A car is a vehicle.
b. The car is a vehicle, but this car does not run anymore.

What happens in (6b) is that the inheritance of hyperonymical features is restricted by the subordinate clause. In this case, it is the generic transportation function that is negated for the particular car referred to in the example.

To consider another example, we can revisit (H) effect-cause:

(10) a. It was raining, so the street is wet.
b. It was raining, but the street is dry (i.e., not wet).

In this case, while (10a) expresses the "natural" or expected entailment relation of the presented state of affairs, (10b) negates the expected consequence. The conjunction "but" implies the contradictory relation between the fact that it was raining and the unexpected outcome of the street still being dry. The original entailment relation in (10a) is thus truncated.

In summary, the examples illustrate how negation of parts of or the enabler's entire proposition correlates with concept truncation. Enablers trigger concept extension, but the extension is constrained by negating selected features of the extended concept. Therefore, truncation is a specification of extension that can be applied to all extension enablers (see Table 2).

3.4.3 *Concept revision*

All enablers can be used for concept revision by replacing parts of the propositional content of an enabler with new information. This works for all enablers alike. We will use the following example for illustration.

(10) a. It was raining, so the street is wet.
c. A fire truck was leaking water, so the street is wet.

Changing (10a) to (10c) revises the original proposition by replacing the cause [it was raining] with the new cause [a fire truck was leaking water]. The second part of the proposition [the street is wet] remains intact.

Now, the type of conceptual change from (10a) to (10c) is totally different compared to the one between (10a) and (10b). While changing (10a) to (10b) causes a complete shift in the quality of the relation expressed in the proposition, in the case of (10a) and (10c) the epistemic relation remains the same. The cause changes, but we are nevertheless still dealing with an effect-cause relation as a whole here.

In the next section, we will consider how language is connected to the enabler-conceptual change patterns, henceforth termed thinking patterns. The main question is: How and what language correlates with which type of thinking pattern? An answer to this question will help us understand how thinking patterns can be instantiated in communication and which linguistic means are available to the dialog partners to facilitate conceptual change learning.

3.5 Conceptual change as perlocutionary effect

So far, we have seen how the enablers are instantiated in the speech acts of the action game. However, what about the conceptual change the enablers correlate with? The conceptual change is part of the so-called perlocutionary effect of the explorative speech act. With the aim of getting a better understanding of what that means, let us take a closer look at perlocution.

In Speech Act Theory, perlocution is defined as the psychological effect a speech act causes in the addressee (Peccei 1999). As for the explorative speech act, it is the particular type of conceptual change correlating with the enabler in the propositional act p that is in the role of the perlocution. Furthermore, the traditional definition of perlocution holds that the psychological effect is beyond the immediate control of the speaker.

This is true in the case of the explorative speech act. The speaker expects the type of conceptual change correlating with the enabler in p to unfold within the hearer. Whether this actually occurs, is, however, outside of the speaker's sphere of direct influence. Other factors also determine the hearer's reaction including her perspectivization of a given problem, her existing knowledge, her comprehension of the problem, the history of the interaction, her learning style including her personal learning preferences, etc.

We can illustrate this view of conceptual change as perlocutionary effect as follows:

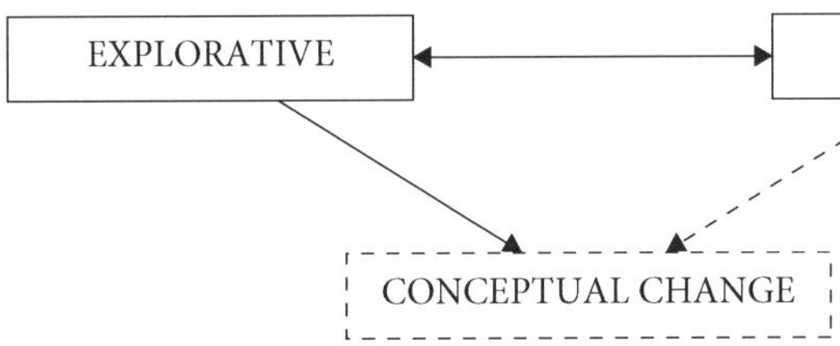

Figure 5. Conceptual change as perlocutionary effect

Figure 5 illustrates the connection between the minimal action game, i.e., the mutually related explorative and discover speech acts, and conceptual change. As indicated by the continuous arrow, the explorative speech act expects that the discover speech act yields conceptual change. On the other hand, if the discover speech act actually results in conceptual change is contingent (therefore the dashed arrow) upon "external" factors.

Action and reaction are mutually related to each other and indirectly linked via conceptual change. The dashed arrow indicates that the link between DISCOVER and conceptual change is indirect, as already discussed above. The link between EXPLORATIVE and conceptual change is stronger in the sense that the speaker expects conceptual change to take place.

4. Guidelines for designing educational technology

There is one central question that I have not discussed so far: what are the implications of explorative action games as a pedagogical model for educational technology? I will answer this question by stating basic principles for the design of educational technology. Ravenscroft has already put forward what he calls Deep Learning Design (DLD) or Situated Learning (2012, 135ff.). In all brevity, DLD is based on the assumption that technology should be designed in accordance with the learner's needs and abilities, not the other way around. Similarly, I hold that the explorative action game as a model for teaching and learning provides important insights into what these needs and abilities are.

In accordance with these considerations, the first design principle is:

1. Educational technology should be dialogic.

This principle can be implemented in different ways. For example, a learning application might function as dialog partner in an explorative action game with the learner. In addition, another application might facilitate and support dialog between two or more learners. To give an example, Pinkwart and McLaren (2012) discuss a number of applications that work in this way. The reader may be referred to their book for a more detailed account.

The second design principle is:

2. Educational technology should be structured around acts of exploration and discovery.

This principle is directly built on top of (1). The important point here is that a learning application should not simply revolve around any kind of dialog, but dialog of a certain kind. As laid out in this chapter, dialog for teaching and learning should have the form of explorative action games. Thus, a learning application should have the communicative faculty to create and interpret directed explorative speech acts.

3. Educational technology should integrate the verbal, perceptive, and cognitive level of communication.

In natural language use, speakers use a potentially open-ended set of communicative means to carry out the explorative and discover speech acts. They integrate words, perceptive input, and cognition including background knowledge and reasoning when engaging in the explorative action game. Educational technology should therefore run along similar lines, incorporating different communicative means. Once again the reader may be referred to Pinkwart and McLaren (2012). For example, tools such as Policy World use graphic representations of meta-linguistic information like argumentation and reasoning structures, highlighting the cognitive level of the interaction. Integrating all levels of communication makes interactions more intuitive and believable. The learning experience becomes authentic and teachers and learners are likely to be more comfortable using this kind of educational technology.

4. Educational technology should be a dialog partner, not a dialog master.

The explorative action game is a game of two or more equal players. In this sense, I believe that educational technology should never play a central role in teaching and learning. It should complement it as a supplementary tool or, at the most, as a player in the game. The other players, i.e., the human users, should always be able to fill out their respective roles without being restricted by the technology.

5. Conclusion

In this chapter, I have developed a communicative model of teaching and learning as explorative action games (TaLEAG). TaLEAG is based on a view of language as dialog and action. I have laid out the basic structure of TaLEAG consisting of the explorative speech act on the one hand, and the discover speech act on the other. The explorative speech act mediates acts of exploring that I connected to 21st century skills and learner-centered approaches in pedagogy. The discover speech act converged with a view of learning as conceptual change learning. On the basis of this communicative framework, I have derived four basic principles for the design of educational technology, namely educational technology should be dialogic, be structured around speech acts of exploring and discovering, integrate different means of communication including perceptive, cognitive and verbal means, and be a partner, not a master in the communication.

I want to conclude with a short glimpse into the future of teaching and learning in general and educational technology in particular. I strongly agree with Precht's claim that teaching and learning should relate more to real life and real life problems. This means that flip teaching or the flipped classroom should definitely become a fixed part of our schools, as should project based learning in groups.

Furthermore, I believe that schools should put more emphasis on showing learners ways to construct, build, and communicate knowledge. How can I structure a discussion in a way, so that different viewpoints are being exchanged, reasons are put forward, and people actually learn something from what is being said? I believe that this is where the future of educational technology lies: technology for teaching and learning should not so much be about content; on the contrary, it should be about highlighting and facilitating ways of knowledge building. TaLEAG is such a way of knowledge building. Educational technology should enable teachers and learners to engage in these knowledge-building techniques, supporting and guiding the cognitive and communicative steps involved.

References

Alexander, R. J. 2006. *Towards Dialogic Teaching: Rethinking Classroom Talk*. 3rd edn. Thirsk: Dialogos.

Aristotle, and William Charlton. 1992. *Physics. Books I and II* (Clarendon Aristotle series). Oxford: Clarendon Press.

Arnett, Ronald C. 1998. *Dialogic Education: Conversation about Ideas and Between Persons*. Carbondale: Southern Illinois University Press.

Feller, Sebastian. 2013. "Conceptual Change in Language Teaching and Learning. Why and How Lexical Concepts Drive Meaning Construction Differently across Languages." *Theory and Practice in Language Studies* 10 (3): 1726–1736.

Hargreaves, David J. 2012. "What do We Mean by Creativity and Creative Thinking?" In *Young Children's Creative Thinking*, ed. by Hiroko Fumoto, 15–26. Los Angeles: SAGE. DOI: 10.4135/9781446250891.n2

Hewson, Peter W. 1992. "Conceptual Change in Science Teaching and Teacher Education." Paper presented at a *Meeting on "Research and Curriculum Development in Science Teaching."* Madrid, Spain.

National Institute of Education, Singapore. 2009. *A Teacher Education Model for the 21st Century*. Online at http://www.nie.edu.sg/files/ aboutnie/ TE21%20online%20version.pdf. (last date of access 6 March, 2012)

Peccei, Jean S. 1999. *Pragmatics* (Language workbooks). London, New York: Routledge. DOI: 10.4324/9780203255773

Pinker, Steven. 2002. *The Blank Slate: The Modern Denial of Human Nature*. New York: Viking.

Pinkwart, Niels, and Bruce M. McLaren. 2012. *Educational Technologies for Teaching Argumentation Skills*. Sharjah, U.A.E: Bentham Science Publishers.

Precht, Richard D. 2013. *Anna, die Schule und der liebe Gott: Der Verrat des Bildungssystems an unseren Kindern*. 1st edn. München: Goldmann.

Ravenscroft, Andrew. 2012. "Highly Communicative e-Learning Communities: Developing a Socio-Cultural Framework for Cognitive Change." In *Education in Cyberspace*, ed. by Sian Bayne, and Ray Land, 130–146. Hoboken: Taylor and Francis.

Searle, John R. 1969. *Speech Acts: An Essay in the Philosophy of Language*. London: Cambridge University Press. DOI: 10.1017/CBO9781139173438
Thagard, Paul. 1992. *Conceptual Revolutions*. 1st edn. Princeton, N.J: Princeton University Press.
Trilling, Bernie, and Charles Fadel. 2009. *21st Century Skills: Learning for Life in Our Times*. 1st edn. San Francisco: Jossey-Bass.
Wegerif, Rupert. 2010. *Mind Expanding: Teaching for Thinking and Creativity in Primary Education*. Maidenhead, Berkshire: Open University Press.
Weigand, Edda. 2000. "The Dialogic Action Game." In *Dialogue Analysis VII. Working with Dialogue* (Beiträge zur Dialogforschung 22), ed. by Malcolm Coulthard, Janet Cotterill, and Frances Rock, 1–18. Tübingen: Niemeyer.
Weigand, Edda. 2010. *Dialogue: The Mixed Game* (Dialogue studies 10). Amsterdam: John Benjamins Publishing Company. DOI: 10.1075/ds.10

Author's address

Sebastian Feller, PhD (Research Scientist)
A*STAR – Institute of High Performance Computing
Social Cognitive Computing
1 Fusionopolis Way, #16-16 Connexis
Singapore 138632
fellers@ihpc.a-star.edu.sg

Index